The Politics of Child Protection

Also by the author

The Politics of Child Abuse

Governing the Family: Child Care, Child Protection and the State

Safeguarding Childhood: Early Intervention and Surveillance in a Late Modern Society

Child Protection: Risk and the Moral Order (with David Thorpe and Corinne Wattam)

Constructive Social Work: Towards a New Practice (with Patrick O'Byrne)

Published by other publishers:

The Political Dimensions of Social Work (edited with Bill Jordan)

Social Work, the Media and Public Relations (edited with Bob Franklin)

Social Theory, Social Change and Social Work (edited)

Child Protection and Family Support: Tensions, Contradictions and Possibilities (edited)

Child Sexual Abuse: Responding to the Experiences of Children (edited with Corinne Wattam)

Constructing Clienthood in Social Work and Human Services: Interaction, Identities and Practices
(edited with Chris Hall, Kirsi Juhila and Tarja Pösö)

Constructive Social Work with Offenders (edited with Kevin Gorman, Marilyn Gregory and Michelle Hayles)

Reforming Child Protection (with Bob Lonne, Jane Thomson and Maria Harries)

Understanding Children's Social Care (with Nick Frost)

Child Protection Reform Across the UK (edited with Anne Stafford and Sharon Vincent)

Child Protection Systems: International Trends and Orientations (edited with Neil Gilbert and Marit Skivenes)

Child Protection Systems in the UK: A Comparative Analysis (with Anne Stafford, Sharon Vincent and Connie Smith)

The Politics of Child Protection

Contemporary
Developments and
Future Directions

Nigel Parton

palgrave
macmillan

First published 2014 by
PALGRAVE MACMILLAN

Palgrave Macmillan in the UK is an imprint of Macmillan Publishers Limited, registered in England, company number 785998, of Houndmills, Basingstoke, Hampshire RG21 6XS.

Palgrave Macmillan in the US is a division of St Martin's Press LLC, 175 Fifth Avenue, New York, NY 10010.

Palgrave Macmillan is the global academic imprint of the above companies and has companies and representatives throughout the world.

Palgrave® and Macmillan® are registered trademarks in the United States, the United Kingdom, Europe and other countries.

ISBN 978–1–137–26929–4

This book is printed on paper suitable for recycling and made from fully managed and sustained forest sources. Logging, pulping and manufacturing processes are expected to conform to the environmental regulations of the country of origin.

A catalogue record for this book is available from the British Library.

A catalog record for this book is available from the Library of Congress.

Typeset by MPS Limited, Chennai, India.

Printed and bound in Great Britain by
TJ International, Padstow

2/10/15

For Sophie, Ada and Euan

Contents

List of Figures and Tables

Figures

Tables

Acknowledgements

Over recent years, I have been privileged to work in a number of national and international projects (see, for example, Lonne et al., 2009; Frost and Parton, 2009; Stafford et al., 2010, 2012; Gilbert et al., 2011a), which have been instructive and have informed my thinking considerably. Numerous people have made suggestions, provided great insights and given tremendous support, which have had a direct impact on this book. I would particularly like to thank David Berridge, Jill Duer Berrick, Chas Critcher, Nick Frost, Mark Furlong, Neil Gilbert, Val Gillies, Maria Harries, Ray Jones, Paul Johnson, Bob Lonne, Phillip Noyes, Sue Peckover, Tarja Pösö, Lorraine Radford, Marit Skivenes, Anne Stafford, Jane Thomson and Jo Warner. The staff at the University of Huddersfield library and Sue Hanson at the Centre for Applied Childhood Studies have provided excellent support; I would particularly like to thank Sue for all her meticulous hard work over many years. Finally, many thanks to Catherine Gray at Palgrave Macmillan for guiding this through to a successful completion after planting the seed in the first place. And many thanks to Maggie Lythgoe, who has, again, given excellent copy-editing support.

I would also like to acknowledge Oxford University Press for permission to reproduce Table 10.1 from N. Gilbert (ed.) (1997) *Combatting Child Abuse* and Table 12.2 from N. Gilbert, N. Parton and M. Skivenes (eds) (2011) *Child Protection Systems: International Trends and Orientations.*

Abbreviations

AARs	Assessment and Action Records
ACPCs	Area Child Protection Committees
CAF	Common Assessment Framework
Cafcass	Children and Family Court Advisory and Support Service
CSJ	Centre for Social Justice
DCSF	Department for Children, Schools and Families
DfE	Department for Education
DfES	Department for Education and Skills
DH	Department of Health
DHSS	Department of Health and Social Security
ECM	Every Child Matters
ICTs	information and communication technologies
JAR	Joint Area Review
LAC	Looked After Children
LSCB	Local Safeguarding Children Board
MoJ	Ministry of Justice
NSPCC	National Society for the Prevention of Cruelty to Children
Ofsted	Office for Standards in Education, Children's Services and Skills
PMQs	Prime Minister's Questions
SCR	Serious Case Review

1
The politics of child protection: an introduction

The initial prompt for this book was a suggestion by Catherine Gray, my long-time commissioning editor at Palgrave Macmillan, in early 2010 that I consider writing an updated edition of *Safeguarding Childhood* (Parton, 2006a), which I had completed the day after the Children Act 2004 had received royal assent in November 2004. We decided we would leave the decision until after the general election in May of that year to assess what was happening in the broad areas of child protection and safeguarding and to see what might be changing. In the event, it seemed prudent to write a completely new book. Not only had a lot been happening since November 2004, including:

- the launch of the *Every Child Matters: Change for Children* (DfES, 2004b) programme
- the scandal associated with the death of Peter Connelly
- the onset of the biggest economic downturn since the 1930s
- the election of the first peacetime coalition government since 1931
- and the establishment of the Munro Review of Child Protection

but it felt that the nature of the changes was not simply to do with the number of developments but their overall import, form and implications. It did not seem that what we were witnessing could easily be covered in a simple update and revision of *Safeguarding Childhood*. So, we decided that a new book was required, hence *The Politics of Child Protection*. As the title suggests, the focus is on a political analysis of child protection and, in the process, I provide a critical appraisal of the developments and their implications.

When the late Brian Corby (2006, p. 199) reviewed *Safeguarding Childhood*, he said that the book, together with *The Politics of Child Abuse* (Parton, 1985) and *Governing the Family* (Parton, 1991), completed a 'trilogy mapping the way in which child abuse, child protection and now safeguarding of children have been shaped by political and social change over time'. In that respect, *The Politics of Child Protection* can be seen as the fourth of a quartet, having similar overall aims to those outlined by Brian Corby for the earlier books.

Histories of the present

The overall approach is to provide a 'history of the present' (Skehill, 2007) in order to advance our understanding of the historical conditions on which the emergence of contemporary policy and practice depends. My focus on the past is motivated by my concern to make sense of the present and thereby engage with it. A major attraction of trying to carry out 'histories of the present', as I have argued previously (Parton, 1998, p. 7), is that, following Foucault (Bell, 1994; Barry et al., 1996), we can introduce an 'untimely' ethos to the present and thereby a sense of its fragility and contingency. We can also think about the present differently and act in new and creative ways. The present is not seen as inevitable or homogeneous but as something to be decomposed, problematized and acted on. The ethos is thus one of a permanent questioning of the present in order to establish the limits of thought and practice and thereby locate the places for their transgression and open up new ways of thinking and acting.

My aim is to provide an analysis of how contemporary practice has been constituted and make explicit the range of complexities, ambiguities and tensions that have fed into it. However, while the focus of *Safeguarding Childhood* was to try and make sense of what, in England, seemed to be a new object of official concern – the *safeguarding* of children and childhood – and which seemed of a different order to what had gone before, the focus of this book, as reflected in the title, is much more concerned with *child protection*. A central theme of the book is that recent years, particularly since late 2008, have seen the re-emergence of official concern with the issue of child protection and the framing of policy and practice much more in those terms; however, this is not to say that the idea of safeguarding has disappeared. What it does suggest is that it is important to think about what these official concerns signify, how they might relate to what came before, how they have come about and with what implications. Although I do provide some background discussion of developments prior to November 2004, my primary concern is the period since late 2004.

While the focus of my analysis is England, I am using England as something of a case study for testing out and exploring some more theoretical concerns. Since completing *Safeguarding Childhood*, much of my time has been spent working with colleagues across the UK, Europe, North America and Australia in studying and comparing child protection systems in different countries. We have compared child protection systems across the four nations of the United Kingdom (Stafford et al., 2010, 2012), across the USA, Canada, England, Sweden, Finland, Denmark, Norway, Germany, Belgium and the Netherlands (Gilbert et al., 2011a), as well as being engaged in a much more normative appraisal of the operation of child protection systems in Australia, England and the USA, as a basis for developing ideas for reform (Lonne et al., 2009). This work has helped me to see the systems and developments in England in much sharper focus. As Richard Freeman (2009) has argued, studying policy and practice in other countries has the effect of seeing things 'back home' and one's own assumptions in a much clearer light. The importance of this work for me has been that, first, it has helped locate developments in England in a much broader context and, second, it has provided the beginnings of an analytic framework for comparing child protection systems in different jurisdictions. However, I have also realized that this framework can be helpful for analysing the more specific changes in England and, hence, adding richness to my 'history of the present'. It helps to further 'question the historical inevitability of existing practices in our own country' (Baistow and Wilford, 2000, p. 344).

It became clear that the ethos I had previously tried to capture in engaging with a 'history of the present' was reinforced by engaging in comparative work and that the framework developed in *Child Protection Systems* (Gilbert et al., 2011a) could be helpful for providing a basis for the critical analysis I wanted to engage with in this book. This comparative work confirmed for me that debates about child protection systems were not at their root technical but were clearly political and concerned with different views about what constituted the good society and, in particular, what the relationship should be between the family, the child and the state, and what the roles and responsibilities of professionals should be in these arrangements. In that respect, I have been taken back to a number of the concerns that were central to *The Politics of Child Abuse* in 1985 (Parton, 1985).

So what are some of the issues that have come out of such comparative research and what are these analytic frameworks on which I will be drawing? To understand why comparative research on child protection systems has developed, it is important to outline the rationales behind this research and why it has been seen as important.

Comparing child protection systems

Child Protection Systems (Gilbert et al., 2011a) aimed to build on the comparative analysis conducted in the early/mid-1990s and published in *Combatting Child Abuse: International Perspectives and Trends* (Gilbert, 1997). Prompted by the rapid increase in reports of child maltreatment from 1980 to the early 1990s in the USA, that study compared social policies and professional practices in nine countries – the USA, Canada, England, Sweden, Finland, Denmark, Belgium, the Netherlands and Germany – in terms of:

- What were the criteria that defined child maltreatment?
- Who was responsible for reporting suspected cases of child maltreatment?
- How were the allegations of maltreatment substantiated, and what was the state's response?
- What were the patterns and make-up of out-of-home placements?

One of the key findings was that there appeared to be variations between countries concerning the extent to which their child abuse reporting systems were characterized by a *child protection* or a *family service orientation* (Table 1.1).

Table 1.1   Characteristics of child protection and family service orientations

	Child protection	Family service
Problem frame	Individualist/moralistic	Social/psychological
Preliminary intervention	Legalistic/investigatory	Therapeutic/needs assessment
State/parent relationship	Adversarial	Partnership
Out-of-home placement	Involuntary	Voluntary

Source: Gilbert, 1997, p. 233.

The two orientations were distinguished along four dimensions:

1 *Problem frame:* the way the problem of child abuse was framed was perhaps most significant. In child protection-oriented systems, abuse was conceived as an act that demanded the protection of children from harm from 'degenerative relatives', usually parents; whereas in the family service-oriented systems, abuse was conceived as a problem of family conflict or dysfunction that arose from social and psychological difficulties but which responded to help and support.

2 *Preliminary intervention:* while a child protection-oriented response operated primarily as a mechanism for investigating deviance in a highly legalistic way, a family service response offered a much more therapeutic response to a family's needs, so that the initial focus involved the assessment of need.

3 *State/parent relationship:* child welfare professionals tended to function in an adversarial way in the child protection-oriented response, while the family service orientation operated much more in a spirit of partnership, particularly with parents but also children.

4 *Out-of-home placements:* while there was a high rate of voluntary arrangements with parents in arranging out-of-home placements with the family service orientation, in the child protection orientation the majority of out-of-home placements were compelled through the coercive powers of the state, usually in the form of court orders.

Combatting Child Abuse (Gilbert, 1997) illuminated the alternative perceptions of child abuse and the quite varied policy and practice arrangements that were in place in the different countries. The book coincided with a flurry of publications that looked at how different countries defined and responded to child abuse and the ways that different systems operated (Harder and Pringle, 1997; Pringle, 1998; Khoo et al., 2002; May-Chahal and Herezog, 2003).

The work by researchers at Brunel University in England was particularly important at this time and acted to reinforce and, in some respects, add to that of *Combatting Child Abuse*. The researchers initially compared the operation of the child protection systems in England and France, focusing particularly on the role of social workers (Cooper, 1992a, 1992b; Cooper et al., 1992, 1995). It was argued that child protection social work had been 'bureaucratised, legalised and systematised' (Cooper et al., 1995, p. viii) in England in a way that was not evident in France, and that the way social workers had been 'pilloried in the press and castigated by government' (1995, p. viii) in England was not present in France. They argued that there were major *cultural differences* between the two countries and that this could be seen to permeate all areas of law, policy and practice. In particular, while the French system seemed to be infused with an *optimism* and *trust* of both families' and social workers' abilities to look after children, this was not the case in England, where *pessimism* and *distrust* seemed to dominate.

These important differences in the cultural contexts in which different countries' child protection systems operated were evident in the further work that the research team carried out, which involved the Belgian Flemish community, the Belgian Francophone community, Germany, Italy, the Netherlands and Scotland as well as England (Hetherington et al., 1997). The major differences were between England and Wales, and, to a lesser extent, Scotland and the other European countries, particularly in relation to the roles, authority and responsibilities of the respective social workers and, again, the overall cultural context in which the work took place.

Some years later, Rachel Hetherington reflected on this body of comparative research. While she felt that the structure of different systems and the overall professional ideology were both important in helping to shape the functioning of different systems, it was the different cultures that were crucial:

> Although culture, structures, and professional ideology all interact to shape the functioning of child welfare systems, their effects are not necessarily equally powerful. There is some evidence from the comparative studies that culture may be the most powerful factor. (Hetherington, 2006, p. 43)

She argued that such a conclusion was thoroughly consistent with the findings in *Combatting Child Abuse* (Gilbert, 1997) that the overall culture and values of a society may be the most powerful factor influencing the functioning of child welfare systems and explaining the main differences. By culture, she meant the nexus of views, understandings, habits of mind, patterns of living and use of language that are built up in a community, nation or state by the shared history, experiences and social circumstances in which people live. The culture of a society was pervasive.

From the late 1990s onwards, when comparing European and Anglo-American countries' approaches, researchers and official government reports invariably drew on the distinction between the child protection and family service orientations outlined in *Combatting Child Abuse*

(Gilbert, 1997). The two orientations seemed to provide something of a touchstone for debates and comparisons. For example, the essential features of the two orientations were drawn on for differentiating and comparing different countries' systems in a report by the Scottish Executive (2002) on possible changes in Scotland and a similar report on Australia by the Australian Institute of Family Studies (Bromfield and Holzer, 2007).

Research at the Faculty of Social Work at Wilfrid Laurier University, Canada (Freymond and Cameron, 2006; Cameron et al., 2007) came to similar conclusions. With *child protection systems*:

> The state is a regulator of social and moral arrangements, with an emphasis on individual rights and responsibilities. There is a clear division between private and public domains that protects the privacy of the family. The primary focus of child protection is to protect children from harm in their own homes. Child protection service providers increasingly rely on adversarial judicial systems to confer authority on their work. (Freymond and Cameron, 2006, p. 9)

The researchers saw England, Canada and the USA as the main examples. In contrast, *family service systems* were characterized as follows:

> The state supports child and family welfare systems that reflect communal ideals about children, family and community. Principles of social solidarity and, in some settings, of subsidiarity (local responsibility) are emphasised. Fostering the proper care of children is seen as a shared responsibility. Providing support for parent-child relationships and the care of children are seen as primary focuses. Demonstrating risks of harming children is not a necessary precursor for families or children to receive assistance. (Freymond and Cameron, 2006, p. 5)

France, the Netherlands and Sweden were seen as good examples of this approach.[1]

By the mid-2000s, there was a broad consensus among researchers and policy analysts about the validity and usefulness of using the child protection and family service orientations as the two broad frameworks for comparing systems in different countries and across different jurisdictions (Thoburn, 2007; Gilbert et al., 2009a; Connolly and Morris, 2012).

It had originally been anticipated that the introduction of mandatory reporting laws had been the main driver for change and the increases in child abuse reports in the USA. However, this proved not to be the case, and mandatory reporting laws did not appear to be linked to either the child protection or family service orientation. It was the important overall differences between the orientations that were key, rather than whether there were reporting laws. The analysis in *Combatting Child Abuse* (Gilbert, 1997) suggested it was possible to group the countries into three broad categories:

1 *Child protection:* USA, Canada, England

2 *Family service – mandatory reporting:* Denmark, Sweden, Finland

3 *Family service – non-mandatory reporting:* Belgium, the Netherlands, Germany.

These groupings paralleled Gøsta Esping-Andersen's (1990) often-cited classification of liberal (Anglo-American), Conservative (Continental) and social democratic (Nordic) welfare state regimes, which was used by Keith Pringle (1998) in his comparison of child welfare systems in Europe.

In 2008, Neil Gilbert, Marit Skivenes and I started a project working with researchers in the different countries to update *Combatting Child Abuse* (Gilbert, 1997). We compared the same countries as before (Belgium, Canada, Denmark, England, Finland, Germany, the Netherlands, Sweden and the USA) plus Norway. The approach followed the same format as the first project 15 years previously and addressed the same questions. The overall conclusion (Gilbert et al., 2011a) was that while the two original orientations, child protection and family service, were still relevant, they needed to be revised in the light of the developments in the various countries during the intervening 15 years up to 2008/09.

The findings suggested that approaches to protecting children from abuse had become much more complex than those operating in the early/mid-1990s. Countries previously identified with the child protection orientation, for example England and the USA, had taken on some of the elements of the family service orientation. At the same time, there was also evidence that those countries that had previously operated according to a clear family service orientation had made efforts to respond to increasing concerns about harm to children. This seemed to be the case in all the Nordic countries (with the possible exception of Sweden) and all the northern European countries studied.

In addition to the various attempts to strike a new set of balances between the child protection and family service orientations, we felt it was possible to discern the emergence of a new approach, which we called a *child-focused orientation* (Gilbert et al., 2011b). This orientation focused on the child as an individual with a much more independent relation to the state. It was not restricted to narrow concerns about harm and abuse; rather, the object of concern was the child's overall development and wellbeing. The programmes aimed to go beyond protecting children from risk of harm to promoting children's overall welfare. With the latter, concerns about abuse became relevant as just one set of factors that might affect a child's development and wellbeing. If, for any reason, there was concern about a child's development, the state sought to intervene to offer support or more authoritative intervention if this was required. With a child-focused orientation, the state took on a growing role for itself in terms of providing a wide range of early intervention and preventive services. The child-focused orientation also often involved arrangements that were adjusted to meet children's needs, competences and maturity by taking into account the views and wishes of the child.

We suggested that the emergence of the child-focused orientation since the mid-1990s was inspired in part by the 1989 UN Convention on the Rights of the Child, which underlined the importance of the social, political and legal rights of children. We also suggested that it was prompted by the changing objectives of modern welfare states from social protection against the vagaries of the market economy towards social activation and inclusion, which sought to enable citizens to be productive workers by, in part, investing in human capital (Esping-Andersen, 2002).

We summarized the key elements of the three orientations in Table 1.2.

This comparative research has demonstrated that there appears to be a clear relationship between the approach to child welfare and protection in a country and the nature and form of the welfare regime in which it is located. Those states that have taken a narrow range of responsibility tend to focus on protecting children from forensic risk of harm and providing a basic social safety net; while those states that take a broad degree of responsibility also attempt to protect children from the risk of unequal life outcomes as a result of their social position or upbringing. The way the responsibilities of the state are constructed – narrowly or broadly – and operationalized are related to how the child welfare system defines responsibility between the private and public spheres and cultural views about children and the family.[2] It is clear that the systems are nested within a broader political and policy context, which helps to define the role of the state vis-à-vis the family and the child, together with the role of professionals. It is the changing nature and form

Table 1.2   Role of the state vis-à-vis child and family orientations to child maltreatment: child focus, family service and child protection

	Child focus	Family service	Child protection
Driver for intervention	The individual child's needs in a present and future perspective; societies need healthy and contributory citizens	The family unit needs assistance	Parents being neglectful and abusive towards children (maltreatment)
Role of the state	Paternalistic/defamilialisation – state assumes parent role; but seeks to refamilialise child by foster home/kinship/adoption	Parental support; the state seeks to strengthen family relations	Sanctioning; the state functions as 'watchdog' to ensure child's safety
Problem frame	Child's development and unequal outcomes for children	Social/psychological (system, poverty, racism etc)	Individual/moralistic
Mode of intervention	Early intervention and regulatory/need assessment	Therapeutic/needs assessment	Legalistic/ investigative
Aim of intervention	Promote wellbeing via social investment and/or equal opportunity	Prevention/social bonding	Protection/harm reduction
State-parent relationship	Substitutive/partnership	Partnership	Adversarial
Balance of rights	Children's rights/parental responsibility	Parents' rights to family life mediated by professional social workers	Children's/parents' rights enforced with legal means

Source: Gilbert et al., 2011b, p. 255.

of these relationships in England that is the primary focus of this book. While similar patterns and developments can be discerned in the other UK nations, it is also important to recognize that the detail and balance of change varies and this has become more evident since devolution in the late 1990s (Stafford et al., 2012).

Central themes and overall argument

A central part of my argument is that debates and concerns about child protection in England have become increasingly politicized over the past 40 years and this has increased dramatically since late 2008, with the scandal arising from the death of Baby Peter Connelly, which

I characterize in terms of a growing 'politics of outrage'. However, this outrage was directed not simply at the perpetrators of the crime but at the professionals and managers responsible for the case and the operation of the child protection system itself. The focus of political concern throughout has been how to reform and improve professional practices and the systems of child protection in which social work and social workers are seen as particularly culpable. The outrage and the focus of political attention were not concerned with how to address the problem of child maltreatment in society but how to improve child protection systems. In many respects, child abuse scandals have become something of a proxy for a variety of debates about a range of political issues concerned with the efficacy of the work of health and welfare professionals, particularly social workers, and arguments about the nature and direction of social policy provision and the state of society more generally.

Ironically, while child protection has become increasingly politicized, rarely has this led to any serious discussion of what we mean by 'child maltreatment' and what are the best ways of trying to do something about it. These are major issues that have rarely received serious political attention and debate. While conceptions about the nature and causes of child maltreatment are often embedded in child protection systems, as summarized in Table 1.1, rarely are these made explicit and the subject of serious attention.

Thus, much of this book is concerned with outlining and critically analysing how the politics of child protection, primarily in England, have played out over recent years and how this has become increasingly interrelated with wider political concerns and agendas. In particular, I look at how policies towards children and childhood were central to the wider New Labour project when it came to power in 1997, leading up to the *Every Child Matters: Change for Children* (DfES, 2004b) programme and the reform of children's services following the public inquiry into the death of Victoria Climbié, and how this was subsequently undermined by a series of high-profile scandals, including that concerning Baby Peter Connelly. I then look in detail at how the Conservative-led coalition government from 2010 onwards took a rather different approach while also keeping some of its key elements, leading up to the publication of the revised and much reduced government guidance *Working Together to Safeguarding Children* (HM Government, 2013) in March 2013.

In many respects, the period after May 2010 can be seen to have been a period of much policy and practice change. I argue that what we have witnessed is the emergence of an 'authoritarian neoliberal state' in child welfare and protection, and that this is changing the relationships between children, parents and professionals, particularly among certain sections of the population. Thus, while the period from the mid-1990s to 2008 can be characterized as shifting policy and practice away from a narrow child protection orientation towards a more family service orientation, together with an emphasis on a particular form of a child-focused orientation, the period since 2008 has seen a clear re-emergence of a child protection orientation. While the current system is now officially defined as a 'child-centred and coordinated approach' (HM Government, 2013) and continues to use the language of 'safeguarding and promoting the welfare of the child' and stresses the importance of 'early help', I argue that this has little in common with the child-focused orientation identified by Gilbert et al. (2011b; and see Table 1.2 earlier). Not only is it now seen as important to 'rescue children from chaotic, neglectful and abusive homes' (HM Government, 2013, p. 22), but it is government policy to take more children into care and to prioritize adoption as a mainstream policy option for those in care. I argue that such an approach is inadequate and that in order to move beyond individualized child protection systems, it is first important to focus attention on what we mean by child maltreatment and seriously address the nature and size of the problem(s) to be addressed. In being so concerned about the operation and failures of the child protection system, we have failed to address what we mean by child maltreatment and what we should do about it. I argue that child maltreatment is a significant *social* problem that cannot be ameliorated by individualized interventions alone.

I return to these issues in Chapter 11, where I try to provide the foundations for thinking about 'the politics of child protection' differently and outline new ways of taking policy and practice forward by moving beyond individualized child protection systems. It begins by arguing that we need to recognize that all studies of the prevalence of child maltreatment suggest that only about one-tenth of the amount of child maltreatment ever becomes known to official agencies and that the current system and assumptions about child maltreatment are clearly inadequate for the task at hand. I argue that a number of policy dimensions should be considered if we are serious about addressing child maltreatment and that issues related to gender, social class and inequality are central.

I argue that a broad public health approach to child maltreatment can provide an important beginning framework for future policy and practice, but that this needs to place a children's rights perspective at its centre and recognize that there are a wide range of significant social harms that cause maltreatment to children, many of which are clearly related to structural inequalities. In doing so, I draw on elements of the approach to child maltreatment first developed in *The Politics of Child Abuse* (Parton, 1985). I also argue that it is important to engage a variety of community-based groups in the process and that the processes of change are as important as the overall aims of what we want to bring about.

2

Children's services in the postwar period

Introduction

The central purpose of this book is to critically analyse recent developments in child protection, together with identifying some of the current challenges. In doing so, it argues that what we now call 'child protection' has a history and line of development that has been influenced by a range of social, economic, cultural and political changes over a century and a quarter, and that a knowledge of this history is crucial to explaining and understanding the current form and function of this area of policy and practice. This is not to suggest that the developments have been straightforward or linear, or that what is referred to as 'child protection' is in any way solid, as a whole range of complexities, tensions and contingencies have fed into its emergence.

At one level, the term 'child protection' refers to the laws, policies and professional practices that have been developed to respond to the problem of child abuse and neglect. For a phenomenon to take on the guise of a social problem requiring some form of state intervention, it first has to be defined and constituted as such and the late nineteenth and early twentieth century were key. What Linda Gordon (1989, p. 20) calls the era of 'nineteenth century child-saving' lasted until the First World War, when child abuse effectively disappeared as a subject of social concern until it was 'rediscovered' by American paediatricians as the 'battered child syndrome' nearly half a century later (Kempe et al., 1962; Parton, 1985).

Gordon (1989) and Parker (1995) argue that child welfare only becomes an issue when women's voices are being heard strongly, and in the latter half of the nineteenth century, middle-class women used their increased leisure time to engage in charitable work, and the welfare of children as well as the fear of delinquency became a focus. The latter, however, remained a major preoccupation (Hendrick, 2003). The huge growth in voluntary organizations followed the riots, famines and hard winters of the 1850s and 60s, which overwhelmed the Poor Law's always limited capacity to provide relief. To regulate all this charitable work, the Charity Organisation Society was set up in 1869, its agents conscientiously investigating the home circumstances of the needy to ensure they were morally deserving.

From such encounters grew a widespread concern (among the middle classes) about child cruelty and neglect (among the poor) and the first Society for the Prevention of Cruelty to Children was established in 1883, modelled on those being established in America. The National Society for the Prevention of Cruelty to Children (NSPCC) was formed in 1889 and was hugely successful in organizing the public and political campaign that produced the first legislation specifically to outlaw child cruelty and give public agencies powers to protect and remove children from home (Behlmer, 1982; Parton, 1985; Flegel, 2009).

The conceptualization of the abused child in England in the 1880s, particularly that represented in the discourse of the NSPCC, reflected a model of childhood that became predominant in the nineteenth century; a model of childhood as a protected time and space to be shared by all children. In the process, the child was transformed from an economically useful member of a household into an economically worthless but emotionally priceless figure in society who was in need or protection (Zelizer, 1985; Cunningham, 1995).

The activities of the NSPCC were of great significance in this period. Ferguson (1990, 2004) has analysed cases drawn from case files and shown how the new discourse of child protection was being constructed. Here were 'social actors actively constructing the foundations of modern forms of knowledge, of therapeutic and cultural practice: in short, a professional culture that would take child protection into the twentieth century' (Ferguson, 1990, p. 135). Indeed, many of the dilemmas of modern practice were here (Ferguson, 1996, 1997), as inspectors advocated for clients, pondered the advisability of rehabilitating children and sought to reform and change abusing parents.

And yet, after 1918, much of this activity disappeared from view. Parker (1995) suggests a number of reasons for this: for example, the decline of the women's movement following the granting of universal suffrage, and changes in the NSPCC, to whom the government was happy to leave the responsibility for child cruelty, which became more bureaucratic and less campaigning. Ferguson (1996, 1997, 2004) has argued that the general approach of the NSPCC to publicizing child deaths shifted during this period. In the nineteenth and early twentieth century, the NSPCC was not afraid to discuss publicly the deaths of children about whom it had direct knowledge and with whom it was working. The child death statistics were always included in its annual report. It seems that, paradoxically, the existence of child death was viewed as a sign that child protection was working well and was publicized because it meant that increasing numbers of vulnerable children were being reached by its workers and hence they were fulfilling a valuable role. Ferguson (1997, p. 223) argues that, by the 1920s, this approach had been transformed so that death in child protection cases ceased to be made public; not because the problem was solved but because the disclosure of deaths 'threatened the authority, optimism and trustworthiness of the expert system'.

The Children Act 1948 and the establishment of local authority children's departments

The period following the end of the Second World War saw considerable change in the organization and principles of delivery of children's services. In particular, it witnessed the establishment of local authority children's departments as the key agency for providing services and carrying out the state's responsibilities in this area of policy and practice. Not only did this mean the demise of the Poor Law but a changing role for child welfare charities, including the NSPCC. Prompted, in part, by the scandal in 1945 of the death of 13-year-old Dennis O'Neill while in foster care and the subsequent inquiry led by Sir Walter Monckton (1946), a campaign for legislative change had started some years previously (Parker, 1983; Holman, 1998). Although the Children Act 1948 was introduced in a period of major change, often characterized as the introduction of the British welfare state (Fraser, 2009), its aim and focus were much narrower than the changes in health, education and social security (Jones, 2009). Importantly, for our purposes, a concern with intrafamilial abuse was hardly on its agenda. This was to become the major driver for change in the 1970s and 80s, when concerns about child abuse re-entered the public and political arenas in significant ways.

The blueprint for the Children Act 1948 was provided by the report of the Curtis Committee, which was established at the end of the Second World War. In particular, it attempted to provide a simplified and unified administrative framework at central and local government level for all children who, for whatever reason, were deprived of a 'normal' home life. While the children came into care via a number of routes and for different reasons, the largest group were those in the care of local authority public assistance committees as 'poor persons in need of relief'. They were either orphans or had been deserted by their parents, or had mentally or physically ill parents who were unable or unwilling to care for them. The number in care categorized as child abuse and neglect was minimal. The total number of children and young people in care at the time was 124,900 (Curtis Report, 1946, p. 8), often accommodated in large institutions.

The new departments tried to lay to rest the Poor Law and embodied the revolutionary principle that they should seek the *best* development of the children they were responsible for. Until 1948, the influence of the 1601 and 1834 Poor Law Acts was explicit and there was no reference to any duties to educate, compensate or care for the children involved.

As Jean Packman (1981) has argued, the aim was that, in future, children in care would be treated as individuals and not as an undifferentiated category of youngsters and should have access to the same range of facilities as other children. The new departments were to be staffed by a new kind of personnel who were professionally trained in the psychosocial sciences and would have a thorough understanding of human relationships and the importance of the family and parental (primarily maternal) attachments for a child's development. However, while the changes were significant, the responsibilities of children's departments were only for children in care. The new service was to play a residual and particular role in the overall context of welfare services.

The postwar welfare state was based on a particular model of the economy and the family. Not only did it assume full male employment, it also assumed a traditional role for the patriarchal nuclear family (Williams, 1989; Pascall, 1997). The idea of the 'family wage' was central, linking the labour market to the distribution of social roles and dependency by age and gender within the family. Within the family, women were to trade housework, childbirth, child rearing and physical and emotional caring in return for economic support from a male 'breadwinner' (Finch and Groves, 1983). It was assumed that most 'welfare work' was carried out within the family either by using the family wage to buy goods and services or by women caring for children. The provision of state welfare was intended to support, not replace, this arrangement. Such an approach was key to the work of the newly established children's departments, which were explicitly designed to provide a residual service for children deprived of a 'normal family life' and therefore in care.

Clearly, however, the work and rationale of the departments would be subject to a whole series of tensions and difficulties if any of these underlying assumptions were to be seriously questioned, or if there were to be significant changes in the key institutions that provided the main pillars for their work – particularly the labour market, the patriarchal nuclear family, or the other universal state welfare services, such as health, education, and social security. Beyond this, further stresses and challenges would be created if the political consensus that underpinned the postwar welfare changes was itself to be put under strain. These were to become important issues from the late 1970s onwards; however, between 1948 and the early 1970s, the focus and rationale of the work was to broaden and develop in significant ways.

The establishment of 'the family service'

During the 1950s, children's departments were finding their role far too narrow and restrictive and they began to expand their operations and reframe their responses (Packman, 1981, 1993). Increasingly, it was felt that waiting until children came into care was doing too little, too late. There was a need to intervene with families earlier in their own homes and thereby prevent children coming into care. Such thinking was given a major boost when influential members of the Fabian Society, prominent academics and senior civil servants made explicit the links between child neglect, deprivation and delinquency, such that providing help to families earlier would not only help prevent admissions into care but would also prevent future delinquency. A new statutory power to provide services to families in the community to *prevent* children being received into care was provided in Section 1 of the Children and Young Persons Act 1963. It provided the legislative backing for what a number of children's departments were already doing in practice.

Moves to expand the remit and rationale of the work developed further in the 1960s. There was an increasing conviction that better services could be provided by reorganizing all local authority children's and welfare services and bringing them together in an enlarged *family service*. This led to the establishment of local authority social services departments in 1971 following the Seebohm Report of 1968 and the Local Authority Social Services Act of 1970 (Hall, 1976; Clarke, 1980; Cooper, 1983). The new department would be generic in nature, with a focus on the family and the community, and the new profession of social work would lie at its core. While the emphasis on genericism reflected a number of issues and was interpreted in a variety of ways, crucially, it was premised on the view that the work drew on certain common values, knowledge and skills and was embodied most clearly in the role of the professional social worker.

The role of the new social services departments was not just to provide a range of services and professional help but to coordinate aspects of other state services, such as health, education, housing and social security, thereby make them more responsive to need, particularly the functioning of a small number of families who were seen as causing a disproportionate number of problems – often referred to as 'problem families' (Philp and Timms, 1962). Social service departments, although residual and small scale compared to the other state welfare services, were established as the 'fifth social service' (Townsend, 1970), after health, education, social security and public housing. They would provide the personalized, humanistic dimension of the welfare state, the primary tool being the professional worker's personality and understanding of human relationships. The early 1970s marked the high point of optimism and confidence in social work, which had been fostered by the approaches developed in the children's departments and its key political and academic advocates. However, during the 1970s, not only were the assumptions on which it operated found wanting, but the social, political and economic contexts began to change significantly.

The growing crisis in child protection

The consensus that had been established in the postwar period, based on the family as the primary mechanism for ensuring the welfare of children, with social workers entrusted with the state's key responsibility for child welfare, began to collapse during the 1970s. What became evident from the mid-1980s onwards was that the problems had become considerably more complex and high profile and were not amenable to easy resolution. Up to this point, social work had been given the key role in mediating and resolving the difficult and sometimes ambiguous relationship between the *privacy* of the family and the *public* responsibilities of the state, so that children could be protected and the privacy of the family was not undermined. However, the tragic death of Maria Colwell and subsequent public inquiry (Secretary of State for Social Services, 1974) was to change all that (Parton, 1985; Butler and Drakeford, 2005, Ch. 5, 2011).

Maria had been in the care of the local authority in Brighton, East Sussex, and at the time of her death at the hands of her stepfather was subject to a supervision order. Although the authorities received numerous calls expressing concerns about her treatment and the home was visited by a number of professionals, she died a tragic and brutal death. The case received considerable media, political and public attention and proved a watershed in the politics of child protection and family social work more generally (see Chapter 10; Butler and Drakeford, 2011).

Between the publication of the Colwell Inquiry report in 1974 and 1985, there were 29 further inquiries into the deaths of children as a result of abuse (Corby et al., 1998). There was considerable similarity between the findings (DHSS, 1982). Most identified:

- a lack of interdisciplinary communication

- a lack of properly trained and experienced frontline workers

- inadequate supervision

- too little focus on the needs of the child as distinct from those of the parents.

The overriding concern was the lack of coordination between the different agencies. The intensity of political and media concern increased further in the mid-1980s with the public inquiries into three other child deaths in different London boroughs – Jasmine Beckford (London Borough of Brent, 1985), Tyra Henry (London Borough of Lambeth, 1987) and Kimberley Carlile (London Borough of Greenwich, 1987). Until this point, all the public inquiries had been concerned with the deaths of children at the hands of their parents or carers. The child welfare professionals were seen as having failed to protect the children and did too little, too late.

However, the Cleveland 'affair', which broke in the summer of 1987, was very different. This time, 121 children were kept in hospital against the wishes of their parents, on place of safety orders, on suspicions of having been sexually abused (Secretary of State for Social Services, 1988; Parton, 1991). Not only was it the first scandal and public inquiry into possible overreaction by professionals, it was also the first when the actions of paediatricians and other doctors, as well as social workers, were put under the microscope and subject to criticism.[1] In the context of the scandals about child deaths and that of the Cleveland affair, it seemed that child protection professionals and agencies were caught between criticisms arising from failures to intervene and criticisms because of overintervention.

The issues articulated through the inquiries into child deaths and the Cleveland affair resonated with a number of developments in the wider political environment, and contributed to the increasing questioning of the welfare consensus around the family. From the 1960s onwards, with the growth of the women's movement and the mounting recognition of violence in the family, it was argued that the family may not be the 'haven in a heartless world' (Lasch, 1977) it had previously been assumed to be. While campaigning was initially concerned with improving the position of women, from the mid-1970s, particularly with the growing attention to sexual abuse, energy was also directed at the position of children (Rush, 1980; Nelson, 1987). Such critiques helped disaggregate the interests of individual family members and supported the sometimes contradictory development of the emerging children's rights movement (Freeman, 1983; Franklin, 1986, 1995).

The period also witnessed the emergence of a more obviously civil liberties critique, which concentrated on the apparent growth of intervention into people's lives in the name of welfare (Morris et al., 1980; Taylor et al., 1980; Geach and Szwed, 1983). Increasingly, lawyers drew attention to the way the administration of justice was unjustly applied to various areas of child welfare and the need for a greater emphasis on individual rights. During the mid-1980s, the parents' lobby gained its most coherent voice with the establishment of Parents Against Injustice (PAIN). Thus, while quite different in their social location and focus of concern, a growing range of constituencies were critical of the postwar consensus in child welfare. These were most forcefully articulated in and through the various child abuse inquiries.

These developments need to be located in the context of the more wide-ranging changes that had been taking place in the political environment. From the mid-1970s, there was an increasing disillusionment about the ability of the postwar welfare state to manage the economy effectively in the context of rising unemployment and inflation, and overcome a range of social problems, such as the growth in violence and crime more generally, via the use of extensive welfare programmes. The growth of the neoliberal New Right (Levitas, 1986) and the election of the Conservative government under Margaret Thatcher in 1979 proved particularly significant in shifting the political discourse in the 1980s. For the neoliberal New Right, the problems in the economic and social spheres were closely interrelated and the approach stressed the importance of individual responsibility, choice and freedom and supported the disciplines of the market against the interference of the state. However, while the vision was of a 'minimal state', when it did intervene the state should be strong and authoritative, particularly to protect the weak and innocent (Gamble, 1988). It had its roots in an individualized concept of social relations, whereby the market was seen as the key institution for the economic sphere and the family was the key institution for the social sphere.

The family was seen as essentially a private domain from which the state should be excluded but which should be encouraged to take on its 'natural' caring responsibilities, particularly for children. The role of the state should be confined to ensuring that the family fulfilled these responsibilities, while making sure that no one suffered at the hands of the violent and abusive. Clearly, however, a fine balance had to be struck between protecting the innocent and weak, and protection from state interference. By 1987/8, it seemed that the state was falling down on both counts; it was failing to protect children in the family (as in the Beckford, Henry and Carlile inquiries), but was also invading the privacy of the family as exemplified by events in Cleveland.

The Children Act 1989

It is in this context that we need to understand the significance of the Children Act 1989. Although the legislation was an explicit attempt to address the wide-ranging disquiet about the practices of health and welfare professionals in the area of child protection (Parton, 1991), it was not simply responding to the recommendations of child abuse inquiries. It was also informed by research and a series of respected official reports during the 1980s, which aimed to update and rationalize childcare legislation, particularly the Short Report (Social Services Committee, 1984) and the *Review of Child Care Law* (DHSS, 1985).

The central principles of the Act encouraged an approach to child welfare based on *negotiation* with families and involving parents and children in agreed plans. The accompanying guidance and regulations encouraged professionals to work *in partnership* with parents and young people. In an attempt to keep the use of care proceedings and emergency interventions to a minimum, the legislation strongly encouraged an approach that emphasized *support* for families with 'children in need'. In the process, the concept of prevention was elevated and broadened from simply the duty to prevent children coming into care to a much broader power to provide services to *promote* the care and upbringing of children within their families. The aim was to establish a new balance in policy and practice between 'family support' and 'child protection', with a much greater emphasis on the former. Section 17 of the Act was key to bringing this change about.

Under s.17(1) of the Children Act 1989:

> It shall be the general duty of every local authority (in addition to the other duties imposed on them by this Part) –
>
> (a) to safeguard and promote the welfare of children within their area who are in need; and
> (b) so far as is consistent with that duty, to promote the upbringing of such children by their families,
>
> by providing a range and level of services appropriate to those children's needs.

And in s.17(10), a child is deemed to be 'in need' if:

> (a) he is unlikely to achieve or maintain, or to have the opportunity of achieving or maintaining, a reasonable standard of health or development without the provision for him of services by a local authority under this Part;
> (b) his health or development is likely to be significantly impaired, or further impaired, without the provision for him of such services; or
> (c) he is disabled.

The Act also introduced a new threshold criterion, which had to be satisfied before compulsory state intervention into the family, via court proceedings, could be warranted. The criterion was: 'that the child concerned is suffering or is likely to suffer significant harm' (s.31(2)(a)), where harm was defined as 'ill-treatment or the impairment of health or development' (s.31(9)). For the first time, the criterion for state intervention included a prediction of what 'is likely' to occur *in the future*. The harm should be *significant* and, where this was concerned with issues of health and development, these should be compared with that 'which could reasonably be expected of a similar child' (s.31(10)).

Thus, while it was not intended that minor shortcomings in health or development should give rise to compulsory intervention (unless they were likely to have serious and lasting effects on the child), it was clear that, in theory, the role of local authorities was broadened, not only because of the much wider notion of prevention but also because of the need to try and anticipate what might happen to a child in the future. The overall duty for local authorities was to *safeguard and promote the welfare of the children* who were 'in need'.

Section 47(1) laid a specific duty on local authorities where they:

(b) have reasonable cause to suspect that a child who lives, or is found, in their area is suffering, or is likely to suffer, significant harm, the authority should make, or cause to be made, such enquiries as they consider necessary to enable them to decide whether they should take any action to *safeguard or promote the child's welfare.* (emphasis added)

Section 47(3) continued:

The enquiries shall, in particular, be directed towards establishing:

(a) whether the authority should make any application to the court, or exercise any of their other powers under this Act, with respect to the child.

The balance that local authorities struck between its new 'preventive' duties under Section 17 'to safeguard or promote the child's welfare' and its responsibilities under Section 47 to investigate whether a child was 'suffering or likely to suffer significant harm' and therefore consider instituting court procedures, was to prove an important issue. Overall, the Children Act 1989 was welcomed on all sides as a progressive piece of legislation, although it was recognized that it was being introduced in a 'hostile climate', out of step with the philosophy and aims of most of the other social and economic policies of the Conservative government at the time, and that its success would be dependent on whether resources were going to be made available for the more extended family support provisions (Frost, 1992).

Developments in the 1990s

By the mid-1990s, it was becoming increasingly evident that the approach envisaged by the Children Act 1989 was only being partially implemented and that the narrow, forensically focused child protection orientation dominated policy and practice (Berridge, 1997). A number of developments and debates took place, which not only illustrated the nature of the difficulties but also suggested how things might change in the future. In the process, they provided key foundations for the way the Labour government might take policy and practice forward following its election in May 1997. I will focus on three areas in particular:

- the 'refocusing' of children's services debate

- the development of the Looked After Children (LAC) project

- the growing emphasis on the importance of early childhood prevention.

The 'refocusing' of children's services debate

A number of reports demonstrated that local authorities were struggling to implement the key principles and aims of the Children Act 1989. The *Children Act Report 1993* argued that:

> A broadly consistent and somewhat worrying picture is emerging. In general, progress towards full implementation of Section 17 of the Children Act has been slow. Further work is still needed to provide across the country a range of family services aimed at preventing families reaching the point of breakdown. Some authorities are still finding it difficult to move from a reactive social policy role to a more proactive partnership role with families. (DH, 1994, para. 239)

A report from the Audit Commission (1994) came to similar conclusions.
However, it was the publication of *Child Protection: Messages from Research* (DH, 1995a), which summarized the key findings from a major government research programme on child protection practices, which was to prove crucial in opening up a major debate about the future shape of child protection policy and practice and children's services more generally (Parton, 1997). It demonstrated that only around 1 in 7 of those referred to as children at risk of abuse were ever placed on a child protection register and less than 1 in 25 was ever removed from home as a result. Thresholds for registration on the child protection register varied between authorities but in all there was a tendency to concentrate on investigating whether there was any risk of abuse rather than assessing whether the child was 'in need'. Even those children who were registered were provided with little treatment, and many children who

were not registered still had considerable difficulties but often received little help.

The report argued that 'if we put to one side the severe cases' (DH, 1995a, p. 19), the most deleterious situations in terms of longer term outcomes for children were those of *emotional neglect* and a prime concern should be the *parenting style* that failed to compensate for the inevitable deficiencies that become manifest in the course of the 20 years or so that it takes to bring up a child. Unfortunately, the research suggested that these were just the situations where the child protection system was least successful. Far too much time and resources were being spent on forensically driven child protection investigations concerned with whether a child had been injured or not and, if so, who was responsible. As a consequence, there was a failure to develop longer term coordinated preventive strategies. The significance of the 'refocusing' debate was that it had the effect of relocating concerns about child protection in a much wider context of providing services to children 'in need', particularly where there were concerns about emotional neglect and parenting style, and thereby arguing for the greater integration of children's services more generally and more emphasis being placed on family support.

Subsequent government research, carried out in the mid-1990s, which reviewed the progress in implementing the Children Act, painted a similar picture. While the overview report was not available until 2001 (DH, 2001), most of the projects had been completed and submitted to government some years earlier. Crucially, it reinforced the message that while there was some progress, local authority social service departments had found it difficult to 'refocus' their services in the way suggested. The essential message was to emphasize the importance of working with families in a way that would keep children in their families and improve their overall 'outcomes'. These outcomes were conceived widely and included the child's education, emotional and physical well-being, their family ties, and their sense of identity and preparation for the future.

The Looked After Children (LAC) project

All these themes were reflected in the Looked After Children (LAC) project. Running alongside the 'refocusing' debate was the development of the LAC project, which aimed to improve the life chances and outcomes for children who were 'looked after' (in care) by the local authority, the first stage of which was the publication of the report by the original working party (Parker et al., 1991). The project was prompted by growing political and professional concerns about the poor outcomes achieved by children who were in care, and the number of scandals concerning the treatment and abuse of children in children's homes, which received wide media coverage from the late 1980s onwards (Corby et al., 2001). It was seen as vital that local authorities fulfilled their responsibilities as 'corporate parents' to the children and young people they 'looked after' (Jackson and Kilroe, 1996). Much of the evidence suggested that not only did 'looked after' children not succeed educationally but also their health, mental health, general wellbeing and integration into mainstream society were poor. Those who had been 'looked after' appeared to make up a disproportionate number of the unemployed, criminals and a variety of other groups later in life. At the heart of the LAC project was an attempt to make explicit what 'good parenting means in practice' (DH, 1995b, p. 22) so that local authorities could fulfil their corporate parenting responsibilities.

Seven 'developmental dimensions' were identified as being key to achieving long-term wellbeing in adulthood:

- health
- education
- identity
- family and peer relationships
- emotional and behavioural development
- self-care and competence
- social presentation.

The key components of the LAC system were a series of six age-related Assessment and Action Records (AARs) and within the seven developmental dimensions the AARs set specific, age-related objectives for children's progress. The AARs were set within a system for gathering information and reviewing children's cases that would provide baseline information about the specific needs of individual children, the situation of their families and the purpose of providing the service. While the AARs were implemented initially as a practice tool, this was secondary to their original purpose, which was to provide local authorities with a systematic means of gathering management information that would enable them to assess the outcomes of 'looked after' children away from home.

Although originally introduced specifically for use with 'looked after' children, local authorities and researchers increasingly began to examine how far the LAC system could be adapted and developed for assessing outcomes in relation to a much wider population of children who came into contact with social service departments and other health and welfare agencies (Ward, 1998). It was to provide a crucial foundation for the development of the *Framework for the Assessment of Children in Need and their Families* (DH et al., 2000), the Integrated Children's System (DH, 2003; Walker and Scott, 2004; Cleaver et al., 2008) and the Common Assessment Framework (DfES, 2006d, 2006e), discussed in Chapter 4.

Early childhood prevention

The third important development during this period was located on the margins of debates in mainstream child welfare and protection and was much more associated with growing concerns about youth crime. Increasingly, a powerful case was made in the 1990s from a diverse set of constituencies, which included the Family Policy Studies Centre (Utting et al., 1993), the Joseph Rowntree Foundation (Utting, 1995) and the National Children's Bureau (Sinclair et al., 1997; Utting, 1998), that early childhood prevention strategies should be placed at the centre of policies for children and families, and that the current approaches were unnecessarily restrictive. The case for prevention was pragmatic and rooted in the changing nature of family life but argued for a higher profile for the state:

> While believing the relationships and choice of lifestyle within families should normally be a private matter, it accepts that this cannot always be the case. The welfare and safety of children, in particular, are viewed as a collective responsibility which can be met through the public provision of preventive services and intervention where necessary. (Utting, 1995, p. 8)

The way children grow up was seen as key to their future attitudes, behaviour and achievements and this was seen as being crucially 'conditioned by their relationships with parents and other members of their families' (Utting, 1995, p. 32). In a rapidly changing world, the role of parents was seen as providing the key mediator between the challenges of adult life and the way children develop.

The importance of prevention for pre-empting future crime was underlined. Over many years, criminological studies had consistently identified a range of family-based factors linked to an increased risk of offending. David Farrington (1996, 2000), perhaps the leading proponent of the theory and practice of youth criminality prevention, identified a number of key 'risk factors', including poor child rearing, hyperactivity, low intelligence, harsh or erratic parental discipline, divorce, low income and poor housing, which significantly contributed to future criminality. Overlapping personal and environmental risk factors were identified not only in relation to drug abuse, criminal behaviour and violence but also for educational failure, unsafe sexual behaviour and poor mental health (Dryfoos, 1990; Mrazek and Haggerty, 1994; Goldblatt and Lewis, 1998).

However, the role of prevention was not only to combat the negatives but also to enhance the positives and opportunities for child development via maximizing protective factors and processes. In such an approach, risk and protection are seen as processes rather than fixed states and protectors are the basis for opening up opportunities (Rutter, 1990). The timing of interventions was crucial, because, if they were to have the most impact, the 'early years' were key and success depended on recruiting parents – usually mothers – into the role of educators. The notion of protection was thus wider than simply protection from harm or abuse. Trying to maximize childhood 'strengths' and 'resilience' was thereby emphasized. Such an approach was seen as providing a major contribution to policies that aimed to tackle the causes of crime and antisocial behaviour.

Importantly, these developments were taking place shortly after the abduction and murder in February 1993 of two-year-old James Bulger by two eight-year-old boys, Jon Venables and Robert Thompson. Media and political responses suggested that not only was childhood in 'crisis' (Scruton, 1997) and in need of serious attention, but also that the relationship between the state, the child and the family was in need of realignment. It coincided with Tony Blair becoming shadow home secretary when he coined the phrase 'tough on crime, tough on the causes of crime' (Blair, 1993), which was to lie at the core of the emergence of New Labour in the mid-1990s. No longer could policy be based on the premise of trying to ensure the privacy of a traditional nuclear family, a central assumption of the Conservative government. If crime was to be taken seriously and social disadvantage overcome, the state would have to take a much more active, wide-ranging and interventionist role in relation to children and their development.

Conclusion

Taken together, the 'refocusing' debate, the development of the LAC project and the growing arguments for the need to emphasize 'early childhood prevention' in order to tackle a number of social problems, particularly in relation to crime and antisocial behaviour, were to provide important foundations for the key developments that were to take place following the election of the Labour government in May 1997. It was also apparent that the nature, focus and aspirations of social services departments had changed considerably from the early 1970s. The various research carried out in relation to child protection and child welfare (DH, 1995a, 2001) clearly demonstrated that social service departments defined their role narrowly and were having to set strict priorities as to what they did. They had moved away from the much more generic, community-based vision of work outlined in the Seebohm Report (1968) and the Barclay Report (1982) towards a narrow concern with child protection. This process had been reinforced by organizational changes following the Children Act 1989 and the NHS and Community Care Act 1990, whereby all departments became much more specialist. In addition, local authority social services had become particularly tarnished by the high-profile child abuse inquiries and, as Jordan and Jordan (2000) have argued, were seen as very much associated with the 'Old Labour' 'statist' approach to welfare – something Tony Blair's 'New Labour' was determined to move beyond. This is the focus of Chapter 3.

3

New Labour, children and childhood

When the Labour Party came to power in May 1997 under the leadership of Tony Blair, it presented itself as being 'new' and different from the 'old' Labour Party. New Labour aimed to introduce a new political philosophy and strategy based on the ideas of the 'Third Way' (Blair, 1998; Giddens, 1998), which would transcend Margaret Thatcher's 'property owning democracy' by combining individualism with egalitarianism in a new way. This involved the reconciliation of two apparently conflicting 'cultural projects' (6, Perri, 2000), one concerned with personal self-realization and rights to autonomy, the other with membership and community. It attempted to do this in part through the introduction of a series of abstract general principles, together with an emphasis on detailed codification, legislation, regulation, prescription, reward and punishment. The approach informed all areas of social policy.

Bill Jordan (2010a) has argued that redistributive systems, government agencies, professional expertise and public provision all underwent fundamental change in line with the idea that individuals wanted choice and were required to be responsible for themselves in the new global economy. They could achieve this independence by borrowing from banks rather than looking to governments and the state for benefits and services. Most people's welfare was seen as best served by controlling their own resources and choosing their own goods and services. Where this could not be done directly via the private market, public services were themselves to be run as if they were businesses with business objectives, strategies and processes. The role of government was to make work pay, to regulate markets in financial products, such as pensions, and to discipline, resocialize or assist those who lacked the skills for such autonomy or were deviant in other respects. Policies in relation to children and young people were key to New Labour's attempts to refashion and modernize the welfare state. It quickly became clear that its emphasis on 'education, education, education', which had been a central theme of its election campaign, was much wider in aspiration than what went on in schools and was concerned with the way children were brought up more generally (Ball, 2007).

The 'Third Way' and the 'social investment state'

At the centre of the New Labour project was an emphasis on the need to establish a new set of values. 'The Third Way is a serious reappraisal of social democracy, reaching deep into the values of the Left to develop radically new approaches' (Blair, 1998, p. 3). Along with the mantra of 'tough on crime, tough on the causes of crime', there was an insistence that rights implied responsibilities so that benefits entailed contributions, for it was asserted that the social citizenship created by the postwar welfare state had a one-sided emphasis on rights. Collective protection in the context of 'social' security was to be replaced by a greater emphasis on individualized compulsion, training and support for those unable to avail themselves of the increasingly open market opportunities. Thus, while people had a right to security, job opportunities and a stable community, they also had a responsibility to act honestly, not violate the rights of other citizens and to actively participate in the workforce.

In addition, the role of the state should shift its focus from *compensating* people for the 'diswelfares' they might have experienced as a consequence of the market to *investing* much more directly and strategically in human capital, so that individuals could compete in the market. Such a social investment perspective frames social policy expenditures as investments rather than expenditures, with the aim of increasing future dividends and improving the economic value and competitiveness of the population by, in particular, improving systems of education and providing income supplements to 'make work pay' and thereby reduce dependency (Dobrowolsky and Jenson, 2005). Social spending in the past was characterized as too passive, too present oriented and insufficiently *focused on anticipated returns on investment*. The term 'social investment state' was coined by Anthony Giddens (1998, p. 117), when he argued that:

> The guideline is investment in *human capital* wherever possible, rather than the direct provision of economic maintenance. In place of the welfare

state we should put the *social investment state*, operating in the context of a positive welfare society.

The role of social investment was to encourage a level of skill and flexibility suited to the labour markets of global capitalism and an ability to withstand and positively negotiate the increasing stresses and complexities of daily life. For social spending to be effective, therefore, it should not be consumed by current needs but should focus on future benefits. The balance of welfare spending should therefore shift from social security to services that would be explicitly preventive, promotional, positive and future oriented – particularly health and education.

In this context, the section of the population that would most benefit from investment for the future was children, particularly very young children. As Tony Blair argued in his Beveridge lecture, where he made a commitment to abolish child poverty within 20 years, there needed to be a refocusing of the objectives and operation of the welfare state:

> If the knowledge economy is an aim then work, skill and above all investing in children become essential aims of welfare ... we have made children our top priority because, as the Chancellor memorably said in his budget, 'they are 20% of the population, but they are 100% of the future'. (Blair, 1999, p. 16)

In a context where social investment for the future in order to compete in the global market was the top priority, policies in relation to children and childhood lay at the heart of the New Labour project to refashion the welfare state (Garrett, 2009a; Langan, 2010).

New Labour and modernization

If New Labour presented its strategy in terms of the Third Way, the manner it characterized its approach was in terms of a process of modernization, whereby the key elements of the state and civil society would be renewed to make them 'fit for purpose' for the globalized economy (DH, 1998a; Cabinet Office, 1999). It aimed to increase opportunity and strengthen community, by combining liberal individualism and a conservative communitarianism (Driver and Martell, 1997). There were a number of important elements to New Labour's approach to modernization, which included an emphasis on communitarianism, managerialism, joined-up government, and prevention and early intervention.

New Labour drew on a version of *communitarianism* informed by the American sociologist Amitai Etzioni (1993, 1997). Appeals to community were seen as a focus for moral renewal in the most deprived communities, asserting the need to restore to communities their moral voices and requiring a much greater sense of individual responsibility towards others. Communitarianism attempted to reactivate the institutions of civil society, particularly schools and families, into vibrant forms of social regulation and opportunity. However, New Labour's main preoccupation was not the centrality of marriage, the unity of the couple or even the permanence of parental relationships, because the nature of 'family' and 'family practices' had clearly changed considerably during the previous generation. Policy shifted from a focus on the traditional nuclear family to an approach that was concerned with childhood vulnerability and wellbeing and, crucially, upholding 'parental responsibility' (Lewis, 2001).

The community was conceptualized as a key site for explaining and intervening in a range of social problems. Central to this were attempts to enhance connections to the labour market and ensure that the control and discipline of children by their parents was strengthened so that children were brought up appropriately. Because the community was rediscovered in the context of moral panic about the collapse of order and the growing lawlessness of the young following the murder of James Bulger, it was deemed necessary for the state to actively take the lead in reinvigorating certain communities.

In practice, its ideas about community were applied only to its public policy initiatives for the most deprived communities, where the attempt was made to mobilize residents in order to improve social order and address problems of crime and antisocial behaviour, and subsequently improve security and combat potential terrorism. All other reforms of public services aimed to encourage individual choice and competition and thereby encourage people to engage in entrepreneurial activities and to leave such areas.

New Labour's emphasis on modernization was also heavily influenced by the *new public management approach* first introduced in the mid-1980s (Horton and Farnham, 1999). Originally, under the Conservative government, the primary impetus was to rein in public expenditure and introduce some of the disciplines of the private sector, particularly via the introduction of the quasi-market and the contract culture, into public services. However, the Conservative changes were not simply concerned with trying to improve 'economy, efficiency and effectiveness', but also emphasized the need to make the actions of professionals and the services they provided more 'transparent' and 'accountable' (Power, 1997). What occurred was a significant shift towards giving managers the right to manage, instituting a variety of systems of regulation to achieve value for money and thereby producing accountability to the taxpayer and the government on the one hand, and the customer and the user on the other (Clarke et al., 2000).

Under New Labour, the changes became even more rapid and intensive with the promulgation of a range of new performance targets, inspection regimes and league tables, with the avowed intent to maximize 'best value' and improve effectiveness. The process of 'audit' increased inexorably (Munro, 2004a; McDonald, C., 2006) and indicators and targets were used to drive and measure improvement (Newman, 2001; Martin, 2005). The techniques were built on the positivist assumption that 'performance', 'outputs' or 'outcomes' could be measured in an objective, rational and quantified manner (Tilbury, 2004, 2005; McAnulla, 2007).

Research and evaluation were drawn on to set standards whereby performance could be measured. While this was used to measure the performance of organizations and practitioners, it was also used to measure the behaviour of the people with whom they worked. Such an approach became increasingly evident in the field of children's services particularly following the lead established by the Looked After Children project. For example, the *Quality Protects Programme* (DH, 1998b), implemented between 1998 and 2003 as a means, primarily, of improving the standards of local authority 'corporate parenting', had a set of specified child welfare outcome measures defined in terms of developmental progress and educational attainment and linked to various organizational targets and indicators. The performance of managers, practitioners and parents was thereby inextricably linked and subject to continual monitoring and evaluation.

Closely associated with the growth of managerialism, and central to the process of modernization, was an emphasis on *joined-up government*, *partnership* and *integration* (Cabinet Office, 1999), which were seen to exemplify the drive to move beyond the old ways of organizing public services in silos in order to address 'wicked problems'. The importance of partnership and interagency coordination had been a key recommendation of all child abuse inquiries since 1973 and was at the centre of the Children Act 1989. However, New Labour saw such approaches as being fundamental to its whole approach to government (Glendinning et al., 2002).

Networks of a variety of agencies drawn from the public, private and voluntary sectors were heralded as alternatives to approaches based on either traditional bureaucracies or markets and were seen as the bedrock of a new form of governance (Clarke and Glendinning, 2002). In the process, information and communication technologies (ICTs) were seen to play a key transformational role in developing new ways of ordering the new and complex governmental systems (Rhodes, 1997). The development of *electronic government* was seen as key to the process of modernization (Hudson, 2002, 2003), where the introduction of a range of new ICTs was given high priority.

Such developments were to prove a particular challenge to practitioners, because, aside from the technical problems involved in their implementation, there was a significant tension. Although such technologies were particularly associated with strengthening the capacities for governmental surveillance and emphasized the importance of sharing citizens' personal information between different public services, there was also an increased expectation that citizens' rights and privacy should be respected (Bellamy et al., 2005; Surveillance Studies Network, 2006).

These issues were sharpened by the emphasis New Labour placed on the importance of *prevention* and *early intervention*. Not only would such an approach be seen as being better for the individuals concerned, it would provide considerable financial savings. An emphasis on *positive welfare* (Giddens, 1994, 1998, 2000) aimed to move beyond simply responding to negative problems to seeing welfare as a crucial component in promoting economic growth and individual wellbeing. It borrowed many of its concepts and technologies of calculation and intervention from the public health model, with its emphasis on primary, secondary and tertiary prevention (Freeman, 1992, 1999). In the process, universal benefits, which individuals previously received on the basis of their citizenship rights, were reconceptualized as primary services designed to maximize their health, wellbeing and employment. More significantly, the approach attempted to identify 'at risk' groups or individuals in the population and engage them in early intervention before the onset of problems or to prevent the problems getting worse. What France and Utting (2005) have called the 'risk and protection-focussed prevention paradigm' provided a key rationale and framework for developing a number of initiatives for children and parents in the first New Labour government, including the Sure Start programme, On Track and projects funded by the Children's Fund (France et al., 2010a). In its second term, there was an explicit effort to make prevention a central focus for mainstream services. For example, in September 2003, John Denham, the then minister for young people, announced that the government required local authorities to develop coordinated local plans for the implementation of preventive strategies for children and their families.

Finally, no discussion of New Labour would be complete without reference to issues of *image* and *news management* (Fairclough, 2000; Franklin, 2003), which had a profound impact on the nature of policies and how they were presented to the media and the wider public. In the process, there was a continual tension between short-termism – where government attempted to respond to public opinion and the media – and the longer term modernization project. As a consequence, New Labour often did not seem confident in the face of high-profile 'bad news' stories and wanted to be seen as authoritative and 'tough'. Such concerns were particularly evident in the arenas of criminal justice, immigration and asylum but also, as we will see in Chapter 5, in relation to child abuse scandals.

Combating social exclusion

While the overall approach of New Labour social policy emphasized the idea of social investment and expanding choice, this did not apply in quite the same way to those sections of the population who were marginalized and posed a threat to social cohesion, either now or in the future. One of the first acts of the New Labour government, in December 1997, was to establish the Social Exclusion Unit, with a strategic relationship to all government departments and located in the Cabinet Office, thus putting it 'at the heart of government'.

A number of underlying assumptions informed the New Labour approach to social exclusion from the outset:

1 Social exclusion was seen as emerging from the major changes arising from increased globalization, which had led to a loss of many extraction and manufacturing jobs and contributed to the collapse of many traditional working-class communities and thus their cultures and values.

2 Social exclusion was seen as a series of linked problems. It did not simply arise because of a lack of money, but referred to what happens when 'people or areas suffer from a combination of problems such as

unemployment, poor skills, low income, poor housing, high crime, bad health and family breakdown' (Social Exclusion Unit, 2001, p. 11), making it necessary to respond in a 'joined-up' way.

3   Social exclusion was addressed in the context of an emphasis on rights and responsibilities, whereby government made 'help available but requires a contribution from the individual and the community' (Social Exclusion Unit, 2001, p. 3).

A particular emphasis was placed on getting people into paid work. Key policies included the introduction of the national minimum wage and alterations to taxes and benefits to increase the incentives to enter the labour market through tax credit and support for childcare through the national childcare strategy. At the centre of government policy on jobs was the New Deal, with its various special programmes for distinct groups, including young people, single parents and the long-term unemployed. While opportunities were offered, a life on long-term benefit was not seen as an option for most. Much stricter tests of availability for work were introduced and unemployment benefit was replaced by jobseeker's allowance. Budgets also contained some redistributionist measures through a series of stealth taxes, which tended to benefit the working poor at the expense of the middle classes.

Addressing social exclusion, however, was not only concerned with trying to get people into work, it was also intimately concerned with improving behaviour and social functioning. A variety of factors associated with certain individuals, families and communities were seen as putting certain people at risk of social exclusion: poor parenting, truancy, drug abuse, lack of facilities, homelessness, as well as unemployment and low income. In particular, an attack on social exclusion also required an attack on the causes of crime as well as crime itself. The behaviour of children and young people was seen as in need of attention and, in particular, it was important that parents took their responsibilities seriously: the introduction of parental control orders, curfew orders and a general concern with antisocial behaviour were all given a high priority, together with the major reform of policy and practice in relation to youth offending (Frost and Parton, 2009, Ch. 5; Churchill, 2011).

Policy was less concerned with redistribution to aid social and material equality and more concerned with integration either by returning people to the labour market or altering the behaviour and characteristics of the excluded themselves. Those who, for whatever reasons, were resistant were subject to increased regulation and discipline (Veit-Wilson, 1998; Byrne, 2005). The emphasis was on equality of opportunity not outcome.

Ruth Levitas (1996, 2005) argued that New Labour's explanation and approach to social exclusion reflected a 'new Durkheimian hegemony', which saw deprivation and inequality as peripheral phenomena occurring at the margins of society, and ignored forms of domination that structure the lives of the excluded and included alike. For New Labour, poverty and disadvantage, as Durkheim argued, were symptoms not of the capitalist market economy, but of pathological deviations from what was essentially a fair and harmonious society. Such a conception of social exclusion implied minimalist reform and was concerned with 'exclusion from access to the ladders of social improvement' (Kruger, 1997, p. 20); it was not a problem related to 'the length of the ladder or the distance between the rungs' (Levitas, 2005, p. 153). 'Concluding the argument in terms of "inclusion of the excluded" constituted an argument for pushing them "just over" the line. They remain borderline' (Goodwin, 1996, p. 348).

Levitas argued that the New Labour approach to social exclusion was poised between the influences of two major discourses. The first, what she called the *social integrationist discourse* (SID), stressed the importance of moral integration and social cohesion, and regarded the economy in general and paid work in the labour market in particular as the necessary means for achieving this. What was absent was any serious recognition of the existence and value of alternative modes of social integration outside the ambit of economic relations of exchange. There was little acknowledgement of the social contribution made by unpaid workers, notably women, and a failure to address the way paid work for many did not provide a strong source of social identity, discipline and self-esteem. This was particularly the case for countless males following the collapse of many traditional industries.

The second discourse identified by Levitas, the *moral underclass discourse* (MUD), deployed cultural rather than material explanations of social exclusion and was particularly associated with the work of Charles Murray (1990, 1994). Murray had argued that an *underclass* had long existed in the USA, but was now spreading in Britain. He likened it to a 'contagious disease', which was spread by people whose values were contaminating the life of whole communities by rejecting the work ethic and the family ethic that were central to the mainstream culture. According to Murray, the existence of an underclass could be diagnosed by three symptoms: illegitimacy, crime, and dropping out of the labour force.

Murray argued that these three factors interacted to produce pathological communities in which the socialization of children, especially boys, was inadequate. The absence of fathers meant there was a lack of role models, particularly for boys, who then felt driven to prove their masculinity in destructive ways. The benefits system encouraged a culture of idleness and welfare dependency, where family structures and socialization processes had broken down, and where only a reinforcement of the work ethic, achieved by means of a continual tightening of the benefit eligibility criteria, could reintegrate the excluded into mainstream society. Such an approach had certain similarities with the communitarianism of Etzioni, and would support approaches that aimed to emphasize 'no rights without responsibilities', and being 'tough on crime and tough on the causes of crime'.

Levitas also outlined a third discourse on social exclusion, what she termed the *redistributionist discourse* (RED), which had its roots in the critical social policy literature, particularly that of Peter Townsend (1979), a number of publications from the Child Poverty Action Group (Golding, 1986; Lister, 1990; Walker and Walker, 1997) and other writers on the left (Jordan, 1996). Here, the prime cause of social exclusion was seen as arising from the increasing inequalities of income, wealth and power. The solutions proposed were explicitly redistributive and included increasing taxation on the rich, a reduced reliance on means-tested benefits and that benefits should be paid primarily on the basis of citizenship rights. Social exclusion was explicitly located in wider issues of power. Such an approach recognized that the problem of social exclusion was as much, if not more, to do with the behaviour and lifestyle of the rich as it was to do with that of the poor and must therefore be subject to change.

New Labour's policy for children and families

New Labour's policies towards children and families were located in the priority given to emphasizing social investment in order to compete in the increasingly globalized economic order, and the importance of attacking social exclusion. The latter was addressed primarily in terms of providing more opportunities and encouragements for paid work, while trying to modify the lifestyles and behaviours of those who were not able to do so, together with ensuring that they did not undermine the rights of others and, in the process, engage in crime and other antisocial behaviours. Policies in relation to children and families were at the core of New Labour's social programme.

After coming to power, it introduced a plethora of new policies and made significant changes to other long-established ones (see Millar and Ridge, 2002; Skinner, 2003; Pugh and Parton, 2003; Fawcett et al., 2004). These included:

- *General support for all parents with children*, including increasing the value of child benefits, the introduction of children's tax to replace the married couple's tax allowance, the introduction of a national childcare strategy, improving maternity and paternity leave.

- *Specific and targeted support for poor families with children*, including the introduction of working tax credit, child tax credit and childcare tax credit; also the special services to aid welfare to work under the New Deal initiative, where personal advisers gave practical advice and support and there was considerable encouragement and finances available to enter the labour market or take up training.

- *Initiatives specifically targeted at disadvantaged children who are 'at risk' of being socially excluded*, particularly the Sure Start programme, Connexions and the Children's Fund.

At the same time, New Labour placed considerable emphasis on the 'responsibilization' of parents (Churchill, 2011). Not only were entitlements and support conditional on the exercise of proper individual responsibility, but adults with children carried extra responsibilities. The idea of 'parental responsibility' lay at the centre of a range of policies in the broad criminal justice, education, health and child welfare areas. Parental responsibility was not only concerned with ensuring that children attended and achieved at school, but also that they did not engage in criminal or antisocial behaviour, and that their health and development were fully supported. Parents were seen to play the central role in creating the 'hard working' and 'prosocial' adults of the future.

Probably the most distinctive New Labour policy initiative in this area was the development of the Sure Start programme – which has been characterized as the 'jewel in New Labour's crown' (Frost and Parton, 2009, Ch. 7; Eisenstadt, 2011) and was announced in 1998. At the outset, the programmes were located in the 20 per cent of areas with the children in greatest need. The aim was to work with disadvantaged parents and children under four to improve social and emotional development, health, the child's ability to learn, and to strengthen families and communities, to be measured, in part, by reducing the number of children re-registered on child protection registers. As Polly Toynbee and David Walker (2001, p. 15) argued: 'Sure Start became an administrative model for other Labour interventions: a small central unit setting targets for local committees, often made up from but not led by councils.' The programme emphasized the importance of early child development and the impact of multiple disadvantages and their relationship to social exclusion later in life. While the success of Sure Start was never easy to measure (see, for example, Rutter, 2006, 2007), the decision was taken to expand it so that by 2010 a national network of 3,500 Sure Start Children's Centres would cover the whole country – a political and economic investment probably unprecedented in the history of child welfare in England.

Conclusion

New Labour drew on a number of ideas to produce a distinctive approach to social policy and its attempts at social and economic renewal more generally. In particular, it brought together an emphasis on the importance of individual autonomy and the mobility of market relations with elements of a socially conservative view of the family and civil society, particularly in terms of its emphasis on responsibility. In practice, the New Labour government's egalitarian aims were always dominated by its concerns to increase methodological individualism, so that its communitarianism was reserved for the socially excluded.

The approach sought to transform the collectivist legacy of the Keynsian period and assumed that not only did individuals want more consumer freedoms and choices, but that they should be required to become more independent and self-reliant than they had been in the welfare state era (Jordan, 2006a). Instead of expecting collective solutions to issues of the life cycle, the economic cycle, change and crisis, they were increasingly required to develop personal resources and material property to cope with all eventualities.

What has now become clear is that while New Labour did have an impact on reducing child poverty, it never seriously delivered on its egalitarian agenda. As Matthew Taylor (2009) has commented, the individualism that triumphed under Margaret Thatcher in the 1980s remained the dominant cultural feature of the New Labour era, and the egalitarian values proclaimed by Tony Blair and the Third Way failed to gain any real purchase in the social order. In effect, the Third Way's attempt to fuse individualism and egalitarianism failed.

Increasingly, New Labour emphasized the importance of individuals choosing among a range of alternative amenities and providers in terms of hospitals, schools and social care resources and encouraged citizens to develop strategies for finding the 'best' facilities. In particular, the 'choice agenda' was promoted as the key mechanism for improving competition and thereby driving up quality in public services (Jordan, 2005, 2006b; Clarke et al., 2006), particularly in its third term of government following its re-election in May 2005. For example, increased freedoms for and greater differentiation between schools, particularly secondary schools, were seen as a major way of improving the performance of the schools themselves and the academic achievements of their students.

Although presented as a coherent and logical mix of principles and policy developments, the potential for tensions and contradictions could never be underestimated. In particular, it was always possible that the emphasis on greater individualism, choice and personal responsibility in order to encourage greater innovation and competition in the global economy would undermine attempts to increase a sense of community cohesion and national solidarity. The emphasis on the need to attract foreign capital by keeping taxation low in order to ensure that the UK, and London in particular, became a global centre of finance was always likely to increase social inequality and thereby undermine attempts to improve social inclusion.

The role of government was to encourage autonomy, choice and risk taking and any external state regulation as was required was ideally exercised through contracts that were seen as mutually beneficial and voluntary. This was the optimistic approach adopted by the private sector – particularly big business, the banks and financial services generally.

However, this was very different to its approach to public services and certain target populations. While the aim was to transform the collective infrastructure and principles of public services in order to meet consumer preferences, what happened in practice was that a tide of increased regulation, micromanagement and audit spread across all public sector organizations. It seemed that frontline professionals could not be trusted to deliver what government required. As a consequence, government agencies did not become more like private businesses and service users did not become more like customers, despite the continual attempts to introduce new terminology and a whole range of new ICT systems. What emerged was not a new morality of self-reflexivity and striving for improvement, but a mechanistic, top-down reliance on rules and procedures on the one hand and commercial logos, symbols and mission statements on the other (Jordan, 2010b). Nowhere were these developments more evident than in the changes in children's services, which were so central to New Labour's attempts to reform social welfare and public services more generally and which I consider in more detail in Chapter 4.

4

The *Every Child Matters* agenda and beyond

As I have argued in Chapter 3, policies towards parents, children and young people lay at the heart of New Labour attempts to refashion the welfare state. Not only were children and young people the focus of attempts to educate and improve the quality of the future workforce, but they were also seen as particularly at risk of social exclusion and were, therefore, identified as in need of special attention. The numbers of children in poverty had trebled between 1979 and New Labour coming to power in 1997, to include a third of all children and young people. Children and young people were seen as particularly vulnerable to the effects of increasing divorce, single parenthood and the growing violence and malaise in certain communities, and they often accounted for a high proportion of crime and antisocial behaviour.

In the first term of New Labour between 1997 and 2001, the policies introduced more specifically in relation to children's services were located in this wider policy context and concerns about child abuse and child protection were not given any significant priority. As the White Paper *Modernising Social Services* (DH, 1998a, p. 41) argued:

> Social services for children cannot be seen in isolation from the wider range of children's services delivered by local authorities and other agencies. The Government is committed to taking action through a broad range of initiatives to strengthen family life, to reduce social exclusion and anti-social behaviour among children, and to give every child the opportunity of a healthy, happy, successful life.

A major emphasis in the White Paper was on the need to introduce a range of new regulations, targets, monitoring and management information systems for social services departments. This was made explicit with the launch of the *Quality Protects Programme* (DH, 1998b), which invested £885 million between 1999 and 2004 on the basis of detailed annual 'management action plans' from each local authority. While a central feature of Quality Protects was improving outcomes for 'looked after' children, following the Utting Report (1997), particularly in terms of their educational achievement and support for care leavers, the programme was much wider in focus. In particular, it was framed in terms of social service departments 'improving the well-being of children in need for whom our local authority has taken on direct responsibility' (DH, 1998b, para. 5.2).

However, following its re-election in June 2001, the government made it clear that it felt progress was slow and that further reform was warranted, such that the 2002 Spending Review (HM Treasury, 2002) argued that despite extensive investment in children's services, most were not having the desired impact on the most disadvantaged children. It recommended that support for children 'at risk' should be better focused on preventive services, the preventive elements of mainstream services should address the 'known risk factors', and improving the 'integration' of services was crucial, which required strong leadership at national and local level, underpinned by 'effective performance management, driving forward reform'. In particular:

> local partners must agree to carry out new functions including: better strategic planning; systematic identification, referral and tracking regimes to ensure children don't fall through the services safety net; and allocating responsibilities for individualised packages of support for these at greatest risk. The Government believes there is a case for structural change to effect the better coordination of children's services, and will pilot Children's Trusts which will unify at the local level the various agencies involved in providing children's services. (HM Treasury, 2002, para. 28.5)

As the above quotation demonstrates, the framework for the 'transformation' of children's services, which would take place from late 2004 onwards, was clearly outlined in the 2002 Spending Review.

However, when the consultative Green Paper *Every Child Matters* (HM Treasury, 2003) was published in September 2003, it was presented as the government's response to a child abuse scandal – the Laming Report (2003) into the death of Victoria Climbié, who had died at the hands of her 'aunt', Marie Therese Kouao, and her boyfriend, Carl Manning, on 25 February 2000. Victoria had been born in the Ivory Coast on 2 November 1991 and brought to London via France in April 1999. In the following 18 months up to Victoria's death, the family were known to four different London social services departments, two hospitals, two police child protection teams and an NSPCC family centre; however, none had been able to intervene to save her life and at no point had the seriousness of her situation been recognized. The case seemed to have many of the similarities of most of the tragic child death scandals of the previous 30 years (see Parton, 2004, for a critical discussion). The government had set up a public inquiry, chaired by Lord Laming, and, following its publication on 28 January 2003, made it clear that to ensure that such a tragedy did not happen again and to avoid having to establish any more expensive, high-profile public inquiries in the future, it was going to engage in a major programme of reform of children's services.

Every Child Matters and the Children Act 2004

It is apparent that while the Green Paper was informed by the Laming Report, it was primarily concerned with taking forward the government's planned agenda for reforming children's services (Parton, 2006a, 2006b), but with a much broader remit than previously envisaged. Rather than being entitled 'Children at Risk', as suggested by the 2002 Spending Review, the consultative Green Paper was entitled *Every Child Matters* (HM Treasury, 2003). This was not to say that the Green Paper was not centrally concerned with 'risk', as clearly it was, but it was framed in recognition that any child, at some point in their life, could be seen as vulnerable to some form of risk. The government therefore deemed it necessary that *all children* should be covered by its proposals. Universal services were seen as offering early (primary) intervention to prevent the emergence of specific risk factors; thus, it was important to ensure the *integration* of universal, targeted and specialist services. Risk was seen as a pervasive, potential threat to all children, and it was in this context that two figures included in the Green Paper (see Figures 4.1 and 4.2) are particularly important in helping to understand how the reform of children's services was conceptualized.

Underpinning the proposals were two basic assumptions concerning the nature of recent social change and the state of current knowledge. First, the Green Paper stated that, over the previous generation, children's lives had undergone 'profound change'. While children had more opportunities than ever before and had benefited from rising prosperity and better health, they also faced more uncertainties and risks. They faced earlier exposure to sexual activity, drugs and alcohol, and family patterns had

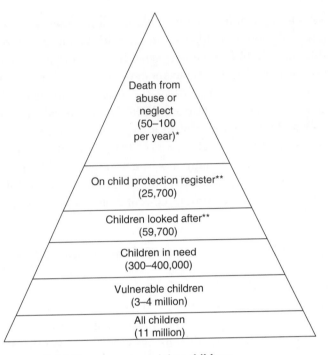

Figure 4.1   *Every Child Matters*: categorizing children

Source: HM Treasury, 2003, p. 15.
Key: * These children may or may not be on the child protection register, nor looked after, nor vulnerable;
** these children are included in the children in need figure, and not all children on the child protection
register are children looked after.

changed significantly. There were more lone parents, more divorces and
more women in paid employment, all of which made family life more
complex and, potentially, made the position of children more precarious.

Second, however, the Green Paper asserted that these changes had
come about at a time when we had increased knowledge and expertise
and were therefore in a better position to respond to these new uncertainties and risks. In particular, 'we better understand the importance
of early influences on the development of values and behaviour' (HM
Treasury, 2003, p. 15). Thus, it was important to ensure that this knowledge was drawn on to inform the changes being introduced:

> We have a good idea what factors shape children's life chances. Research
> tells us that the risk of experiencing negative outcomes is concentrated in
> children with certain characteristics. (HM Treasury, 2003, p. 17)

The more risk factors a child experienced, such as being excluded
from school and family breakdown, the more likely it was they would

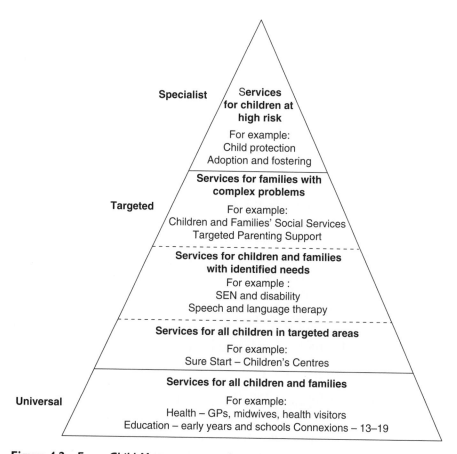

Figure 4.2 *Every Child Matters:* **targeted services within a universal context**

Source: HM Treasury, 2003, p. 21.

experience negative outcomes. Because of this increased knowledge about risk factors associated with a child's development, it was seen as important to intervene at an earlier stage in order to forestall problems in later life, particularly in relation to antisocial behaviour, crime and unemployment. The approach adopted what France and Utting (2005) have called the 'paradigm of risk and protection-focused prevention'. Early intervention in childhood thus provided a major strategy for overcoming social exclusion for children and avoiding problems in adulthood.

The other area where knowledge and expertise had grown, and which was seen as vital in order to take policy and practice forward, was in relation to the major changes that had taken place in the development of ICT systems. The age of electronic government (Hudson, 2002, 2003) was seen as having major implications for the reform and development of children's services. Not only would this provide the potential for identifying problems and enhancing attempts to intervene at an earlier stage, but it would also allow different organizations and professionals to share information in order to ensure that children's problems were not missed and children did not fall through 'the net'.

The government wanted to 'put children at the heart of our policies, and to organize services around their needs' (HM Treasury, 2003, p. 9). The aim was that there should be one person in charge locally and nationally and that key services for children would be integrated within a common organizational focus at both levels, thereby enhancing *integration* and clarifying the lines of *accountability*. At central government level, this would be via the creation of a new minister based in the Department for Education and Skills (DfES), the 'minister for children, young people and families', and at local authority level via the creation of new directors of children's services and a lead council member who would be responsible for children's social services and education in new departments of children's services. It was also planned to further integrate all local services for children and young people via the establishment of Children's Trusts. In many respects, the template for integrating services by Children's Trusts was developed from the way Sure Start programmes had operated (Hawker, 2006). Apart from education and children's social care, Children's Trusts would also include most children's health services and other local services. It was also planned to create statutory Local Safeguarding Children's Boards (LSCBs) and a new office of a Children's Commissioner for England. In effect, the proposals would bring to an end the organizational structures introduced in 1971 with the establishment of a *family* service and would bring about the dissolution of social service departments.

In the spring of 2004, the government announced it was going ahead with the changes and published *Every Child Matters: Next Steps* (DfES, 2004a), together with the Children Bill, which received royal assent on 15 November 2004. It was planned that all the changes would be in place by the end of 2008. While the Children Act 1989 was to continue to provide the primary legislative framework for children's services, the government felt it needed strengthening in certain respects. The key theme of the Children Act 2004 was to encourage partnership and sharpen accountability between a wide range of health, welfare, education and criminal justice agencies. It was described as the most significant change in the philosophy and delivery of children's services in England since 1948, when local authority children's departments were first established (Hudson, 2005a).

Every Child Matters: Change for Children

On 1 December 2004, *Every Child Matters: Change for Children* (DfES, 2004b) was launched under the signature of 16 ministers from 13 government departments. It set out the national framework for the local 'change programme' to 'transform children's services' (Garrett, 2009a; Langan, 2010), together with the timetable for introducing the statutory changes and the publication dates of the statutory guidance.

Outcomes for all children

At the centre of the changes was an ambition to improve the *outcomes* for all children and narrow the gap in outcomes between those who did well and those who did not. The outcomes were defined in terms of:

- being healthy
- staying safe
- enjoying and achieving
- making a positive contribution
- achieving economic wellbeing.

Together, these five outcomes were seen as key to 'wellbeing in child-hood and later life'. Such an ambition required 'whole system' change in local children's services and would be secured through more integrated frontline delivery, processes, strategy and governance. The model of 'whole system change, the children's trust in action' (DfES, 2004b, p. 13) was represented in *Every Child Matters: Change for Children*, as shown in Figures 4.3 and 4.4.

At the core were the 'outcomes for children and young people':

> The outcomes are inter-dependent. They show the important relationship between educational achievement and well-being. Children and young people learn and thrive when they are healthy, safeguarded from harm and engaged. The evidence shows that educational achievement is the most effective way to improve outcomes for poor children and break cycles of deprivation. (DfES, 2004b, para. 2.2)

Figure 4.3 The Children's Trust in action

Source: DfES, 2004b, p. 6.

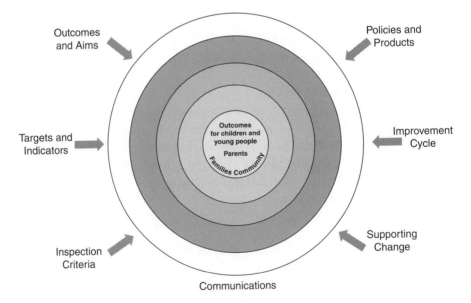

Figure 4.4 National framework for local change

Source: DfES, 2004b, p. 6.

The final sentence of this quotation is of particular significance. Ever since the general election of 1997, with its claims that its main priorities were 'education, education, education', New Labour had given education a central role in its social programme. Not only was it a key element in its aim to prepare the future workforce to participate in a knowledge economy, so that Britain could compete and lead in the increasingly globalized world, but it was also a key element in its policy agenda to tackle social exclusion. As a consequence, education – in its broadest sense, and including early years services – had become the primary vehicle for trying to address a series of social problems.

At the centre of the changes was an explicit performance management approach, which brought together a long-established way of working from the world of corporate business to the improvement and measurement of children's lives. The performance of professionals and parents was to be managed and monitored in the interests of improving outcomes for children (Luckock, 2007). The reforms can be seen to constitute the epitome of rational decision making, with everything flowing from a top-down, outcomes-led approach (Hudson, 2005a, 2005b, 2005c). In practice, the measurement of the five outcomes was restricted to the existing standards, indicators and targets across the partner agencies. As a result, 'enjoying and achieving', for example, was to be judged primarily in terms of school attendance and performance, while 'making a positive contribution' was to be measured primarily in terms of a reduction in offending, school exclusions and antisocial behaviour.

The whole system change was much wider and more ambitious than the concerns that lay at the heart of the Laming Report into the death of Victoria Climbié. Being 'safe from maltreatment, neglect, violence and sexual exploitation' was just one of the six aims seen as important for achieving the 'staying safe' outcome, indicating just how far the changes were trying to ensure that narrowly defined child protection concerns did not dominate day-to-day child welfare policy and practice as they had done in the past. Beyond developing systems for integrating local governance arrangements, there was also an emphasis on integrated frontline delivery and integrated processes.

Integrated frontline delivery

The integration of children's services required that universal services should have easy access to effective targeted and specialist services, following the frameworks outlined in *Every Child Matters* (see Figures 4.1 and 4.2). The *ECM: Change for Children* programme (DfES, 2004b) was introduced alongside the *National Service Framework for Children, Young People and Maternity Services* (DH, 2004), the government's 10-year strategy for early years and childcare (HM Treasury et al., 2004) and the strategy in relation to young people (DfES, 2005a). A central part of the strategy was ensuring that early years and childcare services, schools and health services were integrated into the new arrangements, so that they could identify at an early stage those children who might be experiencing problems or had extra needs.

To achieve this, it was seen as important to develop a strategy for the 'children's workforce' (DfES, 2006a), whereby a single national quali-fications' framework could be established, together with identifying the 'common skills and knowledge' that everyone working with children, young people and families should be able to demonstrate (DfES, 2005b). Developing the role of the *lead professional* was seen as key. The lead professional would act as a single point of contact for the child or family, coordinating delivery and reducing the overlap and inconsistency in the services received. Lead professionals would work with children and young people with *additional and complex needs*, who were therefore deemed to require an integrated package of support from more than one practitioner (as represented in Figures 4.5 and 4.6). The lead professional could be designated from any of the professionals working with the child and did not need to come from any particular professional background – it depended on the particular circumstances and needs (DfES, 2006b, 2006c).

Integrated processes

The development of common processes, a common language and better information sharing were all seen as important for the integration of services, and the introduction of the Common Assessment Framework (CAF) and Information Sharing Index were both to play a key role in this.

The CAF would be used whenever it was felt a child may have 'additional needs' requiring extra targeted support. Such needs may be 'cross-cutting' and, according to the guidance (DfES, 2006d, 2006e), might include:

- disruptive or antisocial behaviour
- overt parental conflict or lack of parental support/boundaries

- involvement in or risk of offending
- poor attendance or exclusion from school
- experiencing bullying
- special educational needs
- disabilities
- disengagement from education, training or employment post-16
- poor nutrition
- ill health
- substance misuse
- anxiety or depression
- housing issues
- pregnancy and parenthood.

It is notable that child abuse and neglect were not listed – these changes were not focused on child abuse but problems and additional needs of lesser significance. The guidance suggested that a CAF should be carried out at any time when someone working with a child or young person felt that they might not progress towards the five ECM outcomes without additional services and it was to include a wide-ranging set of data covering most aspects of a child's health and development, including details about parents and siblings. It followed the format introduced by the Assessment Framework in 2000 (DH et al., 2000). On 25 July 2007, the government announced that the implementation of the CAF would be based on a single national electronic IT system and would, in future, be known as eCAF.

The CAF guidance for practitioners (DfES, 2006d) and managers (DfES, 2006e) provided an important conceptual map of the way services were seen to relate to particular categories of children and the role the new 'processes and tools to support children and families' were to play in the new arrangements. In many respects, Figures 4.5 and 4.6 demonstrate how thinking about the integration of children's services had moved on from ECM in 2003, represented in Figures 4.1 and 4.2 earlier.

In parallel with the CAF, children's services were also expected to improve the practice of sharing information between professionals. Section 12 of the Children Act 2004 required children's services

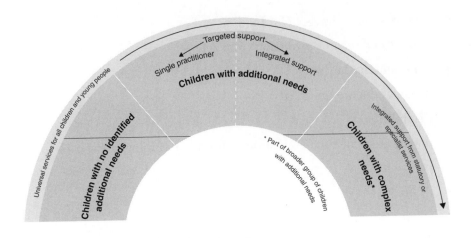

Figure 4.5   Continuum of needs and services

Source: DfES, 2006d, p. 6.

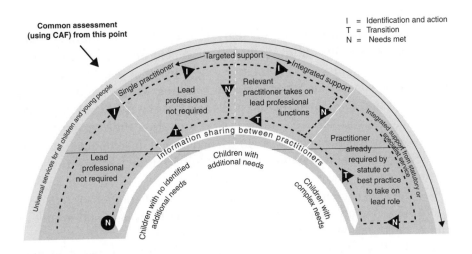

Figure 4.6   Processes and tools to support children and families

Source: DfES, 2006d, p. 7.

authorities (local authorities) to operate a national Information Sharing Index covering all children living in the area. The government intended that this would assist practitioners in achieving the five outcomes. The index was not intended to be narrowly focused on child protection but aimed to improve the sharing of information between professionals, in order to improve the wellbeing of *all* children.

It would contain:

- the child's name, address, gender and date of birth
- a number identifying the child
- the name and contact details of any person with parental responsibility or who had care of the child at any time
- the name and contact details of any educational institution, primary medical services, or any specialist or targeted service, which was, or had been, provided to the person by, or on behalf of, a local authority
- the name and contact details of a lead professional for that child (if appointed).

Section 12 also allowed for the inclusion of any other information, excluding medical records or other personal records, as the secretary of state might specify by regulation. For sensitive areas, that is, those relating to sexual health, mental health and substance abuse, information would only be included on the database with the consent of the parent or young person. The lack of consent could be overridden in certain circumstances to be specified in regulations, but would include cases where there were genuine child protection concerns. Access to the contact details of personnel in sensitive services would be restricted to index management teams. In addition to the information about services in contact with the child, s.12(4)(g) also allowed for inclusion of 'information as to the existence of any cause for concern in relation to him [the child]'.

Both in debates about the Children Bill in the House of Lords and following its passage into law, there was considerable criticism about this element of the legislation, including a report by the House of Commons Education and Skills Committee (2005), which did not feel that it was the most cost-effective way of improving outcomes for children. It also had 'significant concerns' about the security, confidentiality and access arrangements. In addition, the Information Commissioner's Office (2005) raised concerns about children's and young people's rights to privacy and the need to justify the sharing of information. Research exploring the views of young people found they would be reluctant to share information of a sensitive nature and some said they would prefer to forego vital services if their need for privacy was not respected (Hilton and Mills, 2007). These criticisms were developed in detail in a report for the Information Commissioner's Office by the Foundation for Information Policy Research (Anderson et al., 2006). Eileen Munro, from the London School of Economics, was a key member.

What was seen as particularly alarming was the broad and ill-defined concept of 'a cause for concern', which was introduced as the key threshold to share information and depended on the subjective interpretation of practitioners (Munro, 2004b; Penna, 2005; Munro and Parton, 2007). As a result of the criticisms, the database was repackaged in May 2007 as ContactPoint and its objectives stated a little less ambitiously to:

- help practitioners identify quickly a child with whom they have contact, and whether that child is getting the universal services (education, primary healthcare) to which they are entitled

- enable earlier identification of needs and earlier and more effective action to address these needs by providing a tool for practitioners to identify who else is involved with a particular child

- be an important tool to encourage and support better communication and closer working between different professionals and practitioners (DCSF, 2007a)

and any reference to including information on the database in response to 'a cause for concern' was deleted.

ContactPoint was presented as a key element of the *ECM: Change for Children* programme to transform children's services by aiming to support more effective prevention and early intervention. In particular, it would provide a tool to support better communication among authorized users across education, health, social care and youth offending. It aimed to provide a quick, cost-effective way for practitioners to find out who else was working with the same child or young person, allow them to contact one another more effectively, thus making it easier to deliver more coordinated support and identify gaps in service provision, particularly of a universal nature. Because of the concerns about human rights issues and the security of the information, a complex process of managing access to and use of the system was to be established. Each local authority would need to establish a specialist team to support the ongoing migration, matching and cleansing of the data and provide technical support and advice for authorized users. Before being able to access ContactPoint, all users would need security clearance (including enhanced Criminal Records Bureau clearance), a user name, PIN and security token. All ContactPoint users would complete mandatory training, which would include components on the safe and secure use of ContactPoint and would make explicit the importance of compliance with the Data Protection Act 1998 and the Human Rights Act 1998.

While it was to be a national system, the data would be partitioned into 150 parts, each relating to a local authority in England. The total set-up cost was estimated at £224 million, costing £41 million/annum to operate once fully established. It was also estimated that £88 million/annum would be saved on existing services, primarily as a result of the time saved by practitioners trying to identify and make contact with other professionals and services who knew the child concerned (Parton, 2008).

ContactPoint was just one element of the *ECM: Change for Children* programme. However, even in its less ambitious form, it demonstrated the priority that was given to the importance of practitioners sharing information in order to provide a coordinated and integrated range of services to enhance prevention and early intervention. The accumulation and exchange of information about children had taken on a strategic role to ensure that children did not fall through the various 'nets' designed to protect them from harm and to ensure they received early help and thereby fulfil their potential. In the words of Margaret Hodge, then minister for children, in her Foreword to *Every Child Matters: Next Steps* (DfES, 2004a, p. 3), the vision was of 'a shift to prevention whilst strengthening protection'.

Together, the role of the lead professional, CAF and this renewed emphasis on sharing information were seen as key elements in the transformation and integration of children's services. This was represented as the windscreen in Figure 4.6 above, which demonstrates how the integration of universal, specialist and targeted services was conceptualized, the role that the lead professional, the CAF and information sharing would play, and how, in the process, children in the population would be categorized as having either 'no identified needs', 'additional needs', or 'complex needs'.

In addition, the Integrated Children's System, which was designed specifically for children's social care, would include the case records and details of all children and families known to social workers whether they were accommodated in care, subject to a child protection plan, or a 'child in need' (DH, 2003; Walker and Scott, 2004; Cleaver et al., 2008). All these changes were taking place at the same time as the introduction of electronic records in all areas of social care (Information Policy Unit, 2003). The gathering, sharing and analysis of information, particularly in electronic form, lay at the centre of the *ECM: Change for Children* programme (DfES, 2004b). The changes introduced under the *ECM: Change for Children* programme were clearly the most ambitious attempted in the history of children's services in England. In casting its gaze on all children to ensure that 'every child' achieved their potential and trying to integrate universal, targeted and specialist services, there were considerable implications for everyone who worked with children and young people. As I argued at the time, it pointed to a significant shift in the relationships between children, parents, professionals and the state and I suggested we were witnessing the emergence of the 'preventive-surveillance state' (Parton, 2008).

Building on *Every Child Matters*: developments from 2005 to 2008

Although the *ECM: Change for Children* programme was the culmi-nation of a variety of policy developments and debates in the second New Labour government of June 2001–May 2005, the serious process of implementation in local authorities did not start until mid-2005. By then, New Labour had been re-elected for a third term of office and Tony Blair, the prime minister, quickly started making statements that he felt the pace of change, particularly in relation to health, education and social welfare generally, had been too slow and that more radical changes were needed. It was also a period when the divisions within the Labour Party and the government between the 'Blairites' supporting Tony Blair and the 'Brownites' supporting Gordon Brown, chancellor of the exchequer, became more obvious. While part of these divisions arose from personal animosities and difficulties, there were also policy differences, evident in the policies relating to children, young people and families. We can perhaps separate the period from May 2005 to June 2007, when Tony Blair continued as prime minister, with the period from July 2007, when Gordon Brown became prime minister.

Following his re-election in May 2005, Tony Blair made it clear that he felt progress in relation to overcoming social exclusion and antisocial behaviour had not been as successful as he had hoped. On 10 January 2006, he launched the *Respect Action Plan* (Respect Task Force, 2006), which was supported by nine government departments, headed by the Home Office. It aimed to tackle the underlying causes of antisocial behaviour, to intervene earlier where problems occurred, and broaden efforts to address new areas of poor behaviour. It aspired to build 'stable families and strong, cohesive communities', because 'poor parenting' and 'problem families' were seen to lie at the root of the problems.

These themes were made more explicit when, on 11 September 2006, the government launched *Reaching Out: An Action Plan on Social Exclusion* (HM Government, 2006a). The Action Plan examined the reasons why, despite the considerable amount of investment and reform, including the disappointing early results of the Sure Start initiative (Ormerod, 2005; Belsky et al., 2006; Rutter, 2006, 2007), there were still individuals and families who were cut off from the mainstream of society:

> About 2.5 per cent of every generation seem to be stuck in a lifetime of disadvantage. Their problems are multiple, entrenched and often passed down through generations. (HM Government, 2006a, p. 3)

As John Welshman (2006a, 2007) argued, in both the Action Plan and Tony Blair's speech that launched it, the explanations of the problems and the proposals for policy and practice were similar to Sir Keith Joseph's ideas about the 'cycle of deprivation' in the early 1970s. The emphasis of government policies seemed to be shifting to a more muscular interventionist stance towards those deemed to be 'hard to reach' by earlier programmes, particularly where they were perceived as being members of a hard-core underclass. Policy seemed to be heading in a direction increasingly consistent with Ruth Levitas's moral underclass discourse (MUD), discussed in Chapter 3, where the focus of attention should be on trying to change the behaviour, culture and values of a small number of families where the problems were passed between generations.

The Action Plan said that while it aimed to build on the *ECM: Change for Children* programme, it felt that progress was patchy and generally slow and there was a much tougher ring to what was planned. There was a particular concern about those who were hard to reach, not so much because they were not known to services but because they were 'hard to engage' and 'hard to help effectively'. It seemed that from now on, social inclusion was going to mean tougher policies and tougher practices and, in autumn 2006, the Social Exclusion Task Force, based in the Cabinet Office, was established to drive the initiative forward. One of its first jobs was to carry out a Families at Risk Review to report later in 2007.

However, the success of New Labour's policies for children and families, particularly in relation to the 'socially excluded', surfaced as a significant political issue in February 2007 following the publication of the UNICEF report (2007), which placed the UK bottom out of 21 economically advanced nations in terms of the overall wellbeing of children and young people. The publication of the report coincided with the murder of a 14-year-old boy in South London amid escalating concerns about young gangs and knife and gun crime. Political and media comment was considerable, similar to that in 1993 following the murder of James Bulger, and suggested that childhood was in crisis and a terrible reflection on the state of British society. At his monthly press conference on 27 February, Tony Blair spoke at length about social exclusion and launched *Reaching Out: Progress on Social Exclusion* (Social Exclusion Task Force, 2007) in an attempt to address some of the concerns raised and demonstrate the progress that New Labour had made since coming to power.

Essentially, he argued that New Labour policies had proved successful and that since 1997, the bottom 20 per cent of society had seen their incomes rise faster than the richest 20 per cent, although he accepted that this did not apply to the very rich. He also argued that while 1.6 million children had been lifted out of poverty, there still remained a small number of families with multiple problems who were proving particularly hard to reach, and it was these who would need special attention in the future.

On 27 June 2007, Gordon Brown took over from Tony Blair as prime minister and one of his first decisions was to establish a new government department – the Department for Children, Schools and Families (DCSF) – and appoint Ed Balls, his close political ally, to become its first secretary of state. It was clear that this was to be a central plank of Gordon Brown's attempt to renew the New Labour project, while putting his own brand on policy in this now central and high priority field. Ed Balls' first decision was to establish a process of consultation in order to produce a Children's Plan, which would provide the aims and framework for policy change until 2020.

On 11 December 2007, Ed Balls launched the government's *The Children Plan: Building Brighter Futures* (DCSF, 2007b). *The Guardian* reported its publication with the headline 'Fitter, happier and better educated: the hope for 2020', and wrote:

> The government has set a 13-year deadline to dramatically reduce illiteracy and antisocial behaviour and eradicate child poverty in a children's plan which makes a promise from the heart of government that children will be happier by 2020.

The sprawling 170-page document places schools at the hub of an array of measures designed to boost support for parents and provide children and young people with better play and activities to steer them away from crime. (Curtis and Ward, 2007, p. 6)

In many respects, this quotation captures the most significant elements of the plan:

- it came from the heart of government
- it was wide-ranging and ambitious
- it placed schools at the hub
- it signalled a new and more active relationship between the state, parents and children.

While it was particularly concerned with addressing the needs of the most deprived and vulnerable and reducing the wide disparities in children's performance at school, it was also concerned with maximizing the potential of every child. Concerns about child abuse and child protection hardly received a mention.

Although the emphasis was on integration, it was clear that education, schools and Children's Centres lay at the heart of the plan. The government clearly felt that education – in its broadest sense – was the best way of maximizing opportunities and addressing the large inequalities in outcome, because:

Attainment is the biggest single predictor of a successful adult life, but a successful education is not a product simply of what happens in schools and colleges. As our experts and the parents and children we asked told us, we can only succeed by looking at all aspects of a child's life in the round. (DCSF, 2007b, p. 144)

Whenever possible, it was hoped that services could be co-located and schools, extended schools and Children's Centres were seen as central to the plan and, usually, the most accessible places for children and parents. It was vital that universal services were thoroughly integrated into the system so that prevention and early intervention could become a reality.

The plan had considerable ambitions for the '21st century school'. Not only was it to provide excellent education but it was also to actively contribute to all aspects of a child's life in terms of health and wellbeing, safety, and developing the wider experiences and skills that were seen to characterize a 'good childhood' and set a young person up for success as an adult. In addition, schools were a vital community resource that should make a major contribution to maximizing community cohesion.

Under local authority leadership, Children's Trusts were seen as vital in taking the plan forward and maximizing the integration between services and reflecting local needs. There was a clear expectation that Children's Trusts should look beyond direct local authority or other statutory provision to a wide range of potential providers, in the voluntary and community sector and the social enterprise and private sectors. While the plan clearly looked to build on many of the ideas and changes initiated in the *ECM: Change for Children* programme, the increased emphasis on the central role to be played by early years, schools and colleges and the strong education paradigm that informed the whole document was much more explicit.

Tensions and contradictions in New Labour's children's policy

A number of significant tensions and contradictions could be seen to characterize New Labour's policy towards children. In particular, New Labour said that it was determined to reduce child poverty, but this was only partially successful. Throughout, it relied heavily on policies based on a combination of what Ruth Levitas (2005) called the social integrationist discourse (SID) and the moral underclass discourse (MUD). Both were evident in *The Children's Plan* (DCSF, 2007b), which placed a particular emphasis on the importance of education and schools to ensure children fulfilled their potential but also as key to ensuring that a range of social problems could be identified and addressed. In addition, there was a renewed emphasis on the importance of trying to provide more assertive efforts to address the small number of families with multiple problem, who, it was said, accounted for a disproportionate amount of public sector resources. The commitment to Levitas's redistributionist discourse (RED) was confined primarily to improving the position of those just at or below the poverty line. Throughout, New Labour seemed comfortable with trying to attack poverty but much less comfortable attacking inequality.

It is not surprising, therefore, that, while poverty fell during the period, there remained gross inequality between those on the highest and lowest incomes. The inequality was due not so much to the poor falling further behind but because the rich, particularly the very rich, became richer. Brewer et al. (2004) argued that under New Labour, the UK had experienced an unusual combination of slightly rising income inequality and falling relative poverty. This was attributable to two trends: the gap between the very rich, particularly the richest 500,000 individuals, and the rest of the population got wider after 1997, while many lower income families saw their incomes rise faster than average. It was clear that while the gap between those near the top and those near the bottom reduced slightly, the gap between the very top one per cent (and 0.1 per cent in particular) and the rest increased (Sefton and Sutherland, 2005; Brewer et al., 2008). This contrasted with the postwar period until the late 1970s, which saw declining poverty and declining inequality, and the period 1979–97, which saw poverty and inequality increasing. As Orton and Rowlinson (2007, p. 62) argued, it seemed that 'New Labour's combination of falling poverty, increasing riches for the wealthiest and high levels of inequality suggested a "Third Way" was evident'.

Danny Dorling (2014) has argued that the New Labour government did make some significant achievements for children:

- it greatly reduced the numbers living in the very worst of poverty
- it improved education chances and narrowed education divides
- it governed during a period when young people's chances of gaining a job improved, especially in the poorest areas
- national youth suicide rates fell quickly.

However, when it came to assessing the legacy regarding inequality and the access to income and wealth enjoyed by different groups of children, the record was poor. Above all, Dorling argued, the increases in inequality made it easier for people in Britain not to see other people's children as like their own.

The question arises, however, whether the issue of increasing inequality really mattered if poverty was reducing. The person who has made the clearest case that inequalities cause social problems is Richard Wilkinson (1996, 2005), particularly in terms of its impact on health and violence in society. *The Spirit Level: Why More Equal Societies Almost Always Do Better*, written with Kate Pickett (Wilkinson and Pickett, 2009), received considerable publicity towards the end of the decade. They accumulated a range of evidence suggesting it was material inequality rather than poverty that was key, and societies that are poorer but more egalitarian have relatively high levels of good health and less violence because of a higher degree of social cohesion. The *relative* distributions of income, wealth and lifestyle were seen as central factors in influencing an individual's sense of worth and whether they felt valued. Societies that were becoming wealthier but more unequal, for example the USA and the UK, performed poorly as a result. These were just the findings that were evident in the UNICEF report (2007).

Wilkinson and Pickett (2009) argued that in more equal societies:

- there were stronger bonds between people
- public space was treated more as social space
- there was more involvement in social and voluntary activities outside the home and in civic society more generally
- there was less aggressive behaviour
- there was evidence of high self-esteem
- there was less stress, insecurity and depression.

Clearly, absolute levels of poverty were important in determining life chances, health outcomes and behaviour, but it was increasingly evident that the relative inequalities of income and wealth within any society were particularly significant in influencing the outcomes for children and young people and improving their overall wellbeing.

If this was the case, it seemed that the ambitious plans that New Labour had set out in *Every Child Matters* and *The Children's Plan* could only ever be partially successful (Rowlands, 2010, 2011), because issues concerned with the redistribution of resources and reductions in the overall inequalities of income and wealth were never seriously on the agenda. The plans put a particular emphasis on the importance of education and the role of schools as the major vehicles for improving outcomes for children. However, this brings us to another major tension in the New Labour approach. Although it saw schools as, among other things, providing a vital contribution to maximizing community and social inclusion, it also wanted schools to become more autonomous, flexible and businesslike. The White Paper *Higher Standards, Better Schools for All* (DfES, 2005c) emphasized that schools should have greater freedom in order to respond to parental demand in terms of the substance and scale of what they offered. Schools should develop their strengths, such that the range of provision would become more diversified. The emphasis was on competition and a neoliberal set of individualized market relations (Ball, 2007), rather than ideas about cooperation, partnership and integration on which *The Children's Plan* was based.

Not only were these very different rationales for what the primary purpose of schools were about, they also set up some potentially major practical difficulties. If schools were to become semi-independent businesslike operations, it would become difficult to include them at the heart of the new children's services if they did not wish to participate. Similar issues would apply to health trusts and GP practices in particular, which had similarly been set up as increasingly independent, businesslike units (McDonald, R., 2006). Such tensions placed considerable pressures on local authorities and the emerging Children's Trusts and LSCBs.

Beyond this, however, further tensions pervaded *The Children's Plan* and the thinking behind it. These included:

- implementing a top-down agenda while trying to engage the views of the various stakeholders, including children and young people themselves

- attempting to introduce policies and practices concerned with a version of social justice and social inclusion alongside those more concerned with children and young people as social threats and trying to ensure parents fulfilled their parental responsibilities (Gillies, 2008).

A major issue related to the potentially changing nature of the relationship between children, parents and the state. *The Children's Plan* (DCSF, 2007b) went out of its way to argue that the government was not looking to replace or undermine the role of the family but to enter into a new relationship in order to support parents. However, it was not easy to increase the support to families while encouraging early intervention, prevention and the integration of services without creating the image of a 'nanny state', which encouraged dependence and increased surveillance.

Conclusion

In this chapter I have critically reviewed policy developments in relation to children's services after the election of the New Labour government in May 1997, with particular reference to the development of the *ECM: Change for Children* programme. The period was characterized by continual major change, with the creation of new services and agencies and the reconfiguration of older ones. However, there was also continuity throughout in the way problems were conceptualized and explained and the broad policies developed to address these. An emphasis on attacking social exclusion, early intervention and prevention, and trying to ensure that all children achieved their potential were central and were driven forward by a strong top-down performance management approach.

While there was an explicit shift in direction towards a family service orientation and child focused orientation, among the broadening role envisaged for children's services and the increased emphasis on integration, it was less than clear where child protection fitted. Although the government claimed that its *ECM: Change for Children* programme was developed primarily in response to the Laming Report into the death of Victoria Climbié, the nature of and lines of accountability for child protection seemed more complex than ever. More specifically, because the government claimed that the changes were introduced as an explicit response to the Laming Report in order to ensure that tragic deaths like that of Victoria Climbié would be avoided in the future, the government was always going to be vulnerable if and when a similar tragedy occurred in the future, and this is precisely what happened in late 2008 – the moment when all the *ECM: Change for Children* changes were planned to be in place.

5

The tragedy of Baby Peter Connelly and its effects

On 11 November 2008, two men were convicted of causing or allowing the death of a 17-month-old child on 3 August 2007. The child was known simply as 'Baby P', because his identity, and that of his mother and her boyfriend, was being protected for legal reasons. The baby's mother had already pleaded guilty to the charge. During the trial, the court heard that Baby P was used as 'a punch bag', that his mother had deceived and manipulated professionals with lies and, on one occasion, had smeared him with chocolate to hide his bruises. There had been over 60 contacts with the family from a variety of health, police and social care professionals; he was pronounced dead just 48 hours after a hospital doctor failed to identify that he had a broken spine.[1] He was the subject of a child protection plan with the London borough of Haringey.

The media response was immediate and highly critical of the services and professionals involved, particularly local authority social workers and their senior managers. In many ways, the depth of anger evident in the media at the death of Baby P seemed much stronger and more prolonged than anything seen before, including the reaction to the deaths of Maria Colwell and Victoria Climbié. Very quickly, the issue of child protection was politicized and scandalized to a new level of intensity and this continued throughout 2009 and up to the general election of May 2010. It had an immediate impact on day-to-day policy and practice and put considerable pressure on the government, particularly Ed Balls, the secretary of state for children, schools and families. It was to prove to be a watershed in the politics of child protection in England and we can identify clear moves from a family service to a child protection orientation in national and local policy and practice.

Baby P: the key elements

The trial began in early September 2008 and because of the horrific injuries, the fact that these had been missed by a number of professionals and the child had been subject to a child protection plan, it was picked up by the news media. It was reported in the London *Evening Standard*, and received attention in some national newspapers on 10 September. The *Daily Mail* (p. 5) reported the trial with the headline 'Mother "beat to death" baby on at-risk register' and *The Guardian* (p. 4) with 'Injuries from brutal abuse of baby missed, jury told'. In addition, the BBC *Panorama* team had been carrying out research to run a programme on the case when the trial was completed. Although the programme was not broadcast, because of prior scheduling, until six days after the trial finished (17 November 2008), it did mean that BBC news programmes were fully briefed on the case and made it their main news item when the trial was completed.

The political significance of the case was made clear by the London *Evening Standard* on the day the trial finished (11 November), when its huge front-page headline stated 'Boy died just like Climbié: Child was killed after failures by the council in earlier scandal', followed by a double-page spread headed 'Social workers saw him 60 times, and still Baby P died' (pp. 4–5). Some key themes of previous child abuse scandals were immediately repeated: a young defenceless and innocent child being brutalized and being failed by social workers. The added ingredient this time was that this had taken place in the London borough of Haringey, the local authority that had been at the centre of the failures to protect Victoria Climbié.

The full political significance of this was driven home in the late TV news on 11 November and in the national daily newspapers the following day. As *The Guardian* (12 November, p. 5) said:

> The outcome of the Baby P case will prompt questions about the value of the post-Climbié reforms, which aimed to improve multidisciplinary support for children at risk by creating children's services departments in local councils and children's trusts bringing together professionals from different agencies.

In effect, the massive changes brought about by the *Every Child Matters: Change for Children* (DfES, 2004b) programme seemed to have failed, with horrendous consequences.

At a press conference immediately following the end of the trial (11 November), the director of children's services, Sharon Shoesmith, who was also chair of the Haringey Local Safeguarding Children Board (LSCB), which had produced a Serious Case Review (SCR) on the handling of the case (Haringey LSCB, 2008), said that while 'lessons will be learned' and two social workers and a lawyer had been given written warnings, there had been no sackings or resignations and the children's services had recently been given a positive Ofsted (Office for Standards in Education, Children's Services and Skills) inspection.

The press conference ignited the wrath of the tabloid press even more, with the *Daily Mail* (12 November, pp. 4–5) declaring that 'Once again, no one's to blame: Baby P died despite 60 visits from the social services who betrayed little Victoria Climbié', and *The Sun* (12 November, p. 1), under the headline 'Blood on their hands', saying 'First Victoria Climbié then ... Shocking case of Baby P, killed by mum and lover, betrayed by scandal council'.

Initially, the Department for Children, Schools and Families (DCSF) and Ed Balls, the secretary of state, seemed confident they could manage the media criticism, and he immediately appointed Lord Laming (who had chaired the public inquiry into the death of Victoria Climbié) to carry out an urgent review of child protection in England to ensure that this was an exceptional case.

However, on the following day (12 November) at Prime Minister's Questions (PMQs), tempers boiled over and Gordon Brown, the prime minister, and David Cameron, the leader of the Conservative opposition, became emotional and angry and pandemonium broke out in the House of Commons. The prime minister had come to PMQs expecting to talk about the economy and was quite unprepared for David Cameron's questions about Baby P and, in particular, his questioning of the independence of the SCR. In response, the prime minister accused David Cameron of playing 'party politics', whereupon David Cameron lost his temper and they ended up screaming at each other (Treneman, 2008).

From this point, the intensity of political and media pressure, particularly from David Cameron and *The Sun*, increased inexorably. Patrick Butler (2009) has argued that papers submitted to the court as part of Sharon Shoesmith's subsequent appeal against unfair dismissal (see notes 5 and 6) demonstrated that no one in the upper echelons of Haringey Council or the DCSF, including Ed Balls, had any inkling of the scale of the media and political storm that was to ensue. Butler says that straight after PMQs, senior DCSF officials went into crisis mode. David Lammy, local MP for Tottenham, telephoned Sharon Shoesmith to warn her that 'something dreadful' had happened in the House of Commons, and David Bell, the DCSF permanent secretary, telephoned Ita O'Donovan, chief executive of Haringey Council, to demand Shoesmith's suspension. Haringey refused and DCSF press officers sent an email to their counterparts in Haringey informing them that the media would henceforth be handled from Whitehall.

That evening, Ed Balls also:

- ordered Ofsted, the Healthcare Commission and the Police Inspectorate to carry out an urgent Joint Area Review (JAR) of safeguarding in Haringey

- ordered the preparation of a new and independent SCR following the publication of the original one, which he deemed inadequate and insufficiently critical

- established a Social Work Task Force to identify any barriers that social workers faced in doing their jobs effectively, make recommendations for improvements and the long-term reform of social work and report in late 2009.

In an article in the *Evening Standard* on the same day (12 November), David Cameron said that he was 'sickened to the core' by the crime and was further angered by the lack of a proper apology by the professionals involved, particularly the director of children's services, and he called for sackings 'over Haringey council's failure to save Baby P'. He argued that those whose job it was to oversee the system had failed and they must pay the price. However, he said his biggest concern was to stop this ever happening again and a major part of that was about 'reinforcing professional responsibility'. As we will see in subsequent chapters, these were themes David Cameron was to continually emphasize.

What was clear was that the reaction to the death of Baby P was highly charged and emotional. It impacted on the highest level of politics (Ost, 2004), and was stoked by certain sections of the media – the role of *The Sun* was particularly influential.[2] In many respects, the case and concerns about child protection dominated the media and political discourse for the remainder of 2008 and into 2009, even though the economy was facing its sharpest downturn in the postwar period following the banking and credit crisis earlier in the autumn.

On Saturday 15 November, *The Sun* launched a petition under the front-page banner 'Beautiful Baby P: Campaign for Justice', together with what it called 'the first heartbreaking picture of the toddler', which reinforced the innocence of the child and took the spectacle of the suffering involved to a new level (Carrabine, 2012). The hugely photogenic little boy was transformed into an iconic global image. The petition demanded the sacking of four Haringey staff, including the director of children's services – Sharon Shoesmith – and the paediatrician who examined him two days before his death, together with a demand that 'Baby P's killers … be locked away for so long that they never see the light of day again' (*The Sun*, 15 November, p. 6). The paper also announced that four Labour ministers had been sent letters by whistle-blowing Haringey social workers six months before Baby P died saying that Haringey child protection services were a shambolic failure.

The government was clearly on the defensive at a time when it was falling behind the Conservative Party in the political polls and the economic news was bleak. Since the general election of 1992, the support of *The Sun* was seen as crucial for political parties (Curtice, 1999), and these were critical times for the New Labour government of Gordon Brown. Whichever party *The Sun* had supported had won every general election since 1992.

Two weeks after launching its campaign, *The Sun* delivered a petition, containing 1.5 million signatures, to the prime minister demanding justice for Baby P, claiming it was the biggest and most successful such campaign ever. In addition, a large number of Facebook groups, comprising over 1.6 million members, were set up in memory of Baby P and seeking justice for his killers. This weight of expressed opinion put increasing political pressure on Ed Balls who needed to be seen to be acting authoritatively in order to take control of the situation.

On receipt of the JAR on 1 December 2008, which he described as 'devastating', he announced that he was using his powers under the 1996 Education Act to direct Haringey Council to remove the director of children's services, Sharon Shoesmith. Later that month, she was sacked by the council with immediate effect and without compensation. In April 2009, Haringey Council also dismissed four other employees connected to the Baby P case – the deputy director of children's services, the head of children in need and safeguarding services, the team manager, and the social worker. In addition, the paediatrician who examined Baby P two days before his death was suspended from the medical register; and the family doctor who saw Baby P at least 15 times and was the first to raise the alarm about the baby's abuse was also suspended from the medical register.

The sackings, particularly that of Sharon Shoesmith, sent shock waves through children's services. Such summary dismissals had never taken place before on such a scale and certainly no director or senior officer had been dismissed in this way as a result of a child abuse scandal. It engendered a new level of anxiety and insecurity across all levels of children's services and all local authorities. The tensions were felt by officers, politicians and frontline professionals alike. These were most evident in Haringey Council itself and on 1 December, the day Ed Balls demanded that Haringey dismiss Sharon Shoesmith, the leader of the council and the council's cabinet member for children and young people resigned. Events moved at a rapid pace.

In an article in *The Guardian* (Campbell, 2008) on 2 December, it was also reported that Shoesmith had received threats that one of her two daughters would be killed and she had received a wide range of hate mail, including emails entitled '100 ways to commit suicide' and ecards with pictures of Baby P containing messages such as 'forever on your conscience'. Her mother and ex-mother-in-law were pursued by reporters; the police reinforced her doors and windows and offered her protection; and her daughters stayed away from work for a while as they were being pursued by reporters. The level of vitriol directed at professionals and managers in the case was immense and much of it was directed at Sharon Shoesmith. It was notable that even though it became clear that the Metropolitan Police had failed to complete two separate investigations into the case, the media and politicians never focused on the police failures (Jones, 2012).[3]

From 11 November to the first week in December 2008, the scandal about Baby P and the immediate fallout from it received huge media and political attention, often taking up more time and space than that devoted to the economic and financial crisis. Then, just when it seemed the issue might slip down the media and political agendas, it was further fuelled by another major childcare scandal.

On 4 December, Karen Matthews, together with another relative, was found guilty of kidnapping Shannon, her nine-year-old daughter, holding her drugged in the relative's flat in Dewsbury (in West Yorkshire, northern England) and then calling police and making a series of tearful TV appeals. Karen had reported Shannon missing when she did not return home from school on 19 February and over the next four weeks, more than a tenth of Yorkshire's police, together with many volunteers from the local estate in Dewsbury, were involved in searching the area. This included interviewing over 1,500 motorists and the use of sniffer dogs to search over 2,000 houses. It was the biggest such operation since the search for the Yorkshire Ripper 30 years previously and cost £3.2 million.

Panorama, the BBC current affairs programme that had been following the case closely, did not have to wait until its scheduled slot on Monday night but was given an hour at peak time on Thursday 4 December, the day the court case concluded, to broadcast its full detailed exposé on the case. Much of this was concerned with giving a positively framed insight into how the police went about its investigation in finding Shannon, including a lengthy interview with Sir Norman Bettison, the chief constable. Although it was claimed that the case was a positive news story for the police, there were a number of criticisms about the role of the local authority children's services in its work with the family over a number of years.

The following day, Friday 5 December 2008, some of the reporting of the case in the national press was vitriolic. The front page of *The Sun* stated that Karen Matthews was 'Pure evil: Shannon's Mum guilty of kidnap' and a 'Warped, immoral scrounger who lost count of her own children'. The leader column under the headline 'Betrayed again' (p. 8) made an explicit link to the Baby P case and was heavily critical of the role of social workers:

> Like Baby P, Shannon Matthews seems to have been let down badly by the very people who should have protected her. As Shannon's evil mother Karen faces years in jail, The Sun reveals how Kirklees social workers failed to act on warnings from Shannon's teachers and Matthews' sister Julie.

Amid increasing concern being expressed by senior politicians and local MPs, the leader of Kirklees Council in West Yorkshire, where the Matthews family lived, announced it was to carry out an independent SCR into the case, even though there was no evidence that a child had died or had been seriously injured, as required by the then statutory guidance (HM Government, 2006b, paras. 8.5 and 8.6).

Fuelled by the publication of another SCR into the death of five-month-old Alisha Allen in northeast England, the weekend news and comment were dominated by concerns about cases of child abuse, and reaction to the Shannon Matthews case was central. The *News of the World*, the then sister Sunday newspaper of *The Sun*, carried an article by Ed Balls, where he stated that 'social workers do an incredibly tough job in difficult circumstances', and announced that the government was to spend £73 million to improve the training of social workers over the next three years 'in a bid to avert another Baby P tragedy' (p. 2). This seemed to be sympathetically received by the newspaper's leader writer, because, while the leader was critical of social workers, it stated that:

> Victoria Climbié, Baby P and Shannon Matthews are shameful examples of a systematic breakdown and failure in our welfare programme. *Nothing is more important than to get it right.* (*News of the World*, leader: 'To fail just one is to fail us all', 7 December 2008, p. 6)

The *Mail on Sunday* was particularly interesting on 7 December 2008 and clearly demonstrated some of the emerging and sometimes contra- dictory dimensions to the debates. In a major article on the third anni- versary of becoming leader of the Conservative Party, David Cameron launched a trenchant attack on 'our broken society' under the headline: 'There are 5 million people on benefits in Britain. How do we stop them all turning into this?' (p. 27), followed by a large photograph of Karen Matthews with the caption:

> NO MORALS: The verdict on Karen Matthews's vile crime is a verdict on our broken society. It may take a generation to change it.

David Cameron explicitly linked the cases of Shannon Matthews and Baby P to his ideas about 'the broken society', which was becoming central to his analysis of the problems facing British society and his wish to reform welfare and the state more generally. He described the Matthews case in the following terms:

> A fragmented family held together by drink, drugs and deception. An estate where decency fights a losing battle against degradation and despair. A community whose pillars are crime, unemployment and addiction.
> If only this were a one-off story. But Shannon Matthews is just the latest innocent young face to stare out from the front pages.
> Before her there was Baby P, a tiny boy beaten by lower-than-life thugs. (*Mail on Sunday*, 7 December 2008, p. 27)

As the case of Shannon Matthews demonstrated, the anger and concern were not simply to do with children who had died, as with Baby P, but with the major failures of parenting and the circumstances in which some children were being brought up. These were seen as degrading and severely neglectful and typical of a growing 'underclass' (Hayward and Yar, 2006). At its most extreme, certain parents, such as Karen Matthews, were described as 'evil', 'vile' and with 'no morals' – what David Cameron described as symptomatic of 'our broken society' and what others have described as the demonization of certain sections of the working class (Jones, 2011).

I will return to these ideas about 'the broken society' in Chapter 7, but it is also important to note that the *Mail on Sunday* of 7 December 2008 also carried a two-page article by Eileen Fairweather, one of its leading writers, entitled 'Has your child been CAFed?' (*Mail on Sunday*, 7 December, pp. 34–5), essentially a dire warning about the formal launch of ContactPoint, which was scheduled for January 2009, and also the Common Assessment Framework (CAF). The latter was described as a 'creepy, eight-page, 60-section questionnaire', which was being used by hundreds of thousands of state employees on a whole range of children up to the age of 19 (p. 34). The article was sub-headed, with a dour photograph of the prime minister, as 'Brown's police state' and asked:

> How has such a terrifying intrusion into private life crept, almost unnoticed, under the radar? The answer is New Labour has cleverly packaged CAF as an aid to 'child protection' and delivering better services as part of its Every Child Matters project (ECM). (p. 34)

It stated that the Conservative Party was committed to scrapping ContactPoint.

So, in the same paper, we had two major articles, one by David Cameron making an explicit link between the child abuse scandals and the failure of welfare professions to his concerns about 'the broken society'; and the other about how 'Brown's police state' was using concerns about child protection to intervene unwarrantedly into family life and undermining the civil liberties of children, young people and their parents. Both themes were to become central to Conservative Party policy over the next 18 months and its critique of the New Labour policies for children and families and state welfare more generally.

During 2009, reports of child deaths emerged from all parts of the country, usually prompted by the publication of an SCR. In January, reports of seven child deaths in Doncaster, five having died in less than six months, prompted Beverly Hughes, the children's minister, to state that she was considering invoking legal powers so that the government could take control of the council's children's services. This prompted huge political pressure on the mayor and on 13 March he resigned 'over serious child protection failures' (*The Guardian*, 13 March, p. 6).

By early 2009, it was clear that it was becoming difficult to recruit and retain staff nationally to work in children's social care, particularly social workers, and that morale was at an all-time low (LGA, 2009). In addition, a number of influential commentators, including the House of Commons Children, Schools and Families Committee (2009), began to argue that the threshold for admitting children into state care was too high and that if children came into care sooner, a number of the child deaths, including that of Baby P, could have been avoided. Similarly, the Children and Family Court Advisory and Support Service (Cafcass, 2009a) produced figures which demonstrated that:

- there were nearly 50 per cent more care applications to court in the second half of 2008/9 compared with the first half of the year

- demand for care cases was 39 per cent higher in March 2009 compared with March 2008

- the demand for care continued to remain at an unprecedented high level for the first two quarters of 2009/10, with June 2009 having the highest demand for care ever recorded for a single month (see Appendix, Table A1.4).[4]

There was also clear evidence of a large increase in referrals to children's social care, with a growth in the number of children subject to a child protection plan, the number of children being taken into care and Section 47 enquiries (Association of Directors of Children's Services, 2010; Hannon et al., 2010). It seemed that all professionals involved in working with children, including those in children's social care, were operating in a climate of high demand and high anxiety. How far this was because professional social workers and managers were operating at a lower threshold and therefore making decisions to intervene in cases where previously they might not have done, or how far it resulted from a greater willingness by other agencies, such as schools, health and police, to refer cases to children's social care at an earlier stage was not clear.

Whatever the reason, it seemed that all services were operating in a climate of crisis and panic and that the case of Baby P was central to engendering and representing this sense of crisis. In many respects, the case of Baby P marked a watershed in contemporary child protection policy and practice. It seemed that the depth of anger and sense of scandal in the media and among politicians was much stronger and more prolonged than anything witnessed previously and that its impact was wide-ranging and long-lasting. What was it about the case that prompted such a strong social and political reaction?

Baby P and the 'politics of outrage'

I would suggest that a number of key elements came together in the social reaction to the tragic death of Baby P, which had the effect of not simply contributing to a moral and professional panic but generating a 'politics of outrage', never before experienced on such a scale and at such an intensive depth.

The first thing to recognize is that this was not the first case of its kind, and the fact that it had happened so many times before over the previous 35 years made this tragedy seem even more reprehensible. Much of the comment made explicit reference to the deaths of Maria Colwell and Victoria Climbié. However, the case of Baby P was different in one important respect from these earlier high-profile tragedies. The case of Baby P was never subject to a public inquiry in the way the other cases had been. The New Labour government had made it clear when it launched the Every Child Matters reforms in 2003/04 that it was introducing the changes to ensure that a tragedy like Victoria Climbié could never happen again and that there would be no more public inquiries. The death of Baby P seemed to demonstrate the absolute failure of these reforms.

The government had also introduced a revised system of SCRs under the Children Act 2004. Unfortunately, the independence of the SCR process was thought to be seriously flawed in the Baby P case and subject to considerable criticism. But this also meant that there was no public inquiry process to frame and structure the media and political debate as previously. Although public inquiries were seen to have many deleterious effects, it did mean that there was a lengthy time frame and a structured process that often did not take place until well after a court case, with a report published some months, often years, after the event. The case of Baby P was different and the outrage started immediately at the completion of the court case, with no obvious way for the government to manage or control the process. The media was placed in a particularly influential position.

In the context of the influential political position held by the newspaper at the time, the justice for Baby P campaign run by *The Sun* was important not just in contributing to and reflecting the sense of outrage and injustice but also in informing the terms, content and pace of the debate (Burgess, 2010; Jones, 2012; Warner, 2013a, 2013b). There is no doubt that the photographs of Baby P, both from the court case and one taken of him looking so innocent and appealing, were very powerful. We should not underestimate the influence of London's *Evening Standard*, the only daily newspaper to be published in the capital, which, on the day the court case was completed, quickly set the tone of the debate and identified key, highly embarrassing political issues with its front-page headline of 'Boy died just like Climbié: Child was killed after failures by the Council in earlier scandal'. The fact that Baby P, unlike Victoria Climbié, was the subject of a child protection plan only made a difficult situation even worse.

As we have seen, there was an immediate political fallout arising from the case with the highly charged, emotional argument between Gordon Brown and David Cameron. It was as if the frustrations and sense of helplessness being experienced amid the dramatic challenges posed by the dire economic and financial situation were being projected onto this particular case. Increasingly, the Conservative opposition was looking to distance itself from the government and Gordon Brown in particular and to raise the political heat whenever possible. The case of Baby P was one such significant opportunity.

In a debate in the House of Commons on 3 February 2009 called by the opposition, Tim Loughton, the shadow children's minister, set out four changes that tried to demonstrate how the Conservative Party would differ in approach to the New Labour government, which were to become central policies for the coalition government when it came to power in 2010. He stated that in order to restore confidence in the system, it was important that:

- all SCRs should be published in full, appropriately anonymized and redacted, where that would not compromise the welfare of the child and siblings, so that 'all agencies can learn from mistakes made'
- all LSCBs should be independently chaired, in order to increase transparency and accountability
- the Ofsted system for the inspection of children's services 'should be overhauled'

- social workers and other professionals should be freed up to maximize the time available to spend with 'vulnerable families' by scrapping the highly prescriptive template for the Integrated Children's System 'and other cumbersome data systems which have engendered a tick box assessment approach which is undermining child protection'.

It was the last two points that attempted to get to the heart of what were seen as the problems introduced by the Every Child Matters reforms and the New Labour approach to social policy more generally, which had received much critical attention in certain sections of the media (Warner, 2013a). The New Labour approach emphasized the importance of management, audit, meeting targets and using ICT systems to gather, sort and share information, and these had all been found wanting and failed to prevent the death of Baby P. Not only did such an approach seem to encourage the accumulation of misleading information, it had the effect of encouraging perverse incentives – all of which appeared to be evident in the media reporting of the Sharon Shoesmith press conference at the conclusion of the trial into the death of Baby P on 11 November. The press conference and the case more generally seemed to demonstrate that many of the systems put in place to monitor and improve day-to-day frontline management and practice were neither trustworthy nor fit for purpose.

Such criticisms were increasingly being aired in relation to Ofsted – the inspection body for children's services. In October 2006, a joint review by Ofsted and other inspectorates stated that Sharon Shoesmith provided 'strong and dynamic leadership and management at all levels'. Then in November 2007, three months *after* the death of Baby P, Ofsted awarded Haringey children's services a three-star 'good' rating, stating that 'the council's capacity to improve its services for children and young people is good and its management of these services is good'. This was in sharp contrast to the JAR commissioned by Ed Balls that he called 'devastating'. This time, the JAR stated that the leadership and management of safeguarding arrangements in Haringey were deemed to be 'inadequate', but the situation in Haringey was 'exceptional'. It was perhaps not surprising that Christine Gilbert, the then chief inspector at Ofsted, was to come under increasing political pressure, particularly from the Children's, Schools and Families Select Committee of MPs. Barry Sheerman, chair of the committee, stated that he had lost confidence in Ofsted over its handling of inspections in Haringey after the committee questioned Christine Gilbert on 10 December 2008.

Then, in its annual report, Ofsted (2008a) stated that nine local authorities, including Haringey, were found to be inadequate, with eight deemed to be failing to keep children safe – double the number of the previous year. However, the figures prompted questions as to whether any of the findings could be trusted and assertions that the desk-bound, overly bureaucratic inspection system was inadequate. December also saw the publication of Ofsted's report (2008b) outlining its evaluation of its first year evaluating SCRs, where 20 of the 50 reports were deemed inadequate.

Very quickly, therefore, the tragic death was not seen simply as a one-off tragedy but as a case that was symptomatic of a set of system, procedural and practice failures, which could be seen to result directly from the approach to children's services introduced by New Labour and its overall approach to social policy. The nature of the failures operated at a variety of levels. The fact that a series of other high-profile scandals followed in rapid succession in Kirklees, Doncaster and Birmingham all pointed to major institutional problems. The emotional and highly charged nature of the case meant that, from November 2008 through 2009, concerns about child protection continued to be politically high profile and gained considerable media coverage.

What helped keep the scandal of Baby P very much alive was its continual return to the news. From the outset, there had been a large degree of dark mystery about the case, as neither Baby P, nor his mother, nor a man who was her live-in boyfriend found guilty in the case could be named for legal reasons because there were outstanding charges against a second child victim. On 1 May 2009, the 32-year-old man was found guilty of raping a two-year-old girl. However, Baby P's mother was found not guilty in the case. As a result, reporting restrictions were partly removed, so that Baby P could now be named as Peter. When the prison sentences were announced three weeks later on 22 May, they provoked widespread anger. The mother was given a minimum tariff sentence of ten years, thus she could apply for parole after five years. As she had already served two years on remand, this meant that she might only serve three years and her boyfriend eight years. This prompted a front-page headline in *The Sun* of 'Baby P betrayed: Torture tot sentence fury'.

A highly critical SCR was also published on 22 May, which had been demanded by Ed Balls. This second SCR felt that the response of the agencies was 'inadequate' and Baby P should have been taken into care at a much earlier stage (Haringey LSCB, 2009). It emphasized the lack of 'authoritative child protection practice' in the social work with the family and that such an approach should be central in the future. The idea of 'authoritative child protection practice in social work' was to become central from this point.

The outrage continued in June 2009, when the attorney general turned down the demand, backed by *The Sun*, to increase the length of the jail sentences. The case received renewed and extensive coverage in all forms of media when, on 10 August 2009, reporting restrictions were lifted on the identity of the mother of Baby P and his killer – Tracey Connelly and Steven Barker. The complex nature of the case meant that it was continually in the news from November 2008 to August 2009 and, at each stage, the general moral outrage at the level of depravity involved and the horror about fundamental failures of the health and social care agencies to intervene seemed to increase.

In addition, the scandal of Baby P continued to return to the headlines through the actions and sheer doggedness of Sharon Shoesmith, who was clearly determined not to accept her summary dismissal as director of children's services in Haringey.[5]

Her determination to fight her dismissal had the effect of ensuring that the case of Baby P, and all the tensions, concerns and emotions associated with it, continued to maintain a high political and public profile right up until the general election of May 2010. In the process, it ensured that Ed Balls, the minister who was the prime minister's, Gordon Brown, closest political ally, and his role in the case, remained in the public eye.[6]

A number of other cases also received intense publicity in early 2010, with two in particular receiving considerable coverage. On 22 January, two young brothers, aged 10 and 11 at the time of the attacks, were given indeterminate sentences at Sheffield Crown Court, having pleaded guilty to grievous bodily harm, robbery and sexual offences against two boys aged 9 and 11. While they could not be named for legal reasons, they appeared before an adult court because of the severity of the attacks, which took place on 4 April 2009. The attacks took place just days after the boys had been taken into care and placed with a foster family in the village of Edlington, near Doncaster, in South Yorkshire, and the case became known simply as 'the Edlington case'. The front-page headline in *The Times* on 23 January was typical – 'The crimes of neglect: Boy torturers of Edlington: parents face prosecution'. Its main editorial was headed 'The irresponsible society' (p. 2) and argued the case was critical for two main reasons. First, it had many similarities with the murder of

James Bulger by Jon Venables and Robert Thompson in 1993, which, as I discussed in Chapters 3 and 4, had proved key in the transformation of the Labour Party under Tony Blair. Not only did the Edlington case seem to demonstrate that New Labour policies had not worked but it also showed that Britain had a growing 'violent underclass', which seemed to confirm David Cameron's view that Britain had become a 'broken society'. Speaking on the day of the court judgement, David Cameron argued that rather than being an isolated incident of 'evil', it was part of what he described as a 'social recession' and that it was important to debate ways in which society could be strengthened. He argued, as he had done earlier in relation to the cases of Baby P and Shannon Matthews, that the social context of the Edlington case was as depressing and worrying as the crime itself.

However, the second reason why *The Times* editorial considered the case significant was because of the leaked SCR, to which the judge was denied access. It identified 31 separate occasions when nine different agencies had failed to take action about the brothers' behaviour. This was the latest childcare scandal to come out of Doncaster, whose children's services department had been placed on 'special measures' just 12 months before by central government, who had sent in a new senior management team to sort out the problems. For *The Times*, the case exemplified all that was worst about a 'broken society' and what could happen when local authority children's services were themselves 'broken'.

January 2010 also saw the publication of the SCR into the death of seven-year-old Khyra Ishaq in Birmingham (Radford, 2010). She had died in May 2008 after months of neglect and physical abuse at the hands of her mother and her mother's boyfriend. She had been withdrawn from school six months before her death, purportedly to be home educated by her mother. The 180-page SCR found that despite concerns raised by members of the public and school staff, information was not acted on and procedures were not followed. Professionals felt intimidated by the mother and they were not assertive with their investigations. Both the report and press coverage of the case felt it very much echoed the failures found in the case of Victoria Climbié.

Both the 'Edlington case' and that of Khyra Ishaq ensured that concerns about child protection remained high profile and continued to be politicized. Not only were the two main political parties taking different positions as to whether SCRs should be published in full, but it was clear that the media, both print and broadcast, national and local, were finding that SRCs, which were, in most cases, readily available via the internet, could provide an excellent source of information and hence news. At any one time, most local authorities were involved in at least one SCR. In 2007–08, there were 137 cases proceeding to an SCR and 131 in 2008–09 (Brandon et al., 2010). While these reports were officially to ensure that 'lessons could be learned' and that policy and practice, both locally and nationally, could be improved, their existence also helped fuel media criticism and acted as a toxic ingredient in what was a highly unstable and politically charged professional and organizational context. The nature of their production and distribution was increasingly becoming a focus for media and political debate.

It is evident that the case of Baby P marked a watershed in the politics of child protection and, from 11 November 2008 onwards, there was also clear evidence of a 'politics of outrage', where senior managers and practitioners were subject to ongoing, high-profile 'trial by media' (Greer and McLaughlin, 2011). In many respects, this was epitomized by the media treatment of Sharon Shoesmith, director of children's services in Haringey, the local authority at the centre of the Baby P scandal, who was sacked by the local authority on the direction of Ed Balls, the then secretary of state. It is notable, however, that the level of anger and concern continued long after her dismissal. This was prompted, in part, by the continuous flow of high-profile scandals over a number of months and years, beginning with the case of Shannon Matthews.

This increasingly pervasive 'politics of outrage' was not exclusive to child protection but was becoming increasingly typical of the times. Greer and McLaughlin (2010, 2011, 2012a, 2012b), who coined the term, situate their analysis within a range of research exploring the sociology of scandals and the changing nature of visibility (Thompson, 2000, 2005, 2011; Brighenti, 2007; Chouliaraki, 2008; Castells, 2009), which can be seen to add to previous work on scandals and child welfare in the UK (Butler and Drakeford, 2005, 2011) and the USA (Gainsborough, 2010).

Greer and McLaughlin draw on the work of John Thompson (2000, 2005, 2011), who has argued that the increase in 'mediated visibility' is a key factor in explaining the growing prominence of scandals in the news media and that three significant changes have come together to make such visibility possible. In this process, it has considerably shifted the boundaries between the public and the private. First, new forms of electronic surveillance make it harder for public figures to conceal even their most private activities. This was evident throughout the campaign against Sharon Shoesmith, when a photograph of her 'enjoying' herself at the Ascot racecourse was in wide circulation.[7] There were also numerous occasions when the behaviour of Ofsted and the secretary of state was called into question regarding the existence and whereabouts of certain emails and whether important documents had been 'interfered with'.

Second, Thompson argues there is a new journalistic culture which, driven by the need for economic survival and severe media competition, has amplified the pressure to deliver dramatic headlines. Greer and McLaughlin (2012a, 2012b) see this as a particular pressure on the print media, which, more than ever, needs to increase the shock/dramatic effect of its stories for sheer commercial reasons. In a hypercompetitive 'do what it takes' 24/7 news mediasphere, it is the British national press that has most proactively embraced the combined cultural and commercial appeal of scandals, so that the news press increasingly try to construct their stories in a populist way. And few scandals generate as much high-profile, emotionally charged news coverage and public outcry as the abuse of young children. As Moeller (2002, p. 37) has argued, 'in today's competitive news environment, children are perceived to be one of the few sure fire ways to attract eyeballs – online, in print and on television'. In addition, not only have we witnessed the growing scandalization of news stories but the boundaries between the news and drama has become blurred. While such developments mean that the print media continues to play a key role in setting the news agenda, broadcast media is also important. As the *Panorama* TV programmes on the BBC in relation to both Baby P and Shannon Matthews demonstrated, the broadcast media also try to take the initiative. Greer and McLaughlin (2012a, p. 277) argue that while the dramatization of scandals has always been newsworthy and, on that basis, made good business sense, 'today, we would suggest, it has become an economic imperative'. As Castells (2009) points out, news as 'infotainment' encourages stories to become scandalized in order to attract and hold an audience.

The third reason why Thompson suggests 'mediated visibility' has become a significant issue is that we have witnessed the rise of a 'performative politics of trust', which places a premium on the individual integrity of public figures, and correspondingly invests scandal with greater journalistic and public significance. Increasingly, it also seems that public figures are expected to show humility and demonstrate their emotional sensitivity, particularly in situations of death and serious illness, and the public apology has become required practice, something the media suggested Sharon Shoesmith wanted to avoid.

Greer and McLaughlin (2012a) argue that it is not only individuals whose integrity, competence and credibility has increasingly been subjected to intensive journalistic exposure and critique, but public institutions are also subjected to such exposure and critique. 'Institutional failure' has now become a defining explanatory trope and a key determinant of newsworthiness in contemporary reporting:

> Unlike individualised scandals, institutional failure results from systemic problems that cannot be explained away by a few 'rotten apples', or resolved through tokenistic apologies, dismissals or reforms ... Whilst the practice of pursuing individual miscreants has forever been a part of the press agenda, the practice of assailing entire institutions with accusations of systemic institutional failure constitutes a more ambitious form of agenda-setting journalism. (Greer and McLaughlin, 2012, p. 277)

In the immediate post Baby P era in child protection, both levels of scandalization were evident – the individual and the institutional. A part of the process involved various parties trying to defend themselves and trying to blame others. However, these battles had the effect of prolonging and making the scandal appear worse. This was clearest in the ongoing allegations between Sharon Shoesmith and Ed Balls, but it was also evident in the way Ed Balls and David Cameron attempted to 'use' the media as well as simply respond to its agenda(s).

Conclusion

In this chapter, I have argued that the case of Baby P marked a watershed in the contemporary politics of child protection in England. Not only did it have an impact on day-to-day policy and practice but it raised concerns about what to do about child neglect to a new political level and the case quickly came to represent all that seemed to be wrong with contemporary managerial and professional decision making. It also provided a salutary view of the state of society more generally.

I have argued that a major influence on policy and practice after 11 November 2008 was the 'press politics of outrage'. This reflected the hyper-adversarial, highly normative style of reporting, which was motivated by a deep belief that 'institutional failure' was endemic in children's services and child protection, of which social workers were particularly culpable. While such views have been evident in media reporting of social work and child abuse for many years (Franklin and

Parton, 1991, 2001), a subject I will return to in Chapter 10, the outrage following the death of Baby P reached new levels, was extensive and lasted for much longer. Whereas individualized scandals and previous cases of 'trial by media', usually via a public inquiry, were seen as exceptional, the 'press politics of outrage' following the scandal of Baby P had the effect of normalizing and routinizing the deep distrust and adversarialism represented in the media in many of the institutional contexts in which day-to-day professional work was being carried out. How to move beyond this would clearly provide a major political, policy and practice challenge. It was also clear that the cases of Baby P and Shannon Matthews and the Edlington case acted to exemplify and crystallize a number of issues concerned with 'the broken society' and the 'underclass', while also bringing about a growing emphasis on the need for 'authoritative child protection practice' with certain children and families. As Critcher (2009, p. 27) has argued, when evil is unambiguously identified, as it was with the cases of Baby P and Shannon Matthews and the Edlington case, it permits state intervention at its most aggressive, because 'evil represents a challenge to the moral order of such magnitude that it must be identified, named, cast out'.

6

Central government guidance and child protection: 1974–2010

Government guidance has been at the core of the development of child protection in England from 1974 onwards, providing the framework for policy and practice that local authorities and other social care, health, education and criminal justice agencies are required to implement in their local areas. The guidance represents official thinking and priorities at any one particular time, while also playing a key role in trying to bring about policy and practice change on the ground. The changes in the guidance result from a variety of legal, social, media and political influences, which are the focus of this book.

The central aim of this chapter[1] is to describe and outline the growth and development of this guidance up until 2010. I return to the changes after 2010 in subsequent chapters. I argue that such an analysis provides important insights into the changing nature and aims of child protection policy during the period, particularly in terms of its priorities, focus and organization. It will become apparent not only that the guidance grew enormously and became much more detailed and prescriptive in the process, but also that the object of concern broadened from 'battered babies', to 'non-accidental injury to children', to 'child abuse', to 'safeguarding and promoting the welfare of children'. Further detailed analysis of this is provided in summary form in Table A1.1 in the Appendix. It also becomes evident that the guidance and procedures, as we saw in Chapter 5, were increasingly seen as a major contributor to the problems to be addressed and therefore in need of reform and serious attention. Such issues came to a head via the responses to the scandal of Baby P.

The beginnings of the contemporary child protection system

The contemporary child protection system in England was effectively inaugurated with the publication of the DHSS (1974) circular entitled *Non-Accidental Injury to Children* in the wake of the public inquiry into the death of Maria Colwell (Secretary of State for Social Services, 1974) and was just seven pages long. It followed earlier guidance in relation to battered babies (DHSS, 1970, 1972). The system was refined in a series of further circulars throughout the decade (DHSS, 1976a, 1976b, 1978) and by 1980 the problem to be addressed had been officially reframed as 'child abuse' (DHSS, 1980), which was made up of physical injury, physical neglect, failure to thrive and emotional abuse but did not include sexual abuse.

The primary focus of the system was to ensure that a range of key professionals were familiar with the signs of child abuse and that mechanisms were established so that information was shared between them. Coordination between agencies and professionals was seen as key for improving practice, and the roles of paediatricians, GPs, health visitors and the police were seen as vital. However, social service departments were constituted as the 'lead agency' and local authority social workers identified as the primary statutory professionals for coordinating the work and operating the system.

There were a number of key elements. Area Review Committees, subsequently retitled Area Child Protection Committees (ACPCs) (DHSS, 1988), were established in all local authority areas as policy-making bodies in order to:

- coordinate the work of the relevant agencies
- develop interprofessional training
- produce detailed procedures to be followed where it was felt a child had been abused or may be at risk of abuse.

In such situations, there was to be a system of case conferences so that the relevant professionals could share information about a particular child and family, make decisions as to what to do and provide an ongoing mechanism for monitoring progress. Where it was felt a child protection plan was required, the child would be placed on a child protection register. The register could then be consulted by other professionals to establish whether the child was currently known.

The first central government guidance that had the title 'Working Together' was published in 1988 (DHSS, 1988), on the same day as the publication of the public inquiry into the events in Cleveland (Secretary of State for Social Services, 1988). While it explicitly built on the consultation document published two years previously (DHSS, 1986), it had been considerably redrafted to take account of the Cleveland Inquiry, where a major concern had been the inappropriate and possibly excessive intervention of state welfare professionals into the privacy of families on the basis of uncertain and questionable evidence of sexual abuse (see Parton, 1991, pp. 121–35). While the guidance broadened the definition of child abuse to include sexual abuse, it was primarily concerned to ensure that professionals maintained a balance in their work between protecting children from abuse and protecting the privacy of the family from unnecessary and unwarranted intrusion – the issue which was to lie at the heart of the 1989 Children Act (Parton, 1991). The 1988 Working Together was 72 pages long, and was a much more substantial document than the DHSS (1974) circular *Non-Accidental Injury to Children*, which had begun the process of establishing the contemporary child protection system.

In addition, it established a new element to the system, which would grow in significance 20 years later. Part 9 of the guidance introduced a system of 'case reviews' to be carried out by the senior management of the relevant agencies, conducted under the auspices of the ACPC, which would become Serious Case Reviews (SCRs) in the 2006 guidance. The case reviews were introduced to try and pre-empt and perhaps avert the need for time-consuming, expensive and high-profile public inquiries, such as the Cleveland Inquiry, in the future.

From the protection of children from abuse to the safeguarding and promotion of children's welfare

Central government guidance on Working Together was revised twice during the 1990s. A comparison of the two documents clearly demonstrates the impact of New Labour and how official thinking about the nature of the problem and the best way of addressing this changed during the decade. There were clear moves to try and move policy and practice from a child protection orientation to a family service orientation.

The 1991 *Working Together under the Children Act 1989* (Home Office et al., 1991) was published to coincide with the implementation of the Children Act 1989 and had many similarities to the 1988 version (DHSS, 1988) and, following the aims of all the guidance since 1974, was framed in terms of responding to child abuse and improving the child protection system. This was evident in the document's subtitle: *A Guide to Arrangements for Inter-Agency Co-operation for the Protection of Children from Abuse*. The emphasis was on the need to identify 'high-risk' cases so that they could be differentiated from the rest. Thus, children could be protected from abuse while ensuring that family privacy was not undermined and scarce resources could be directed to where, in theory, they were most needed. While working in partnership with parents and children was seen as important, the focus was 'children at risk of significant harm', such that the whole document was framed in terms of when and how to carry out an 'investigation' in terms of Section 47 of the Children Act 1989. The key 'threshold' criterion to be addressed was whether the child was 'suffering or likely to suffer significant harm' (s.31(91)(9)). While the essential principles of the Children Act 1989 provided the legal framework, the focus was quite specific:

> The starting point of the process is that any person who has knowledge of, or suspicion that a child is suffering significant harm, or is at risk of suffering significant harm, should refer their concern to one or more of the agencies with statutory duties and/or powers to investigate or intervene – the social services department, the police or the NSPCC. (Home Office et al., 1991, para. 5.11.1)

There was no mention of any of the more wide-ranging preventive duties that local authorities had in terms of s.17(1) of the Children Act 1989 'to safeguard and promote the welfare of children in their area who are in need'.

As the title indicated, the 1999 Working Together was very different – *Working Together to Safeguard Children: A Guide to Inter-Agency Working to Safeguard and Promote the Welfare of Children* (DH et al., 1999). Not only was this the first time that the word 'safeguarding' was used in official guidance about child abuse but the subtitle explicitly framed the issue in terms of s.17(1) of the Children Act.

The 1999 Working Together had been revised in the light of *Child Protection: Messages from Research* (DH, 1995a), the 'refocusing' debate (Parton, 1997) and the research on the implementation of the Children Act, particularly in relation to the difficulties that local authorities were having in developing their 'family support' services (DH, 2001), and was framed – as indicated in the subtitle – in terms of the general duty placed on local authorities by s.17(1) of the Children Act 1989. The guidance underlined that local authorities had wider responsibilities than simply responding to concerns about 'significant harm' and was explicitly located in the wider agenda for children's services being implemented in the early years of the New Labour government. Social exclusion, domestic violence, the mental illness of a parent or carer, and drug and alcohol abuse (Cleaver et al., 1999) were all identified as 'sources of stress for children and families which might have a negative impact on a child's health, either directly, or because they affect the capacity of parents to respond to their child's needs' (DH et al., 1999, para. 2.19).

While the 1999 guidance continued to make it clear that if anyone believed that a child may be suffering 'significant harm' they should always refer these concerns to the social services department, it also stressed that these should be responded to by social services departments in the context of their much wider 'responsibilities towards all children whose health or development may be impaired without the provision of support and services, or who are disabled' (described by the Children Act 1989 as children 'in need') (para. 5.5). In order to take this forward, a more differentiated and holistic approach to assessment was introduced.

The publication of the 1999 edition of Working Together was combined with the publication of the *Framework for the Assessment of Children in Need and their Families* (DH et al., 2000) and the two documents needed to be read and used together. The Assessment Framework, like Working Together, was issued as guidance under Section 7 of the Local Authority Social Services Act 1970, which meant that it 'must be followed' by local authorities unless there were exceptional circumstances that justified a variation. Thus, it had the same legal status, and was, in effect, incorporated into Working Together.

The Assessment Framework replaced the previous guidance on *Protecting Children: A Guide for Social Workers Undertaking a Comprehensive Assessment* (DH, 1988), which had only been concerned with comprehensive assessment for long-term planning where child abuse had been confirmed or strongly suspected. In contrast, the Assessment Framework moved the focus from the assessment of risk of child abuse and 'significant harm' to one that was concerned with the possible impairment to a child's development. Both the safeguarding and promotion of a child's welfare were seen as intimately connected aims for intervention, so that it was important that access to services was via a common assessment route. The critical task was to ascertain whether a child was 'in need' and how the child and the parents in the context of their family and community environment might be helped. The effectiveness with which a child's needs were assessed were seen as key to the effectiveness of subsequent actions and services and, ultimately, to the outcomes for the child (Gray, 2002).

The framework explicitly built on the Looked After Children (LAC) system, which I discussed in Chapter 2, and was presented in terms of three dimensions: the child's developmental needs; parenting capacity (of both mother and father); and family and environmental factors. It was only by considering all three and the interrelationships between them that it would be possible to assess whether and in what ways a child's welfare was being safeguarded and promoted.

The different levels of assessment within the framework had different timescales attached to them. It was expected that within one working day of a referral to the social services department, there would be a decision about what response was required. If it was felt that more information was required, this constituted an initial assessment and should be completed within seven working days. It should address the three dimensions of the Assessment Framework and thereby determine whether the child was in need, the nature of any services required, from where, within what timescales and whether a further, more detailed core assessment should be undertaken.

A core assessment was defined as an 'in-depth assessment which addresses the central or most important aspects of the needs of a child and the capacity of his or her parents or caregivers to respond appropriately to these needs within the wider family and community context' (DH et al., 2000, para. 3.11) and should be completed within a maximum of 35 days from the point that the initial assessment ended.

While primarily a practice tool for social services departments, the Assessment Framework also aimed to provide a common language, shared values and commitment among a much wider range of agencies and professionals. In addition, it would assist the development of an Integrated Children's System, which would provide the basis for a unified approach to collecting and producing management information data for central and local government departments (Cleaver et al., 2008). Taken together, the 1999 Working Together (DH et al., 1999) and the Assessment Framework were much more substantial and complex documents than the 1991 Working Together (Home Office et al., 1991) (see Table A1.1 in the Appendix). Not only had the objects of concern broadened, but different timescales were also introduced for different types/levels of assessment, thereby providing the key criteria for judging and inspecting the performance of local authority children's services.

Working Together in the context of *Every Child Matters*

There was a clear attempt in the 1999 Working Together (DH et al., 1999) to reframe the object of concern away from a narrow, forensically driven conception of child protection towards the much broader notion of safeguarding, to the point where some commentators argued that child protection had disappeared and the idea of safeguarding was wide-ranging and vague (Munro and Calder, 2005; Smith, 2008). Certainly, the document did not provide a clear definition of safeguarding and its relationship with child protection, and a report produced jointly by eight child inspectors argued that while the idea of safeguarding children had become a major government priority, the term 'safeguarding has not been defined in law or government guidance' (DH, 2002, para. 1.5). This was to change with the publication of the 2006 Working Together (HM Government, 2006b), where:

Safeguarding and promoting the welfare of children is defined for the purposes of this guidance as:

- protecting children from maltreatment
- preventing impairment of children's health or development
- ensuring that children are growing up in circumstances consistent with the provision of safe and effective care

and undertaking that role so as to enable those children to have optimum life chances and to enter adulthood successfully. (para. 1.8)

While the 2006 Working Together had the same title as the 1999 version (DH et al., 1999), this was the first guidance authored by HM Government (2006b) rather than by particular government departments as previously. Although it built on the central principles and mechanisms laid out in the 1999 guidance, it was updated to take account of the Laming Report (2003) on the death of Victoria Climbié, the major changes being introduced by the *Every Child Matters: Change for Children* programme (DfES, 2004b) and the Children Act 2004.

A key element of the government's strategy was to strengthen the framework for single and multi-agency safeguarding practice. Under Section 11 of the Children Act 2004, a new statutory duty was placed on certain agencies (including the police, prisons and health bodies) to make arrangements to ensure that they had regard to the need to safeguard and promote the welfare of children. In addition, as from April 2006, local authorities were required to replace ACPCs with statutory Local Safeguarding Children Boards (LSCBs). The core membership of LSCBs was set out in the Children Act 2004 and was to include senior managers from different services, including the local authority, health bodies, the police, any secure training centre or prison in the area and other organizations as deemed appropriate.

The guidance (HM Government, 2006b) was framed in terms of supporting *all* children and families in terms of the five ECM outcomes of being healthy, enjoying and achieving, making a positive contribution, achieving economic wellbeing, and, particularly, staying safe, which were seen as 'key to children and young people's wellbeing' (para. 1.1). The guidance was presented as part of 'an integrated approach', so that effective measures to safeguard children were seen as those which also promoted their welfare, and should not be seen in isolation from the wider range of support and services to meet the needs of all children and families. The idea of safeguarding was explicitly located in the wider New Labour government policy agenda on tackling social exclusion.

While protecting children from maltreatment was seen as important in order to prevent the impairment of health and development, on its own, it was not seen as sufficient to ensure that children were growing up in circumstances that ensured the provision of safe and effective care, which could bring about the five outcomes for all children. The guidance was centrally concerned with trying to ensure that all agencies and professionals fulfilled their responsibilities both in relation to prevention and child protection, as well as safeguarding and promoting the welfare of all children, and where professionals and managers were held accountable for their actions.

Simply comparing the page length of the 1999 Working Together (DH et al., 1999) with that of 2006 (HM Government, 2006b) (see Table A1.1 in the Appendix), there was:

- an increase from 119 to 231 pages

- the number of pages on managing individual cases increased from 15 to 56

- the number of pages on SCRs increased from 4 to 15
- the number of footnotes increased from 12 to 43
- the number of references increased from 50 to 78.

For the first time, references were also in the form of internet links/ web addresses, accounting for 69 of the 78 references. The Assessment Framework (DH et al., 2000) continued to be fully incorporated into the 2006 guidance. Not only had the guidance nearly doubled in length and became much more detailed, but the objects of its concern had broadened considerably.

Staying Safe

These developments became even clearer in mid-2007. One of the first things that Ed Balls did when he became minister at the new Department for Children, Schools and Families (DCSF) was to publish a consultation document on *Staying Safe* (DSCF, 2007c). It clearly stated that:

> For some, safeguarding may have a narrow definition, focused on protecting children from abuse and neglect. But safeguarding used here covers a range of things we all need to do to keep children safe and promote their welfare. (DCSF, 2007c, para. 1.9)

Safeguarding had a broad remit and was 'everybody's business'. This was represented in the document on the 'roles, responsibilities and principles for improving children's safety' (Table 6.1).

It is interesting to note that 'children's social care' was one of just a number of agencies and its role was summarized as to 'act on child protection referrals, assess need, coordinate responses from local agencies to keep children safe *and* promote welfare'.

When *The Children's Plan* (DCSF, 2007b) was published later in 2007, with Chapter 2 entitled 'Safe and Sound', 11 areas were identified for new or additional action with various proposals for action. These were wide-ranging and were represented in terms of 'universal', 'targeted' and 'responsive' safeguarding (Figure 6.1).

However, while the idea of 'safeguarding' was much broader than 'child protection', it made no reference to a whole range of community, institutional and social structural factors that impact on a child's welfare, which I will discuss in Chapter 11. What becomes clear is that while the

Table 6.1 Roles, responsibilities and principles for improving children's safety

Children and young people, parents and families
Know what acceptable/unacceptable behaviour towards children and young people is, how to identify and manage risk of harm (and for parents, to help their children do so), and who to approach if they have concerns

The **general public** help ensure children and young people are safe, including by their own behaviour, identify unacceptable behaviour by others towards children and act on any concerns

Everyone **working with children and young people**, whether in paid employment or as volunteers, are alert to risks and indicators of harm, and know when and with whom to share information

Children's social care	Police Services	NHS organisations and staff	Services for vulnerable adults	Other services
Act on child protection referrals, assess need, coordinate responses from local agencies to keep children safe and promote welfare	Identify and act on child protection concerns, carry out criminal investigations, enforce road traffic laws and help to prevent harm	Actively promote health and well-being of children, identify and work in partnership with agencies on safeguarding concerns, and provide timely, therapeutic and preventative interventions	Prisons, adult mental health, adult substance misuse, domestic violence intervention projects recognise the links between service users who are parents, and risks to their children's safety, and safeguard children	Schools, including extended schools, FE colleges, housing, planners, parks/green spaces managers, road safety officers create a safe environment for children and young people, educate children and young people about how to keep themselves safe, and refer child protection concerns

We should create safe environments for all children and young people to help prevent harm, including employers checking the suitability of those who work with children – but take additional action for vulnerable groups of children. Services should intervene where necessary, in the most effective way, at the most effective point. Actions chosen should be proportionate to the needs of the child, the risk faced by children, and the impact they will have

Local Safeguarding Children Boards and children's trusts
Lead the whole system locally including safe local environments, providing and promoting child protection training for service providers, safe roads, building effective partnerships, working within specific legislative frameworks, leading enquiries on specific cases and providing services for children in need

Inspectorates
Ensure regulated services for children have effective child protection and safeguarding policies in place, and an ethos of safeguarding

Central Government
Formulate policy and lead on strategy to safeguard children and young people, ensure a clear national framework is in place, develop the legislative framework, raise awareness of the issues and responsibilities, support local implementation, review policy and performance through inspection, support research and allocate resources

Where it is more appropriate to work in partnership to address concerns, efforts will be co-ordinated across Government and local services, including the private and voluntary sectors where necessary.
A culture of evaluation and learning will be embedded in all services.
There is no excuse for abusing, exploiting or neglecting a child, whether suggested for cultural or religious reasons, or reasons of income or social exclusion

Source: DCSF, 2007c, p. 24.

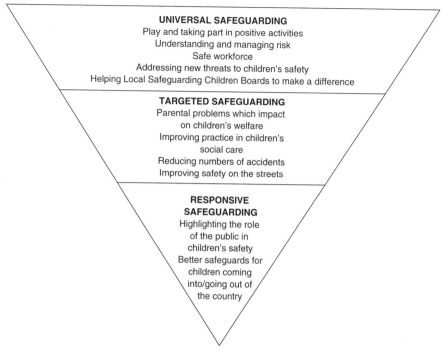

Figure 6.1   Safeguarding in *The Children's Plan*

Source: DCSF, 2007b, p. 42.

new systems being set in place to safeguard and promote the welfare of children were far more complex and wide-ranging than the much narrower and forensically driven child protection system of the early 1990s, child protection still inhabited the core of the new arrangements. Similarly, it continued to be local authority children's social care and social workers who were given the lead responsibility for carrying out the key assessment tasks in relation to who may be a child in need and which children may be suffering significant harm. It was 'experienced and qualified social workers' (HM Government, 2006b, Ch. 5) who were given the key responsibilities for decision making at the point of referral, initial assessment and core assessment and who were expected to operationalize and coordinate responses under Sections 17 and 47 of the Children Act 1989. As I argued over 20 years ago, it was social workers who were given the key role in deciding whether a child was safe or not and negotiating the boundaries between, and respective responsibilities of, the state and parents, particularly where compulsory intervention into the privacy of the family was being considered (Parton, 1991).

While the *ECM: Change for Children* programme was ambitious and aimed to transform children's services, social workers continued to play the key role in relation to the statutory responsibilities of the state and the specific operation of the child protection system.

Beyond this, however, and as we saw in Chapter 4, it seemed that many of the principles, systems and processes of the child protection system had been taken up, developed and applied to a much wider proportion of the child population and those who had responsibilities for them, whether these be parents or other health, welfare and educational professionals. The importance of interagency coordination, multidisciplinary work, early intervention and prevention, and the sharing of information was now seen as providing the key elements for the transformation across the continuum of children's services and not just where there are concerns about significant harm. In many ways, the formalized interagency approaches that had been developed in relation to child protection for over 30 years were to be applied to all children's services. In the process, the mechanisms whereby these various elements would be integrated became much more complex and considerable reliance was being placed on new ICTs to make these work. Not only were such systems aimed to improve and integrate the work of frontline practitioners but also to provide aggregate data so that the nature of the work could be measured, audited and managed. It was planned that the various elements of the *ECM: Change for Children* (DfES, 2004b) would all be in place for late 2008. However, particularly in the light of the claim by the government that the huge changes had been prompted to ensure that a tragic case like Victoria Climbié could never happen again, the new arrangements were always likely to be open to criticism and subject to major strain if and when another high-profile child death came to light; and such a possibility was never far away (Devo, 2007).

Working Together in the post-Baby P era

In Chapter 5, I analysed the case of Baby P and attempted to assess its impact on policy and practice. I argued that it marked a watershed in the politics of child protection in England. In many ways, the term 'Baby P' came to represent and characterize much that appeared to be wrong with contemporary policy and practice, not only in relation to children's services but also in relation to the problems in society more generally. Immediately after the completion of the court case, the government had established a series of initiatives to try and contain the political fallout from the tragedy. One of these was the appointment of Lord Laming to carry out an urgent review of child protection in England. A part of the motivation was to establish that the problems evident in Haringey were not common in other parts of the country. Another, and perhaps more significant, reason was to demonstrate that the New Labour reforms introduced as a direct response to the death of Victoria Climbié (Laming Report, 2003) under the *ECM: Change for Children* programme (DfES, 2004b) were working and, crucially, were fit for purpose.

When he reported in March 2009, Lord Laming's conclusions in relation to the latter were somewhat equivocal:

> The Government deserves credit for the legislation and guidance that has been put in place to safeguard children and promote the welfare of children over the last five years. *Every Child Matters* clearly has the support of professionals, across all of the services, who work with children and young people. The interagency guidance *Working Together to Safeguard Children* provides a sound framework for professionals to protect children and promote their welfare ... However, whilst the improvements in the services for children and families, in general, are welcome it is clear that the need to protect children and young people from significant harm and neglect is ever more challenging. There now needs to be a step change in the arrangements to protect children from harm. It is essential that action is now taken so that as far as humanly possible children at risk of harm are properly protected. (Laming Report, 2009, pp. 3–4)

It seemed that while Lord Laming was generally supportive of the changes introduced post-Climbié, he also felt more needed to be done to strengthen, what he saw, as its core business and his report was explicitly framed in terms of 'child protection'.

The government responded quickly and positively – again in terms of 'the protection of children in England' (HM Government, 2009) – and accepted all of his 58 recommendations. It stated that the reforms would be driven forward by a new cross-government delivery unit, the National Safeguarding Delivery Unit, which would work alongside Sir Roger Singleton, who was appointed as the first ever chief adviser on the safety of children. The government's *The Protection of Children in England: Action Plan* (HM Government, 2009) responded to the Laming Report by allocating recommendations to a number of work programmes. While 10 of the recommendations would be the responsibility of the Social Work Reform Board to take forward, 20 would be accounted for by a major revision to Working Together, the official government guidance. In addition, a further 6 of the changes were to be dealt with by changes to the statutory guidance on SCRs, which would be included in Chapter 8 of the revised Working Together.

Following a public consultation, the revised Working Together was published on 17 March 2010 (HM Government, 2010a), just before Parliament was dissolved prior to the general election. While the new guidance explicitly attempted to respond to the Laming Report (2009) and the Action Plan (HM Government, 2009), it also attempted to reflect and respond to a whole variety of other changes in research, policy and practice evident since the publication of the previous Working Together in April 2006 (HM Government, 2006b). The document followed the detailed, proceduralized format of previous documents, but because of the increased demands and challenges it was attempting to address, its length and complexity grew considerably. Concerns about this were a significant issue and commented on by numerous respondents to the consultation (HM Government, 2010b). The government said it planned to address this in due course by producing a navigable, web-based version and a short practitioner guide, and identifying ways in which the statutory requirements would not be obscured by the non-statutory guidance.

The expansion and growing complexity of the 2010 Working Together (HM Government, 2010a) were not only reflected in the increased page length, from 231 to 390 pages (see Appendix, Table A1.1 for further details), but in the huge increase in the number of references (from 78 to 200), internet links (from 69 to 124) and footnotes (from 43 to 273) since 2006. While the 'Managing individual cases' chapter only increased by one page, to 57 pages, the 'Serious case reviews' chapter increased from 8 to 23 pages. In addition, Chapter 6 outlined and provided links to 10 other statutory supplementary guidance documents which, together, added a further 424 pages.

It seemed that government had found itself in a major dilemma. The guidance needed to reflect the government's policy, following ECM, of providing a wide-ranging preventive, early intervention and integrated range of services for children and young people, while also needing to be seen to be strengthening its explicitly child protection focus and the fact that practitioners and managers needed to be held accountable for what they did and the decisions they made. Such changes were being introduced in the emotionally charged post-Baby P political climate. In the process, the length and complexity of government guidance grew enormously. The guidance had come a long way since the publication of the original seven-page memorandum on 'non-accidental injury to children' in 1974 which had, in effect, established the modern child protection system. New and ever more detailed procedures were being introduced in an attempt to repair what appeared to be an increasingly bankrupt system. It was difficult to see how such a bureaucratic response was going to overcome what the media, politicians and the wider public had come to see as major, wide-ranging institutional failures.

It seemed that many of the procedural and institutional changes that had been introduced over the previous 40 years, particularly those introduced after 1999, had become major problems. These problems were made explicit by a number of papers published at the time based on empirical research, which were critical of many of the complex new IT systems that had been introduced, particularly in relation to the Integrated Children's System (Shaw and Clayden, 2009; Shaw et al., 2009a, 2009b; White et al., 2009a, 2010). The changes seemed to have had the effect of deflecting frontline practitioners from their core task of working directly with children, young people and parents (Hall et al., 2010), thus increasing the bureaucratic demands of the work and the possibilities for greater error (Broadhurst et al., 2010a, 2010b; White et al., 2010), and catching practitioners in an 'iron cage of performance management' (Wastell et al., 2010), unable to exercise their professional judgement in order to safeguard children and promote their welfare (Peckover et al., 2008; White et al., 2009b). In the process, major concerns were raised about the future development of the ECM programme of change (Broadhurst et al., 2009; Ayre and Preston-Shoot, 2010; Simon and Ward, 2010). It seemed that while the changes were introduced with the best of intentions, they had a number of unintended, and even dangerous, consequences, and the overproceduralized, micro-managed and bureaucratized nature of the child protection system seemed to lie at the heart of the problems.

Conclusion

In this chapter, I have summarized the growth and content of government guidance on child protection policy and practice from 1974 to 2010. In doing so, I have argued that such guidance can be seen to represent official thinking and priorities at any one particular time, while also playing a key role in trying to bring about policy and practice change on the ground. Not only did the size of the guidance grow and become more complex but it also became more prescriptive, while the objects of concern broadened from 'battered babies', to 'non-accidental injury', to 'child abuse', to 'safeguarding and promoting the welfare or children'. By 2010, the guidance was being subjected to increasing criticism as it seemed to represent much that was problematic with the child protection system itself. I will return to these issues in Chapter 8, after discussing some of the key elements of change introduced by the Conservative-led coalition government, which came to power in May 2010, in Chapter 7.

7

'Social breakdown', the 'big society' and the Conservative-led coalition government

In May 2010, Britain had a new government. Following many days of intense negotiations and against the backdrop of the worst financial crisis and economic downturn since 1929, Britain had its first peacetime coalition government since the 1930s. While the Conservative Party had the largest number of seats in the House of Commons (307), it required the support of the Liberal Democrats (57 seats) to form a government. David Cameron became prime minister and Nick Clegg deputy prime minister.

In their Foreword to *The Coalition: Our Programme for Government* (HM Government, 2010c), forged during those negotiations, the two leaders made it clear that while the overriding and most urgent task facing the new government was to reduce the public debt, they also believed the coalition:

> can deliver radical, reforming government, a stronger society, a smaller state, and power and responsibility in the hands of every citizen. Great change and real progress lie ahead.

The government set itself a major agenda for reform that would aim to:

- reduce the role and size of the state
- reduce the top-down bureaucratic demands of the performance management regime established under New Labour

- improve civil liberties for the individual
- devolve as much power and decision making via an emphasis on 'localism'.

In the process, the government would embark on a major programme of public spending cuts and far-reaching restructuring of the public sector, which would involve significant transfers of responsibility for providing services to the private and third sectors and to communities and individuals themselves (Taylor-Gooby and Stoker, 2011; Taylor-Gooby, 2012). Such radical reforms were not simply a response to the financial and economic crisis. The ideas informing such changes had been developing over a number of years, partly in response to the policies of the New Labour government and partly as attempts to develop an approach that could be seen as distinctive and, for the Conservative Party of David Cameron, different from those of the Thatcherite view that there was 'no such thing as society'. I will look at a number of themes that can be seen to have had a significant influence on the approach of the coalition government.

The coalition government: some key background ideas

Total politics: Labour's command state

In 2003, the Conservative Party Policy Unit published a substantial document edited by Greg Clark, who was appointed 'minister of state for decentralisation' in the new government, and James Mather called *Total Politics: Labour's Command State*, which included chapters by different members of the Conservative Policy Unit.

The argument was clearly stated:

> It is Labour's state centralism which causes failure in government, holding back everyone's quality of life. Public services and local communities are being stifled by a command state that forces front-line professionals to deliver the sort of services bureaucrats, rather than ordinary people, want to see. (Clark and Mather, 2003, p. vii)

They identified four key drivers of this 'command state' that needed to be changed:

- targets imposed from Whitehall
- centrally controlled inflexible funding

- bureaucratic audit and inspection
- rigid terms and conditions.

It was argued that it resulted in squandering taxpayers' money on wasteful bureaucracy, led to unintended consequences, undermined a local sense of belonging, and devalued the professional judgement and discretion of frontline professionals.

The vision for the future rested on freeing frontline services from this total politics and delivering choice to citizens and communities. Such an analysis was to become a central element of the Conservative critique of New Labour policies and would have resonated with many of the emerging criticisms of the child protection and child welfare reforms introduced under New Labour, summarized at the end of Chapter 6.

The Centre for Social Justice and the threat of 'breakdown Britain'

In 2004, Iain Duncan Smith, who had briefly been leader of the Conservative Party, established an independent think tank, the Centre for Social Justice (CSJ), to find some effective solutions for the 'poverty and blight' that he felt were evident in many parts of Britain. The CSJ's mission was to put justice at the heart of British politics and build an alliance of poverty fighting organizations in order to see a reversal of 'social breakdown' in the UK. Such a development seemed to demonstrate that the Conservative Party was keen to show it had changed from the 'nasty party' and wanted to develop a social policy that attempted to address the problems associated with poverty and social justice. When he became leader of the Conservative Party, David Cameron asked Iain Duncan Smith to establish a Social Justice Policy Group to make recommendations to the Conservative Party. It produced a number of important reports, where it characterized the social problems facing certain parts of the country in terms of 'social breakdown'.

The first report was called *Breakdown Britain* (Social Justice Policy Group, 2006) and argued that the margins of society had been breaking down and the social fabric of many communities was being stripped away. It argued that while material deprivation should be dealt with, poverty was not just an issue of money. It was the 'quality of the social structure of our lives' (p. 3) that was key. It identified five 'pathways to poverty' that needed to be addressed: family breakdown; educational failure; worklessness and economic dependence; addictions; and indebtedness.

In its report the following year, called *Breakthrough Britain*, the group made its explanations of the problems even more explicit, as well as outlining some of its policy recommendations. The notion of an 'underclass' became central:

> As the fabric of society crumbles at the margins what has been left behind is an *underclass*, where life is characterised by dependence, addiction, debt and family breakdown. This is an underclass in which a child born into poverty today is more likely to remain in poverty than at any time since the late 1960s. (Social Justice Policy Group, 2007, p. 5, emphasis added)

The report advocated a new approach to welfare for the twenty-first century:

> We believe that, in order to reverse social breakdown, we need to start reinforcing the Welfare Society. The Welfare Society is that which delivers welfare beyond the State. At the heart of the Welfare Society is the army of people, who, for love of neighbour and community, shoulder the massive burden of care. (p. 6)

In many respects, this idea that there was a welfare society 'beyond the state' prefigured the idea of 'the big society', which was to crystallize as David Cameron's 'big idea' in 2009. In doing so, it argued that while the overall approach was based on the belief that people must take responsibility for their own choices, government also had a responsibility to help people make the right choices. Two specific areas were said to underpin the overall approach. First, a range of policies that aimed to break 'the cycle of disadvantage' in the early years of a child's life, and, second, policies that aimed to strengthen 'stable families'.

These ideas were reinforced in a publication the following year written by Iain Duncan Smith and Graham Allen, the Labour MP for Nottingham North, and published jointly by the Centre for Social Justice and the Smith Institute (Allen and Smith, 2008), on the importance of *early intervention*, a theme Graham Allen was to be closely associated with in the first two years of the coalition government. In the report, the two MPs warned that unless concerted action was taken to transform parenting skills and revitalize the upbringing of

> poor children on the worst council estates, Britain would be saddled with a new generation of disturbed and aggressive young people doomed to repeat and amplify the social breakdown disfiguring their lives and others around them. (Allen and Smith, 2008, p. 1)

Underpinning the report was the view that since the 1960s, Britain had witnessed a considerable decline in the institution of the family, with an increasing divorce rate, a growing number of children born outside marriage, and increased numbers of single-parent families. What happens inside the family when a child is very young 'strongly determines how they will react to people outside the home, how ready they will be to learn and ultimately what kind of a citizen they will become' (p. 12). In particular, the first few months and years were crucial to how children were nurtured and ensured that their brain developed properly (p. 12). Neuroscientific research demonstrating that the first 12 months of a child's life were key to maximize appropriate brain development was seen as crucial, particularly the work of Bruce Perry and Rima Shore in the USA (Perry, 1995; Shore, 1997). Parenting in some poor families needed to be transformed, otherwise the 'dysfunctional base' (the underclass) of society would grow further. At the centre of policies to counteract such developments should be a much greater emphasis on early intervention:

> The philosophy of Early Intervention goes much further than prevention. It is about breaking the intergenerational cycle of underachievement. (Allen and Smith, 2008, p. 4)

Such a view had a number of connections with some of the pronouncements and policy developments of the later years of the New Labour government and its increasing emphasis on the importance of 'the cycle of deprivation', discussed in Chapter 4. One of the central aims of the document by Allen and Smith was to try and attract cross-party support for such an initiative.

The CSJ report developed the idea of 'the broken society' and had quite specific ideas about how this had come about and how it should be addressed (Hayton, 2012). As we saw in Chapter 5, this informed David Cameron's overall view of social policy and his response to the child abuse scandals of 2008/09. While such an approach did have a view that there was such a thing as society, it was a particular view, consistent with what Ruth Levitas (1996, 2005) has termed the moral underclass discourse (MUD), discussed in Chapter 3.

Red Toryism and the move to 'the big society'

While the CSJ was influential in informing Conservative Party thinking in the late 2000s, other think tanks also had influence, such as the

Adam Smith Institute, the Institute for Economic Affairs and the Centre for Policy Studies – all of which had been operating for some years – together with those that had been established more recently, such as Policy Exchange and the Social Market Foundation. However, it was probably the newest think tank, ResPublica, which had the most influence on David Cameron's idea of the importance of 'the big society', where the case for decentralization and the rejuvenation of civil society played a central role.

Phillip Blond, director of ResPublica, developed a critique of contemporary society and the role of the state. While he was scathing about the impact of New Labour policies, he was also highly critical of neoliberalism and the impact of the market (Blond, 2009, 2010). He combined a demand for the remoralization of the market with a call for the breakup of central state power. He argued that the neoliberal emphasis on the market had become the site of monopolistic practices and corporate privilege that disadvantaged the poor. At the same time, state welfare, in attempting to protect people from damaging exposure to the market, had induced dependency and undermined mutual support and community self-help. There needed to be a much greater emphasis on rejuvenating civil society. With state welfare much reduced and the market free of corporate monopolies, conditions could be created for the emergence of an associative democratic arena in which citizens could become more active in commissioning services and/or running them themselves.

While Blond never used the term 'the big society', his thinking was clearly influential and potentially radical. As Nick Ellison (2011) has argued, while the CSJ focused on poverty and its version of social justice and 'responsibilization', Blond complemented these ideas, first with a much more trenchant critique of the deleterious effects of markets on the poor, increasing inequalities and the overall quality of social life and, second, with a much more idealized vision of the potential for creating a mutualized 'good society'. Under Cameron's leadership of the Conservative Party, the idea was stressed so that the importance of 'the big society' became central to the Conservative Party's 2010 election campaign and its election manifesto (Conservative Party, 2010).

Probably the first time Cameron (2009) used the term was in the 2009 Hugo Young lecture, when he attempted to reframe the way the Conservative Party was perceived and remake the case for an up-to-date version of 'one nation conservatism'. The lecture heavily criticized New Labour's attempt at 'big government' and contrasted this with the new Conservative vision of a one nation 'big society' based on the principles of decentralization, neighbourhood, empowerment and mutuality, and largely organized by voluntary organizations, social enterprises and individuals themselves. Interestingly, while the social conservatism of Blond and the CSJ was evident, there was no reference to Blond's critique of neoliberalism and the negative impact of corporations and the private market (Corbett and Walker, 2013). The emphasis was on the need to break up state monopolies and the importance of charities, social enterprises and private companies providing public services so that individuals' needs could be met and a greater sense of social responsibility could grow (Lister, 2011).

The Orange Book: Reclaiming Liberalism

For many years, the Liberal Democrat party seemed much closer politically and in policy terms to the Labour Party, and on numerous social policies was the most left wing of all three main political parties, so that a coalition with the Conservatives seemed unlikely. However, under the leadership of Nick Clegg, who became leader in 2007, this began to change. It was obvious that Nick Clegg's personal relationship with Gordon Brown, the leader of the Labour Party, was poor and he made it clear during the post-election negotiations that he could not join a coalition government with the Labour Party while Gordon Brown remained leader.

The potential for a link-up between the Conservatives and the Liberal Democrats had been signalled by the publication of *The Orange Book: Reclaiming Liberalism* (Marshall and Laws, 2004). Contributors to the book included a number of Liberal Democrat politicians who were to play leading roles in the negotiation of the coalition agreement and would become members of its inaugural Cabinet, namely Nick Clegg, David Laws, Vince Cable and Chris Huhne. Central themes of the book were that 'whenever possible "command and control" regulation should be replaced by self-regulation reinforced by statute' (Cable, 2004, p. 153), and that the reform of public services should be informed by a vision in which a mixture of public sector, private and mutually owned enterprises should compete to provide mainstream services. The book identified four strands of liberalism that needed to be built on – personal, political, economic and social – and argued that economic liberal principles were needed to deliver social liberal goals. It argued that it was important to accept that competition, consumer power and private sector innovation offered the best way for increasing wealth and reducing poverty, so that for social liberalism what was important was:

- introducing more choice, competition and consumer power into public services such as health, while preserving the principle of access for all on the basis of need, not ability to pay

- reforming our welfare system to give people more control and involvement in their own security, in exchange for more personal responsibility

- breaking the cycle of deprivation, which is caused by family breakdown, poor parenting and child poverty; improving the standards of our education system to help address inequalities of opportunity (Laws, 2004, pp. 41–2).

Many of these ideas would have been attractive to David Cameron who, in 2007, had claimed he was a liberal Conservative 'because I believe in the freedom of individuals to pursue their own happiness, with the minimum of interference from government' (Cameron, 2007).

Viewed in the light of the economic liberalism of *The Orange Book*, the willingness of the Liberal Democrats to negotiate a coalition with the Conservative Party and the agreement of the five Liberal Democrat Cabinet members with cuts to public spending and the introduction of radical, market-based reforms of public services becomes comprehensible, and demonstrates that there was potentially much in common between the leaderships of the Liberal Democrats and the Conservatives.

The Coalition: Our Programme for Government

The ideas of 'the big society' and 'social breakdown' framed much of the Conservative Party's election manifesto (Conservative Party, 2010). The Foreword (p. viii) stated:

> we need fundamental change: from big government that presumes to know best, to the Big Society that trusts in the people for ideas and innovation ... Mending Britain's broken society will be a central aim of the next Conservative government.

It went on to say:

> We will give people much more say over the things that affect their daily lives. We will make government, politics and the public services much

more open and transparent. And we will give the people who work in our public services much greater responsibility. But in return, they will have to answer to the people. (p. ix)

The Labour government, and Gordon Brown in particular, was blamed for Britain's main economic problem – the record size of the public deficit. A crisis that had its origins in the banking and financial centres of the USA and the UK was transformed into a political problem concerned with the size of the public debt, the overblown size of the public sector and the overintervention of the state (Clarke and Newman, 2012). Conservatives sought to reduce the bulk of the 'structural deficit' in one parliamentary period from 2010 to 2014/15 and set out a 'new economic model' (Conservative Party, 2010, p. 3) based on low levels of public borrowing, pro-business tax regimes and productive investments, which would promote private sector-led economic growth (Gamble, 2012). They planned to reduce the size and scope of state welfare and ensure there would be fewer top-down rules and regulations and micromanagement of public services, together with more private finance initiatives, outsourcing of services, payment by results, citizen involvement, use of volunteers and third sector initiatives. They would 'give public sector workers back their professional autonomy' (Conservative Party, 2010, p. 35) and claimed that their approach was 'absolutely in line with the spirit of the age: the post-bureaucratic age' (p. 35). Proposals included a range of policies to reduce welfare dependency and a refocusing of initiatives such as Sure Start and extended schools to more targeted services for the people who need it most – 'disadvantaged and dysfunctional families' – including the provision of '4,200 more Sure Start health visitors' by 'refocusing Sure Start's peripatetic outreach services' (p. 43). The manifesto also asserted that 'strong families are the bedrock of a strong society' (p. 41) and wanted to promote pro-marriage policies by ending the 'couple penalty' (p. 41) in the benefits system, review the law and legal processes on family justice, and support couple relationship services.

In comparison, the Liberal Democrats (2010) framed their manifesto around the idea of 'fairness':

• fair taxes

• a fair chance for every child

• a fair future by creating jobs for making Britain greener

• a fair deal by cleaning up politics.

They agreed with the Labour government about seeking less severe spending cuts, pledging to halve the public deficit by 2014/15. Their manifesto criticized prior Conservative and Labour governments for overseeing widening inequalities and infringements to civil liberties, and advocated tax reforms to reduce taxation on lower paid workers and increase taxes on the wealthy. It included detailed plans for a 'pupil premium' to provide additional funds to schools to support under-achieving disadvantaged children and more extensive free and part-time preschool provision and family-friendly employment measures. Both the Conservative and Liberal Democrat manifestos made it clear that they would scrap ContactPoint and ensure that SCRs were published in full 'to ensure that lessons are learned'. The Liberal Democrats (2010, p. 50) also committed themselves to 'support the objective of at least a 70 per cent reduction in child maltreatment by 2030'.

Following the initial agreement from the Conservative–Liberal Democrat negotiations (Conservative/Liberal Democrats, 2010), the new government published *The Coalition: Our Programme for Government* (HM Government, 2010c, p. 7), in which it stated that 'the most urgent task facing this coalition is to tackle our record debts' and that there would be an emergency budget within 50 days of any agreement and a full Spending Review reporting in the autumn. Such a statement seemed to be given added significance by the rapidly deteriorating financial situation in Europe and the apparent imminent bankruptcy of the Greek government.

The emergency budget was announced on 22 June (HM Treasury, 2010a), which identified an additional £40 billion of 'fiscal consolidation' to that planned by the previous Brown government. The Spending Review (HM Treasury, 2010b) was published on 20 October and planned:

- the biggest squeeze on overall public expenditure since 1945

- the tightest settlement for spending on public services since the mid-1970s

- the tightest squeeze on NHS spending since April 1951–March 1956 (Crawford, 2010).

The Spending Review envisaged a total of £80.5 billion of expenditure savings by 2014/15, with overall public expenditure falling from 47.3% of GDP in 2010/11 to 41% of GDP in 2014/15. There would be a total fiscal tightening of £110.3 billion by 2014/15, made up of 73% in spending cuts and 27% in tax rises (HM Treasury, 2010b). The UK economy was forecast to grow by 2.7% in 2014/15, and the state was planned to contract by around 6.3% of GDP. It anticipated that, as a result, the private sector would grow by the equivalent of 9% or £180 billion of output by 2015. The coalition approach to macroeconomic policy seemed to revive the 'crowded-out' thesis, which had been implemented, and failed, during the first Thatcher government in the early 1980s. This was based on the assumption that if the frontiers of state investment and intervention were rolled back and state regulation reduced, the frontiers of the market and enterprise would inevitably and spontaneously roll forward to fill the vacuum; private sector jobs would be created and the fiscal deficit reduced. As Simon Lee (2011) argued, it had not worked in the 1980s and it was unlikely to work in the current situation.

It was not simply the size of the planned cutbacks that marked out the approach of the coalition to the public debt from other Western governments, including the USA, but the speed of their introduction. It was also in sharp contrast to its relative inactivity in relation to private debt and the ongoing and potentially destabilizing deficit in the finances of UK banks.

The coalition claimed that while the Spending Review did make choices, these were unavoidable in order to secure economic stability (HM Treasury, 2010b, p. 5). However, many of the choices had not appeared in either of the coalition parties' general election manifestos. Some choices, most notably the increase in student fees for students attending English universities, contradicted both manifestos' commitments, and the Liberal Democrats had signed undertakings to oppose any increases. Others, most significantly the coalition's plans for the reform of the NHS in England, not only had *not* appeared in either party's manifesto, but had not been specified in *The Coalition: Our Programme for Government* (HM Government, 2010c).

It became apparent that the government was not simply concerned with responding pragmatically to the major economic and financial challenges but was engaged in a major programme of public services reform. It was a government in a hurry, which, in the first 12 months, introduced legislation and policy change that would have a major impact on all areas of state activity, particularly in relation to the major areas of welfare. It engaged in a far-reaching restructuring of state services, which aimed to transfer significant areas of responsibility from the state to the private sector and the citizen. How far these changes were simply a reversion to a Thatcherite neoliberal approach, or arose from a new ideology based on a fusion of modern liberal Conservatism and social/orange liberal democracy, which sought to reduce the state's provider role (although not necessarily its funding obligations) while also trying to bolster localism, is not easy to assess. However, the two approaches were not incompatible as both wished to reduce the role of the state.

From 'the big society' to open public services

While 'the big society' was perhaps the major narrative that attempted to frame the approach to government of the Conservative Party and the early days of the coalition government and was clearly ambitious in its aims, it was also an idea that did not grab the imagination of the electorate and did not receive the support of all members of the Conservative Party. At various points after 2009, David Cameron made attempts to relaunch the idea (Ellison, 2011) and it became increasingly clear that its central concern was the reform of public services.

The ideas about public services reform were laid out in a speech by David Cameron (2011a) to the Royal Society of Arts on 17 January 2011, where he argued that his aim was to empower not only service users, but professionals and would not only strengthen existing providers but new ones in the private and voluntary sectors. The coalition programme would:

> Free professionals from top down control and bureaucracy. Give choice to the user. Encourage competition between the suppliers. Pay by results wherever appropriate. Publish information available wherever you can. Make public service professionals answer to people, rather than the government machine. (Cameron, 2011a, p. 8)

The link between the reform of public services and the politics of 'the big society' were developed further in a speech on 15 February (Cameron, 2011b). He said that while he knew that the first task of the coalition government was to sort out the debt and bring about economic recovery, that was not what he was passionate about:

> What is it I am really passionate about? It is actually social recovery as well as economic recovery. I think we need a social recovery because as I have said lots of times in the past, there are too many parts of our society that

are broken, whether it is broken families or whether it is some communities breaking down; whether it is the level of crime, the level of gang membership; whether it's problems of people stuck on welfare, unable to work; whether it's the sense that some of our public services don't work for us – we do need a social recovery to mend the broken society. To me, that's what the Big Society is all about. (Cameron, 2011b, p. 2)

He argued that it was crucial that people took more responsibility. For those who were not able to exercise their responsibility appropriately and thereby exercise their freedom, it may be necessary to limit that freedom and reduce their choices. For those who could act responsibly, it was important that they were given more power and control to improve their lives and communities. As Ben Kisby (2010, p. 485) has argued, underlying Cameron's idea of 'the big society' was the view that 'the state is bad and almost anything – the free market, charities or volunteers – is better'.

In order to reform public services to overcome these problems, Cameron (2011b, p. 2) argued that there were three key ingredients:

1 It was important to devolve more power, and here the legislation on localism was important.

2 It was important to open up services 'to make them less monolithic'.

3 It was important to have more philanthropic giving and more volunteering.

The opening up of public services was a vital part of dismantling big government in order to build the big society.

In July 2011, the government launched its White Paper *Open Public Services* (HM Government, 2011a), which was to provide the policy framework for all public services. In order to overcome 'the old, centralised approach to public services', where it was assumed that 'the man in Whitehall really does know best' (p. 7), the White Paper outlined 'five principles for modernising public services':

- Wherever possible we will increase choice.
- Public services should be decentralised to the lowest appropriate level.
- Public services should be open to a range of providers.
- We will ensure fair access to public services.

- Public services should be accountable to users and to taxpayers (p. 8).

In relation to the final principle, the White Paper stated that:

> If people are to exercise real choice they need timely and easily accessible information about what services are available and how good they are … we will ensure that the datasets government collects are open and accessible in order to support individuals to make informed choices about the services they use. (HM Government, 2011a, p. 19)

The publication, via the internet, of information and data gathered by government, particularly on the performance of different services such as schools, hospitals and police forces, was seen as a major way of improving quality and increasing accountability to the wider public. Not only would it improve transparency, it would support user choice.

It was clear that the government was committed to opening up the public sector to competition in order 'to drive up standards'. It argued that apart from those public services where it saw that government had a special reason to operate a monopoly (for example the military), every public service should be opened up to delivery by a diverse range of providers, which it saw as a better way of meeting people's complex needs and narrowing the gap between rich and poor (p. 39). At all levels, the role of government would thereby change; rather than trying to run and provide public services, government should increasingly become funders, regulators and commissioners.

When reviewing the progress of its reforms in March 2012 (HM Government, 2012a), the coalition made it clear that the reform of all public services – including schools, welfare benefits, health, the police and local government – was central to its political strategy. The full radicalism of the changes became increasingly evident in the review and that the government had only just begun the process so that:

> open public services deliver effective choice to citizens, are decentralised to the most appropriate level, are supplied by a diverse range of innovative providers, ensure fair access for all citizens, and are transparently accountable for the service levels and outcomes they deliver. (HM Government, 2012a, p. 4)

If a significant thrust of the Thatcher/Major governments of 1979/1990 had been to sell off and privatize a wide range of nationalized industries and public utilities, it was clear that the aim of the coalition government was to commercialize and marketize as many core state activities as possible.

Conclusion

We can see that while there were a number of similarities in the approach of the coalition government to that of New Labour, there were also some important differences. The emphasis on choice and the opening up of services to different providers and the overall sympathy with introducing market principles into the public services had been introduced by New Labour. However, the rate of change, particularly in the first two years of the coalition government, was tremendous and, crucially, its reforms were being carried out at the same time as introducing major public expenditure cuts. The New Labour reforms were carried out at a time of growth for the economy and public finances (Prabhakar, 2011), and there was an emphasis throughout on top-down control, micromanagement and the importance of centrally generated and monitored targets and performance indicators, all of which the coalition government claimed it wanted to move beyond.

While New Labour attempted to base its approach on a Third Way and talked in terms of social exclusion and the importance of investing in public services via 'the social investment state', the coalition and the Conservatives in particular used the language of 'social breakdown', 'the big society' and the importance of opening up public services. The latter was absolutely central for its strategy for the reform of public services at all levels of government and was pursued with particular vigour. It was also notable that children and childhood did not lie at the centre of the coalition government in the same way as that pursued by New Labour. If the initial dominating focus of the New Labour government when it came to power in 1997 had been 'education, education, education', for the coalition in 2010 its stated, overriding priority was the 'reduction of the public debt'.

8

Reforming child protection: a child-centred system?

On taking office, the coalition government immediately changed the name of the Department for Children, Schools and Families (DCSF) to the Department for Education (DfE), with Michael Gove appointed as the minister for education. Initially, it was not clear whether it was simply a name change and rebranding of a recently established central government department that had been closely associated with Gordon Brown and Ed Balls, or something more significant. It quickly became evident that it did point to something much more significant. From the beginning, the coalition government made no reference to Every Child Matters and the departmental web pages changed overnight. It became clear, in the first two years, that the primary driver and focus for the recreated DfE was to be radical changes in the governance and funding of schools, particularly the expansion of academies and the introduction of free schools. In the process, most schools would be removed from local government control, be given greater independence, and be accountable directly to the DfE. This was a rather different role for schools to that which had been envisaged by New Labour in its Children's Plan (DCSF, 2007b).

In the process, the New Labour emphasis on the integration of children's services and the establishment of a whole variety of new technologies, processes and practices to improve a wide range of child outcomes all but disappeared from sight as being major priorities for central government. No longer would there be a requirement for local authorities to establish Children's Trusts and produce annual Children and Young People's Plans, and the 'duty to cooperate' in promoting pupil 'wellbeing' for schools was removed (DfE, 2010).

The Conservative Party had been opposed to a number of New Labour developments for some years, including the technological demands and timescales of the Integrated Children's System and the electronic Common Assessment Framework (eCAF) and was determined to reform both. Perhaps of greater immediate political significance was the decision to scrap ContactPoint as from August 2010, seen as important on financial and civil liberty grounds, together with the disbanding of the National Safeguarding Unit, which had only been in existence for a few months. The coalition government was also committed to publishing SCRs in full in order to improve transparency and accountability, and this was required of all new SCRs after April 2011.

However, after the major scandal following the death of Baby P and the many criticisms voiced about child protection policy and practice, summarized in Chapter 6, there was also a commitment to have a full review of the child protection system itself. While this was not a major priority for Michael Gove at this time, it was something that Tim Loughton, junior minister for children and families, had been committed to for some time. He had established the Conservative Party Commission on Social Workers, which had produced two influential reports, the second of which, *Response to Lord Laming's Inquiry* (2009), had provided the basis for the Conservative Party's submission to the Laming Report (2009) *The Protection of Children in England*. Early in 2010, Eileen Munro, a qualified, experienced social worker who was Professor of Social Policy at the London School of Economics, was approached to lead a review of the child protection system in England, if the Conservative Party was successful in the general election. The review was announced within two weeks of the election and was the first announcement of a number of reviews on related themes, including those on child poverty (Field, 2010), early intervention (Allen, 2011a, 2011b), early years services (Tickell, 2011) and family justice (Norgrove, 2011).

Over the years, Eileen Munro had articulated a number of major criticisms of the child protection system in England. These included that it:

- was overly complex

- overextended the surveillance role of the state, potentially undermining the civil liberties and rights of children and parents

- was overly bureaucratic and unnecessarily driven by a desire to introduce inappropriate information technology

- and, because of the much broader range of child welfare concerns that health and welfare professionals were now expected to give attention to, there was a real danger that a central focus on child protection had got lost (Munro, 2004a, 2004b, 2005, 2007a, 2007b, 2009, 2010a, 2010c; Munro and Calder, 2005; Anderson et al., 2007; Munro and Parton, 2007).

The Munro Review of Child Protection

In his letter to Eileen Munro announcing the establishment of the review, Michael Gove (2010) said that while it would be broad in scope, he hoped it would address three central issues: early intervention; trusting frontline social workers; and transparency and accountability. He seemed to see the improvement of the child protection system as intimately connected to and dependent on the support and improvement of frontline professional social work, because he said that, in order to improve the system of child protection in England:

> My first principle is always to ask what helps professionals make the best judgment they can to protect a vulnerable child? I firmly believe we need reform to frontline social work practice. I want to strengthen the profession so social workers are in a better position to make well-informed judgments, based on up to date evidence, in the best interests of children, free from unnecessary bureaucracy and regulation. (Gove, 2010, p. 1)

It seemed that a major priority was to reverse a trend that had been evident for many years, whereby the dominating response to tragedies in child protection had been to substitute *confidence in systems* for *trust in individual professionals*, particularly social workers (Smith, 2001). The review was produced in three parts in order to invite ongoing comment.

The Munro Review of Child Protection: Part One, A Systems Analysis (Munro, 2010b) was published in October 2010 and identified what were seen as the main problems with the current system. The analysis and theoretical framework drew on an approach Eileen Munro (1998, 2007a, 2008) had been developing over a number of years, which was laid out in an article in the *British Journal of Social Work*, entitled 'Learning to Reduce Risk in Child Protection' (Munro, 2010a). The article argued for a systems approach to learning how to improve performance and conceptualized child protection services as complex, adaptive systems, where the role of professional judgement was key and the current strategies for managing risk were, paradoxically, making it harder for professionals to learn how to protect children better.

The review's second report was published in February 2011 (Munro, 2011a) and was framed in terms of 'the child's journey' through the child protection system. It concluded that instead of 'doing things right', that is, following procedures, the system needed to focus on 'doing the right thing', that is, checking whether children and young people were being helped. The aim was to 'develop a system which was more child-centred and about learning rather than compliance driven and blaming' (Munro, 2011a, p. 93). The review received considerable evidence that the growth of central government guidance, targets and rules had severely limited the ability of practitioners and managers to stay 'child centred' and reduced their capacity and time to work directly with children, young people and families. For example, the core government guidance, *Working Together to Safeguard Children* (HM Government, 2010a), was 55 times longer than when it had been first introduced in 1974 (Parton, 2011a; Chapter 6).

It was no surprise, therefore, that the overall aim of the final report (Munro, 2011b) was to develop a system that valued professional expertise. It recommended that the government should revise Working Together to 'remove unnecessary or unhelpful prescription and focus on essential rules for effective multi-agency working and on the principles that underpin good practice' (p. 7), including the removal of the prescribed timescales for social work assessments (DH et al., 2000). Inspection was also a key influence on frontline practice and needed to be reformed. In future, inspections should be conducted on an unannounced basis and should inspect the effectiveness of *all* local services, including health, education, police, probation and the justice system, and not just local authority children's services.

The review was clear, along with the other independent government reviews (Field, 2010; Allen, 2011a, 2011b; Tickell, 2011), that it wished to emphasize the importance of 'early help', because 'preventative services can do more to reduce abuse and neglect than reactive services' (Munro, 2011b, p. 7), and recommended that government should place a duty on local authorities and their statutory partners to secure sufficient provision of local 'early help services' for children, young people and families.

In addition, the review made a number of recommendations designed to improve accountability. In the light of a range of policy changes being introduced by the coalition government, the review argued that it was vital that the responsibilities of health, education and the police for safeguarding and child protection should not be lost, and that the statutory role of directors of children's services and the local authority lead member for children should not be watered down. The lead role for the local authority was confirmed, together with a strengthened role for LSCBs.

But perhaps the most significant recommendations related to the role and practice of social workers. If there was to be a reduced reliance on procedures, central guidance and targets, the authority and practice of professionals needed to be improved and strengthened, and it was social workers who were seen as the key professionals in the newly reformed child protection system.

The review saw itself building on the report from the Social Work Task Force (2009) and the ongoing work of the Social Work Reform Board (2012). In particular, it recommended that:

- each local authority should designate a principal child and family social worker at senior manager level to represent the views and experiences of frontline staff to all levels of management

- a chief social worker should be appointed to advise government and inform the secretary of state's annual report to Parliament on the workings of the Children Act 1989

- local authorities should review and redesign the way child and family social work was delivered

- a range of changes should be introduced by local authorities and higher education to improve the training, capabilities and professional development of social workers.

The overall aim of the review was to bring about a paradigm shift in child protection policy and practice:

> This final report sets out the proposals for reform which, taken together, are intended to create the conditions that enable professionals to make the best judgements about the help to give to children, young people and families. This involves moving from a system that has become over-bureaucratised and focused on compliance to one that values and develops professional expertise and is focused on the safety and welfare of children and young people. (Munro, 2011b, p. 6)

The review was purposefully analytic and stated from the outset that it recognized that the way child protection operated was highly complex and that uncertainty and risk were key features of the work. It was warmly welcomed by child welfare organizations, the relevant professions and the main political parties, including the British Association of Social Workers, the Association of Directors of Children's Services and the National Children's Bureau (Butler, 2011).

Of the 15 recommendations, the government accepted 9 outright, and 5 'in principle' (DfE, 2011). It said that it wanted to 'consider further' whether the current methodology for carrying out SCRs should be scrapped in favour of a systems approach and that Ofsted evaluations of SCRs should end. The government wanted to have time to consider the outcomes of a number of pilots using the systems methodology as well as wanting to plan any transition to any new arrangements carefully. The government also rejected the review's recommendation that a new duty should be placed on local authorities and statutory partners to secure sufficient provision of local early help services, as it claimed there was already sufficient existing legislation to realize the recommendation.[1]

However, the government appeared supportive of the review and saw it as consistent with its overall approach to the reform of public services:

> The government is determined to work with all involved with safeguarding children to bring about lasting reform … that means reducing central prescription and interference and placing greater trust in local leaders and skilled frontline professionals in accordance with the principles set out in the Government's Open Public Services White Paper. (DfE, 2011, p. 5, para. 2)

In many ways, the review confirmed a development that had been evident since the highly critical reaction to the death of Baby Peter Connelly from November 2008 onwards – the re-emergence of 'child protection' as a significant governmental concern and the key role allotted to social work in this (Parton, 2011b). As we have seen, a major development during the period of the New Labour government from 1997 onwards was the framing of policy in this broad area in terms of 'safeguarding and promoting the welfare of children'. Local authority children's social care had wider responsibilities than just forensically responding to concerns about significant harm and was explicitly located in the broad agenda for children's services promulgated by the New Labour government associated with social exclusion. This policy priority had been taken further with the launch of the *Every Child Matters: Change for Children* programme in 2004 (DfES, 2004b).

This emphasis on safeguarding and developments in children's social care more generally did not mean that child protection and social work had disappeared, but it had meant that they were placed more in the background and seen as elements of the much broader responsibilities of the newly created departments of children's services. Developments since the Baby Peter scandal had meant that social work and the term 'child protection' were again placed at the core of governmental concerns, as was evident in the title of the review itself – the Munro Review of Child Protection.

However, the review did not make it clear what it meant by 'child protection' nor what it identified as the main aims of the child protection system. Although it stated that 'the measure of the success of child protection systems, both local and national, is whether children are receiving effective help' (Munro, 2011b, p. 38), it did not state what it meant by 'effective' nor 'effective' in relation to what? If effectiveness was to be judged by a reduction in the number of child deaths, it was possible that the current system could have been seen as a success. For example, research by Pritchard and Williams (2010) analysed the changes in the rate and number of 'child abuse-related deaths' between 1974 and 2006. They argued that the number and rate of such deaths had declined in England during the period and fell significantly more than 'all causes of death' during the same period, and that the improvement was greater than most other major developed countries. On this basis, the period could be seen as a relative success story for child protection services in England. However, it was clear that the review did not see the aim of the child protection system simply in terms of reducing 'child abuse-related deaths' but something rather broader.

One would assume that the aims of a child protection system were primarily, if not exclusively, concerned with protecting children from child abuse and neglect or – in the words of the statutory guidance – 'children who are suffering or at risk of suffering significant harm' (HM Government, 2010a, para. 1.23). What had become evident over the previous 20 years was that such harm could take place in a variety of contexts and could have a variety of perpetrators. Certainly, some of the biggest changes in policy and practice in relation to protecting children from abuse and neglect in England since the mid-1990s had been in terms of the growth of the multi-agency public protection arrangements, led by the police and probation services, for violent and sex offenders in the community (Kemshall, 2010); together with the growth of Criminal Records Bureau checks and the expansion of vetting and barring arrangements for both employees and volunteers who come into regular contact with children (Stafford et al., 2012, Ch. 9).

However, such developments were not seen as part of the child protection system for the purposes of the review, because it stated:

> Children and young people's problems arise from many factors other than poor or dangerous parental care, but it is the latter cause that is most relevant to this review. (Munro, 2011b, p. 69)

Thus, the focus of the review was how to ensure that the state protected children from 'poor or dangerous *parental* care', what I have previously called state policies and practices for governing the family (Parton, 1991), which I discuss further in Chapter 10, rather than with protecting children and young people from abuse and neglect 'in society' more generally.

In many respects, the review seemed to take us back to the debates in the mid-1990s in England about the appropriate balance between child protection and family support in child welfare services (Parton, 1997), discussed in Chapter 2. Crucially, the review's estimate of the size and nature of the problem(s) the child protection system was designed to address was not based on estimates of the prevalence of child abuse in society, but on the official statistics on the operation of local authority children's social care and the number and types of cases known to it. It stated that referrals to children's social care had risen steadily from 547,000 children in 2008/09 to 603,500 in 2009/10 and that the figures for 2009/10 also showed 13 and 14% rises in initial and core assessments respectively from 2008/09. In both years, 6% of children referred to children's social care became or continued to be the subject of child protection plans, while the number of children being 'looked after' by local authorities had increased from 60,900 to 64,400. The review stated that:

> The overwhelming majority of referrals concerned children who were subsequently judged not to be suffering, or likely to suffer, significant harm . . . this level of demand for responding to referrals diminishes the ability of children's social care to provide effective protection to those children who are suffering, or likely to suffer, harm. (Munro, 2011b, p. 80)

A central focus for the review was, therefore, to improve the way thresholds into children's social care operated and the way children's social care responded. If 'early help' was available, cases could be dealt with more appropriately so that statutory interventions could be more measured and effective. However, there was nothing to suggest that the number of referrals to children's social care provided any insight into the prevalence of abuse and maltreatment experienced by children and young people and the best way of responding (Hooper, 2011; Radford et al., 2011). I return to these issues in Chapter 11.

In May 2012, 12 months after the publication of her final report, Eileen Munro (2012) published a progress report, which assessed how far the review recommendations had been implemented. It noted that:

- Ofsted (2012) was introducing a revised child protection inspection framework

- the government was in the process of appointing a chief social worker

- there was wide sector-led activity to support the reforms, including the establishment of the Children's Improvement Board, the appointment of principal social workers in many local authorities, and the establishment of the College of Social Work in early 2012.

It also noted that a number of authorities had been granted exemption from the statutory guidance in order to experiment with different and more flexible approaches to assessment.

However, the report also identified a number of important challenges. In particular, the changes in child protection were taking place at the same time as major reforms in health, education and policing, and these might put at risk the importance of professionals and agencies 'working together' to help children, young people and their families. The cuts in public sector funding were also of clear significance (Munro, 2012, para. 1.10). The overall conclusion was therefore somewhat sanguine:

> The overall conclusion of this report is that progress is moving in the right direction but that it needs to move faster. There are promising signs that some reforms are encouraging new ways of thinking and working and so improving services for children. There are, however, a number of reforms that still require implementation; as this happens over the next 12 months, the pace of change should be hastened further. (Munro, 2012, p. 3)

One of the problems was that the proposed changes to the statutory guidance had not yet been circulated for consultation. Originally, the government had said that a new Working Together would be in place by the end of 2011, but then said that a draft would be published for consultation in March 2012, but this was also delayed. The consultation on the revisions to Working Together was eventually launched on

12 June 2012 following the publication of three draft statutory guidance documents, totalling just 68 pages.[2]

Working Together to Safeguard Children (2013)

Following a further lengthy delay, the final revised version of Working Together (HM Government, 2013) was published as one single document on 21 March 2013 and came into effect on 15 April 2013. It had the same title as previous guidance going back to 1999 (DH et al., 1999; HM Government, 2006b, 2010a) and did not change the definition of the key concepts in the 2010 version (HM Government, 2010a): safeguarding and promoting the welfare of children; child protection; abuse; physical abuse; emotional abuse; sexual abuse; neglect; children; and young carers. However, in other respects, it had a number of important differences. Significantly, the document had been reduced from 399 to 95 pages and the number of footnotes had been reduced from 273 to 43 (see Appendix, Table A1.1).[3] In addition, the Assessment Framework no longer had the status of statutory guidance. There was a clear view that the growing bureaucratization of the work was a direct result of the growing central prescription and complexity of Working Together and, in the written Ministerial Statement (Hansard, HC Deb, 21 March 2013, c52WS) at the time of publication, it was claimed that the revised guidance clarified the core legal requirements and made it much clearer what individuals and organizations should do to keep children safe and promote their welfare:

> We want social workers and other professionals to focus on the needs of individual children and families and take decisive and effective action to help those children. Today's guidance will support that. It makes absolutely clear the legal framework and the expectations on different professionals. (www.theyworkforyou.com/wms/?id=2013-03-21a.52WS.3)

Whereas the 2010 guidance (HM Government, 2010a, para. 1.1) was explicitly located in the *ECM: Change for Children* programme and began by stating the five ECM outcomes and emphasizing that 'all children deserve the opportunity to achieve their full potential', this was not the case with the 2013 Working Together. At no point was ECM and its five outcomes mentioned or referenced, nor was the idea of 'integration' given any importance.

The 2013 guidance stated that it adopted 'a child-centred and coordinated approach to safeguarding':

Effective safeguarding arrangements in every local area should be under-pinned by two key principles:

- safeguarding is everyone's responsibility: for services to be effective each professional and organisation should play their full part; and

- a child-centred approach: for services to be effective they should be based on a clear understanding of the needs and views of children (HM Government, 2013, p. 8).

Thus, while the focus continued to be 'safeguarding and promoting the welfare of children', this was no longer in the context of the wide-ranging and ambitious *ECM: Change for Children* programme of New Labour. Although the document clearly drew on a number of the ideas evident in *ECM: Change for Children* and the earlier guidance (HM Government, 2006b, 2010a), these were reframed in the context of the Munro Review (Munro, 2011b) and the political priorities of the coalition government. This was particularly evident in the chapters concerned with assessment, LSCBs and SCRs.

Chapter 1 'Assessing need and providing help' drew on the Munro Review idea of 'early help', as well as making important changes to the statutory requirements for assessment. While the requirement to use the CAF was removed, the new Working Together (HM Government, 2013, p. 14, emphasis added) clearly stated that 'the provision of *early help services* should form part of a *continuum of help and support* to respond to the different levels of need of individual children and families'. It identified the need for 'early help assessments', undertaken by a 'lead professional', which would identify the help the child and family required in order to prevent the needs escalating to a point where a statutory assessment under the Children Act 1989 was required. The lead professional should provide support to the child and family, act as an advocate on their behalf and coordinate the delivery of the support services. 'Early help' should be 'targeted' to address the assessed needs of a child and their family 'which focuses on activity to significantly improve the outcomes for the child' (p. 11).

The guidance outlined what it meant by a 'continuum of help and support' for:

Where need is relatively low level individual services and universal services may be able to take swift action. For other emerging needs a range of early help services may be required, coordinated through an early help assessment. Where there are more complex needs, help may be provided under section 17 of the Children Act 1989 (children in need). Where there are child protection concerns (reasonable cause to suspect a child is suffering or likely to suffer significant harm) local authority social care services must make enquiries and decide if any action must be taken under section 47 of the Children Act 1989. (HM Government, 2013, p. 14)

The guidance made it clear that LSCBs should publish a *threshold document*, which stated clear criteria for taking action and providing help across the full continuum.[4] Anyone who had 'concerns about a child's welfare' should make a referral to local authority children's social care: 'Within one working day of a referral being received, a local authority social worker should make a decision about the type of response that is required and acknowledge receipt to the referrer' (HM Government, 2013, p. 23). There was no longer a requirement to conduct separate initial and core assessments, although the maximum timeframe for the assessment to conclude should be no longer than 45 working days from the point of referral. Within this:

> The speed with which an assessment is carried out after a child's case has been referred into local authority children's social care should be determined by the needs of the individual child and the nature and level of any risk of harm faced by the child. This will require judgements to be made by the social worker in discussion with their manager on each individual case. (p. 23)

Apart from the removal of key assessment timelines, it was clear, particularly in light of the coalition government's removal of the statutory obligation for local Children's Trusts to operate, that the role of LSCBs in coordinating, overseeing and providing challenge and leadership in the area of children's services was emphasized. It was also notable that while the statutory authority of the Assessment Framework (DH et al., 2000) had been removed, its basic principles and conceptual framework were still evident and it was included in Appendix C as a 'further source of information' if local areas wanted to continue using it. However, while the concept of risk had been consciously removed from the Assessment Framework from the outset (Seden et al., 2001) and hence from Working Together in 1999 (DH et al., 1999), 2006 (HM Government, 2006b) and 2010 (HM Government, 2010a) in order to ensure the centrality of the concept of 'need', it was explicitly introduced into the 2013 document (HM Government, 2013). The understanding, assessment, management and balancing of risk factors and the risks of harm were seen as key for child protection and the safeguarding system generally and central for local authority social workers and their managers.

Another notable development in the guidance was the increased concern about neglect and this was clearly connected to the importance of acting decisively and authoritatively – a failure highlighted in a number of SCRs, including the second SCR into the death of Baby P (Haringey LSCB, 2009), and it was in this context that the meaning and significance for professionals, particularly social workers, being child centred became clear:

> Social workers, their managers and other professionals should always consider the plan from the child's perspective. A desire to think the best of adults and to hope they can overcome their difficulties should not trump the need to rescue children from chaotic, neglectful and abusive homes. Social workers and managers should always reflect the latest research on the impact of neglect and abuse when analysing the level of need and risk faced by the child. This should be reflected in the case recording. (HM Government, 2013, p. 22)

The idea of 'rescuing children from chaotic, neglectful and abusive homes' could be seen to lie at the heart of many of the high-profile scandals of recent years – particularly those of Baby P, Shannon Matthews, Khyra Ishaq and the 'J' children in the Edlington case. The theme of 'rescuing children' from possible abuse or neglect ran through the guidance.

The Edlington case in Doncaster had clearly proved influential. Michael Gove had made it plain that he had found the SCR into the case 'highly unsatisfactory' and had asked Lord Carlile to provide an independent report on the case, which he did in November 2012 (Carlile, 2012). In the Foreword to the government's response to Lord Carlile's report (DfE, 2013a), published on the same day as the new Working Together, Michael Gove, secretary of state for education, said that he had wanted to know 'why no-one acted sooner to address the damage being caused by the offending children's faulty upbringing', and that Lord Carlile's report demonstrated that 'we must get better at responding to the needs of children who are suffering neglect' (p. 2). But he also said that he felt there had been insufficient progress in Doncaster to improving services for children, and had appointed Professor Julian Le Grand, from the London School of Economics, Alan Wood, director of children's services in Hackney, and Dame Moira Gibb to consider 'the most appropriate structure of governance arrangements for delivering improvements' and whether the management of the service in Doncaster should be taken over by an external private body. Clearly, the private sector was seen as potentially playing a key role in the future management and delivery of core child protection services.[5]

It seemed that the idea of a child-centred safeguarding system was premised on the twin ideas of listening to the views of children and child rescue. The importance of being 'timely' and 'decisive', particularly in cases of neglect, was emphasized:

> The assessment of neglect cases can be difficult. Neglect can fluctuate both in level and duration. A child's welfare can, for example, improve following input from services or a change in circumstances and review, but then deteriorate once support is removed. Professionals should be wary of being too optimistic. Timely and decisive action is critical to ensure that children are not left in neglectful homes. (HM Government, 2013, p. 24)

Thus, while the language of safeguarding and promoting the welfare of the child was retained, we can see a significant shift in the guidance – when compared with that of 1999 (DH et al., 1999), 2006 (HM Government, 2006b) and even 2010 (HM Government, 2010a) – towards a much more explicit child protection orientation.

It was not simply that any reference to the *ECM: Change for Children* programme had been dropped, but that the idea of supporting families, which had been seen as important ever since the refocusing debate in the mid-/late 1990s, had disappeared. For example, the Working Together published in late 1999 (DH et al., 1999) located concerns about child protection and safeguarding within a clear family service orientation. Chapter 1 was entitled 'Working together to support children and families' and the opening paragraphs were concerned with 'supporting children and families' (paras. 1.1–1.7) and emphasized that the guidance was based on an 'integrated approach' (paras. 1.8 and 1.9). This orientation was no longer present in the 2013 Working Together (HM Government, 2013). As I demonstrated earlier, the 2013 guidance was premised on 'a child-centred and coordinated approach to safeguarding' and began by stating that 'safeguarding children – the action we take to promote the welfare of children and protect them from harm – is everyone's responsibility' (HM Government, 2013, p. 7).

In the process, the idea and practice of early help was framed within this clear move to a child protection orientation and the emphasis was placed on the importance of 'timely and decisive action [which] is critical to ensure that children are not left in neglectful homes' (HM Government, 2013, p. 24).

As Norman (2013) has demonstrated, any notion of partnership or working with parents in the context of the assessment of need (Section 17 of the Children Act 1989) by a local authority seemed to have disappeared:

> Each child who has been referred into local authority children's social care should have an individual assessment to their needs and to understand the impact of any parental behaviour on them as an individual. (HM Government, 2013, p. 21)

It seemed that the local authority had become the routine arbiter of 'parental behaviour', which seemed far removed from a language of partnership that might encourage parents to become empowered and to come forward for support; and which had been clearly reflected in previous Working Together's interpretation of Section 17 of the Children Act 1989. While clearly at a lower threshold to assessments carried out under Section 47 of the Children Act 1989, in the 2013 Working Together (HM Government, 2013), Section 17 had now become the basis for statutory assessments and was explicitly presented as such in the guidance.

Chapter 3 of the guidance was concerned with the statutory objectives, functions, membership, accountability and resourcing of LSCBs. It stressed that a part of their statutory function was to 'assess the effectiveness of the help being provided to children and families, including early help' (HM Government, 2013, p. 60). Not only had the role and significance of LSCBs grown – particularly in the context of the demise of Children's Trusts – but it was clear that 'early help' was very much a safeguarding issue. Not only had any notion of family support been lost from the guidance, but early help had become a key element in the reconfigured child protection system, which was to be authoritative, decisive and timely and, as will become clearer in Chapter 9, should not be afraid to take children into care.

The guidance also made it clear that every LSCB should have an independent chair (p. 63) who would play the central role in the operation of SCRs. SCRs were seen as playing a major role in ensuring accountability and transparency by being published on the internet, and thereby maintaining local learning and improving the system:

> These processes should be transparent, with findings of reviews shared publicly. The findings are not only important for the professionals

involved locally in cases. Everyone across the country has an interest in understanding both what works well and also why things can go wrong. (HM Government, 2013, p. 65)

Each LSCB was to maintain a 'local learning and improvement framework' (p. 65), which would be shared across local organizations that worked with children and families. The local framework should cover the full range of reviews and audits. The reviews would be conducted regularly and would not be restricted only to cases that met the statutory criteria for an SCR. There was clearly concern that the number of SCRs being carried out had dropped since the requirement to publish them had been introduced (Brandon et al., 2012; Timpson, 2013). In future, reviews should be carried out on cases 'which can provide useful insights into the way organisations are working together to safeguard and protect the welfare of children' (HM Government, 2013, p. 65), and should include:

- Serious Case Review: where abuse or neglect are believed to be a factor (statutory requirement)

- child death review: a review of all child deaths up to the age of 18 (statutory requirement)

- review of child protection incident that falls below the threshold for an SCR

- review or audit of practice in one or more agencies.

Reviews 3 and 4 above were additional to those in previous government guidance (HM Government, 2010a) and signalled the increased significance allotted to reviews and the role of LSCBs in these. There was to be a national panel of independent experts on SCRs, who would advise LSCBs about the initiation and publication of SCRs and who would try to ensure a degree of national consistency of practice.[6]

Beyond this, there was the potential for much greater local discretion as to how SCRs were carried out and LSCBs could draw on approaches consistent with the systems methodology recommended by Eileen Munro (2011b, recommendation 9). Although the review process was to include appropriate representation from a range of organizations that might be required to submit written information about their involvement with the child who was the subject of the review, there was no longer the requirement, as previously, for organizations to undertake Individual Management Reviews. The final reports of the SCRs' findings were to be published on the LSCBs' website for a minimum of 12 months. Thereafter, the report should be made available on request. The guidance stated that final SCR reports should:

- provide a sound analysis of what happened in the case, and why, and what needs to happen in order to reduce the risk of recurrence;
- be written in plain English and in a way that can be easily understood by professionals and the public alike; and
- be suitable for publication without needing to be amended or redacted (HM Government, 2013, p. 71).

While slightly revised in the light of the consultation, including bringing the three draft consultation documents together into one set of guidance, the focus of Working Together (HM Government, 2013) was on the core legal requirements in terms of:

- assessing need and providing help
- the key responsibilities of the main organizations
- the key role of LSCBs, particularly in relation to SCRs and other forms of review.

It was perhaps surprising that there was no reference to the Jimmy Savile[7] case in the light of its high profile since the publication of the consultation in June 2012, and the key role of the police and other criminal justice agencies, particularly in terms of the multi-agency public protection arrangements and systems of vetting and barring. In the 2010 Working Together, there had been a whole chapter (Ch. 12) on 'Managing individuals who pose a risk of harm to children', which had been removed in the 2013 Working Together (HM Government, 2013). However, Appendix C listed and provided links to 45 other websites, making up over 3,500 pages of other guidance that LSCBs and others would need to be aware of. This included a link into the Ministry of Justice *Public Protection Manual* (nearly 700 pages long), and guidance on safer recruitment practices in education and more widely (nearly 200 pages long). The 'supplementary guidance' in Appendix C was of clear significance.

Conclusion

In many respects, the 2013 Working Together (HM Government, 2013) seemed to succeed in taking on board many of the central principles and recommendations of the Munro Review (Munro, 2011b) with its emphasis on early help and being child centred. It certainly seemed to succeed in concentrating on what it deemed to be the core legal requirements. While it returned the guidance to the size it had been over 20 years previously with the implementation of the Children Act 1989 (Home Office et al., 1991), in many other respects it was quite different and clearly reflected the particular time and political context in which it had been produced and the various policy and practice developments that had taken place in the intervening 22 years.

As I demonstrated in Chapter 6, the focus and starting point of the 1991 Working Together (Home Office et al., 1991) was 'children at risk of significant harm', such that the whole document was framed in terms of when and how to carry out an 'investigation' in terms of Section 47 of the Children Act 1989. There was no mention of any of the more wide-ranging preventive duties that local authorities had in terms of s.17(1) of the Children Act 1989 'to safeguard and promote the welfare of children in their area who are in need'. The 2013 Working Together (HM Government, 2013) was very different. Not only was it explicitly framed in terms of s.17(1) and, following all guidance since 1999, was titled *Working Together to Safeguard Children*, its remit had been broadened even further to include the provision and assessment of early help. However, while the language of safeguarding and promoting the welfare of children continued, this was now framed in terms of a much more authoritative and decisive child protection orientation, where concerns about early intervention into cases of neglect were central. Thus, while the focus of the guidance was broad, it was very much located within a child protection orientation.

Similarly, while the 2013 Working Together succeeded in reducing the size of the guidance to 1991 proportions, it could only succeed in doing so by including 45 links to supplementary guidance (over 3,500 pages) in its Appendix C. It seemed complexity could only be reduced so far, for such complexity had arisen as a direct result of a wide range of developments in research, policy and practice and, crucially, as a result of the increasing growth in understanding about the nature of child maltreatment, issues I return to in Chapter 11. However, to understand the implications and possible impact of the 2013 Working Together, it is important to locate the developments in the wider political and policy priorities at the time, particularly in relation to the coalition government's policy approach to children and families. This is the focus of Chapter 9.

9

Child welfare reform and the authoritarian neoliberal state

The reform of the child protection system signalled by the Munro Review and the 2013 Working Together (HM Government, 2013) was taking place in the context of major changes in all areas of public services and the role of the state. In Chapter 7, I discussed some of the main ideas and influences on the coalition government and outlined its early aims and policy changes. I argued that while ideas about 'the big society' provided much of the rhetorical framework for the Conservative Party of David Cameron and the coalition government in its early days, these were quickly sidelined.[1] Ideas outlined in the *Open Public Services* White Paper (HM Government, 2011a) and concerns about 'the broken society' became central. In this chapter, I will develop this analysis further and outline the impact of government changes for children, families and child welfare and protection services more specifically. What emerges is a clear agenda to establish, what I will call, an 'authoritarian neoliberal state'. While this development had clear links to the approach of the earlier Conservative governments of Margaret Thatcher and John Major (1979–97) and to some elements of the New Labour approach of Tony Blair and Gordon Brown (1997–2010) (Levitas, 2012), it can be seen to take neoliberal ideas further into the heart of government and to the reform of the state itself, what Soss et al. (2009, 2011) and Wiggan (2011) have called 'neoliberal paternalism'.

Neoliberal paternalism

Under neoliberal paternalism, the reform of the state, and state welfare in particular, is informed by the new public management practices of contracting out and 'payment by results', together with a much greater emphasis on a coercive paternalism that strives to strengthen labour discipline and social behaviour, particularly among the underclass.

While classical liberal thought from the early nineteenth century onwards was concerned with the intimate relationship between political freedoms and market freedoms, Soss et al. (2009, 2011) argue this should not be confused with contemporary neoliberal thought, which goes much further and attempts to extend the reach of market logic so that it becomes the organizing principle for all social and political relations. Crucially, it is not simply a revival of the drive to limit the state, as claimed by Cameron and the coalition government, but to considerably extend markets, understood as the natural mode of human relations, throughout civil society so that they can flourish independently. It is a movement that aims to integrate state and market operations, mobilize the state on behalf of the market agenda, and reconfigure the state on market terms (Brown, 2006). Rather than seeking to limit the state, contemporary neoliberalism envisions the state as a site for the application of market principles. Through contracting, decentralization and competitive performance systems, it aims to reconstruct the state's operations to mimic market forms and promotes market standards for evaluating performance. It argues that neither the market nor economic and social behaviour can be left to their own devices and thus assumed to be 'natural'. They need to be 'constructed' and therefore organized by law and political institutions; they require political intervention and orchestration.

Ideologically, although it is claimed that the aim is to reduce the big, overblown state, this only applies to certain elements of its operations. While it embraces ideas of increased laissez-faire, freedom and deregulation to reduce restraints on capital and entrepreneurial activity, it is far from embracing laissez-faire and deregulation in other areas. Particularly in relation to the poor and the marginalized, it is argued that government should be directive, supervisory and disciplinary and there needs to be a shift from a 'nanny state' to a 'muscular state'. The link between neoliberalism and this emphasis on coercive paternalism lies in a common definition of freedom as a practice of efficient living that requires an inner discipline, so that those who fail at this freedom must be trained into it (Segal, 2006).

Such an approach is particularly evident in relation to the reform of income support and employment services, where the unemployed and others in receipt of sickness and disability benefits are presumed to be responsible for their situation and lack the competence, willingness or support to reconnect with the labour market. It therefore falls to policy via a range of 'workfare' and other interventions to instil in benefit recipients an understanding of what constitutes 'good behaviour' and a moral obligation to work and manage their family's affairs competently (Wiggan, 2011). The existence of large numbers of long-term benefit claimants is not seen as evidence of market failure but of the failure of benefit and employment services, thereby justifying further economic liberalization.

The coalition government's reforms in this area have led to the intensification of a number of the changes introduced by New Labour and, in the process, increased the residualization and marketization of state services. A whole range of services, previously provided directly by the state, are contracted out to a variety of providers who are required to deliver against certain criteria and are reimbursed on the basis of 'payment by results', which, for income support and employment services, are essentially based on getting people back into work or on to some sort of training scheme.

At the same time, the value of working-age benefits has been reduced and a financial cap placed on others, demonstrating the coalition government's determination to strengthen the principle of less eligibility so that it becomes increasingly difficult for individuals and families to exist outside the labour market (Finn, 2011). The problem of unemployment is located in a breakdown in the work discipline of the poor and the gap between their stated desire to work and their apparent capacity to do so. A combination of 'help and hassle', grounded in personalized support and monitoring of client behaviour by various welfare advisers, together with mandated activation and threat of sanction is used to instil and maintain work discipline (Mead, 1997, 2007).

Policies and services for children and families

It became evident that families with children and young people were no longer considered a priority group in the way they had been under New Labour (Stewart, 2011). After May 2010, it was only older people who received any exemptions from the welfare cuts. Their universal benefits were protected and they were granted more generous uprating rules for pension credit and the basic state pension compared with benefits for working-age households and those with children. An analysis by the Institute for Fiscal Studies of changes in the first 12 months of the coalition government indicated that households with children would lose by more than those without children at all levels of the income distribution as a result of the government's changes to tax and benefits (Brewer et al., 2011). The changes demonstrated that it was not only that children and families were no longer a priority group but that even where benefits continued to be available, there was a clear shift towards targeting.[2]

The government made it clear that it felt that the provision of a wide range of financial and material benefits had the effect of encouraging dependency and undermining incentives and failed to come to grips with, what it saw as, the main causes of poverty (Wiggan, 2012). It carried out a major reform and rationalization of benefits with the introduction of universal credit, which attempted to amalgamate and simplify a whole range of benefits and tax credits for those of working age, which were to be withdrawn at a rate of 65 per cent as income went up (Bennett, 2012), but in the context of the £18 billion welfare cuts.[3] A major change was that people who were also receiving income from the state would be caught in the administrative and supervisory net of the benefit system in a way they were not when tax credits were separate. With universal credit, they would be expected to increase their hours and earnings if the benefits office deemed that suitable opportunities were available. Universal credit reinstated coercion for many households that had previously found their own way through the labour market and complex benefit system (Mabbett, 2013).

It was clear that the coalition government had a new approach to child poverty, which was somewhat different to that of New Labour. Although it formally supported the Child Poverty Act 2010, which set a target to eradicate child poverty by 2020, it did not see the problem of poverty as primarily arising from a lack of money. It made it clear that it saw its approach as 'tackling the causes and not the symptoms of poverty' (HM Government, 2011b, p. 11). In future, it was planned to measure child poverty in terms of how long children had two birth parents looking after them, the length of worklessness in households and school achievement, rather than measuring poverty relative to the rest of the population (Bamfield, 2012). The approach was clearly developed from many of the ideas promulgated by Iain Duncan Smith and the Centre for Social Justice prior to the election of the coalition government, which I discussed in Chapter 7, and the view of David Cameron and Nick Clegg that 'what matters most to a child's life chances is not the wealth of their upbringing but the warmth of their parenting' (Cameron, 2010). They were also informed by two independent reviews established by the government in its early weeks.

Long-time Labour MP Frank Field (2010) argued that children's learning, emotional and physical abilities were largely determined by the age of five and outlined the research evidence that demonstrated the wide differences in cognitive development between advantaged and disadvantaged children by the time they went to school. He was clear that allocating financial benefits to the poor would not address the problem, what was required was a greater investment in high-quality preschool opportunities and parenting programmes – what he called the 'foundation years' early education and family services. While this had much in common with the New Labour approach, it was the de-emphasis on the importance of income benefits that was significant. He argued that the income measures in the Child Poverty Act 2010 should be supplemented by life chances, family context and child development indicators, which included indicators for monitoring a child's physical, emotional and cognitive development at ages three and five.

The second independent review, by Graham Allen, also a long-standing Labour MP, had much in common with Frank Field's report and built on his earlier report with Iain Duncan Smith for the Centre for Social Justice (Allen and Smith, 2008). His review was published in two parts and the first, *Early Intervention: The Next Steps* (Allen, 2011a), provided a review of early intervention approaches and initiatives and stressed the importance of recent research, which argued that the first three years of a child's life were the most critical for emotional, cognitive and intellectual development – with the first 12 months of life being particularly significant. The research also argued that the social environment was key and that the behaviours of parents and immediate carers and the quality of their interactions with their children were crucial. As a result, it was claimed that the size of the brain of a child brought up in a 'normal' environment was considerably bigger and more developed than one from a 'neglected' environment – which was starkly illustrated by a picture comparing two such brains on the cover of the report. The report emphasized that 'early intervention' at this stage could make a considerable difference and in the long run would lead to major savings in public spending by reducing welfare and criminal justice expenditures, while encouraging more productive employment and higher tax revenues.[4]

In his second report, Allen (2011b) developed proposals for trying to attract private finance into the early years and family welfare services by the establishment of an Early Intervention Fund and Early Intervention Bonds. The basic idea, which was also being developed in other areas of state activity including criminal justice and health and welfare, was that private investment bonds would receive a return on investment based on the performance of the scheme invested in. This would require clear outcomes-based contracts that would demonstrate how early intervention had saved public money in other areas – such as by reducing unemployment, criminal or antisocial behaviour – and that these savings would provide the basis for showing a profitable return on the investment. Such a development was a clear example of how the New Labour emphasis on the 'social investment state' was being shifted towards an emphasis on 'the social investment market' (Allen, 2012; Churchill, 2012).

Allen also called for the establishment of an Early Intervention Foundation to provide easy access to the relevant research on early intervention programmes and promote policy change, including advice on how to bring about his suggested new funding arrangements.[5] This was to be a rather different model and approach to early intervention compared to that in the New Labour ECM programme. While ECM was driven by central government, was top down, very wide-ranging, had statutory backing in the 2004 Children Act and considerable state investment, the Early Intervention Foundation was different. Although it had government support, there was little central government funding, considerable latitude as to whether and how local areas might pursue the initiative, and it was to be funded primarily by private finance.

The overall approach of the government to child poverty was summarized by Iain Duncan Smith, the secretary of state for work and pensions, in his Foreword to the Government White Paper *A New Approach to Child Poverty* (HM Government, 2011b), when he said that the focus was on 'fairness and personal responsibility, not cash handouts' and that the long-term strategy was to 'protect the most vulnerable and reform welfare so *work pays* as a sustainable route out of poverty' (p. 3). The idea of fairness was to ensure that those out of work were never better off than those in work, in effect a contemporary notion of 'less eligibility'; it was not concerned with fairness between rich and poor or reducing overall inequality. As a consequence, because the standard of living of the vast majority of the population had declined since 2007, it was important to ensure that the position of those out of work also declined and they were also subject to 'personalized' support and conditions in order to get them into the labour market or be subject to extra disciplines, caps and interventions if not. While there was no mention of social exclusion, there was, as with New Labour in its latter years, a clear commitment 'to break the cycle of deprivation' (p. 4). The White Paper also confirmed plans to reform early years, including revising the funding arrangements of Sure Start Children's Centres, and increasing the number of health visitors.

However, while the coalition claimed it wanted to promote early intervention, such services were subject to major cuts. From April 2011, the separate ring-fenced funding streams for a range of preventive programmes, such as those for health promotion, parenting support, youth crime prevention, family intervention projects and Sure Start programmes, were abolished and repackaged into a new 'early intervention grant' for local authorities to decide how to allocate but with an overall 11 per cent reduction in the total grant. A year later, ring-fencing of the grant was removed and it became part of the general allocation to local authorities to spend as they felt most appropriate. Local authorities were encouraged to use the kinds of evidence-based interventions highlighted in Allen's reports and sustain the continuation of any universal services by introducing charges. There was also the aim of increasing the involvement of voluntary and private agencies, particularly in the commissioning and delivery of Sure Start Children's Centres, which were to become a service for 'vulnerable families' with children and young people up to the age of 18, rather than a universal service for a whole community primarily for younger children. In addition, the White Paper confirmed that it would provide £60 million funding for 2011–13 to support a small number of voluntary organizations to continue to provide various forms of parenting advice and family support services. This emphasis on *targeting* services on *vulnerable families* and drawing on a *marketized* model for funding based on 'payments by results' was reinforced in the latter part of 2011.

In the first week in August 2011, many of England's major cities experienced a violent and prolonged period of rioting. Looting of city shops was widespread and for a number of days the forces of law and order struggled to cope. In his speech on the 'fightback after the riots' on 15 August 2011, David Cameron (2011c) made it clear that the riots resulted from 'pure criminality' and 'moral decline', and insisted that such behaviour reinforced his view that it arose directly from the factors that contributed to 'the broken society', and it was the broken society agenda that would be central to the government's 'social fightback' and 'fixing the welfare system' lay at its heart. There needed to be an accelerated focus on improving parenting and ensuring that parents took full responsibility for their children and he gave a commitment to 'turn around the lives of the 120,000 most troubled families in the country' in the lifetime of the Parliament. He particularly praised the work of Emma Harrison, chief executive and chair of the social enterprise company A4e (Action for Employment), who had received major government contracts as part of the work programme, and who he had appointed as the government's 'family champion' in December 2010.[6]

On 13 October 2011, the government established the Troubled Families Team to be headed by Louise Casey, who had previously headed up the Anti-Social Behaviour Unit and the Respect Task Force under the New Labour government. Based on the approach of Family Intervention Projects introduced by New Labour in 2008 (HM Government, 2008), the idea was to cut across bureaucracy and red tape to provide intensive intervention with families who were seen to have entrenched and complex problems and who were estimated to cost public services £9 billion at an average of £75,000 per family per year, with £8 billion of that 'spent on reacting to, rather than getting to the root causes of, their problems' (Pickles, 2012). The overall aim was seen as: 'getting kids off the streets and into school; getting parents off benefits and into work; and cutting youth crime and anti-social behaviour' (Pickles, 2012) and was based on 'payments by results'.[7]

As well as being a central plank of the government's 'fightback' to the riots, the Troubled Families programme provided an excellent exemplar of the government's overall approach to the 'social deficit'. As Ken Clarke (2011, p. 34), then minister of justice, wrote at the time: 'The coalition has a renewed mission: tackling the financial deficit, for certain. But also, importantly, addressing the social deficit that the riots have highlighted.' He argued that there were a number of elements to addressing the social deficit. It certainly meant building 'stronger families by gripping the 120,000 most problematic ones and really addressing their problems, not leaving them in touch with, but untouched by, dozens of different agencies' (p. 34). But it also included pressing ahead with the welfare reforms and the work programmes, together with the 'liberalizing' of the school system so that more students could benefit 'from high standards and discipline'. However, he argued that the most radical step of all, which underpinned everything else, was paying those who provided the services, including the private and voluntary sectors, by the results they achieved and 'not (as too often in the past) for the processes of box-ticking' (p. 34). 'Payments by results' was a central part of the coalition strategy for reforming public services (NSPCC, 2011; Audit Commission, 2012a).

The various threads to the approach were brought together in March 2012 with the launch of *Social Justice: Transforming Lives* (HM Government, 2012b), which set out the government's 'social justice strategy', outlining how family breakdown, low educational attainment, worklessness, problem debt and addiction combined to cause the entrenched poverty affecting many communities. It aimed to complement the child poverty strategy published the year before (HM Government, 2011b) and emphasized how tackling these prime causes of entrenched poverty required an emphasis on early intervention and new forms of social investment by 'securing millions of pounds of private capital in pursuit of social goals' (HM Government, 2012b, p. 4).

While the Troubled Families programme was located in the Department for Communities and Local Government and the main driver for the child poverty strategy and social justice strategy was the Department for Work and Pensions, both had considerable significance for children's social care, although the Department for Education had the central government responsibility for children's social care.

During the first two years of the coalition government, it was becoming increasingly evident that the Department for Education was almost exclusively focused on radical changes in the funding and governance of schools, particularly the expansion of academies and free schools, with the result that policy for children and families – which had been the central rationale for the previous Department for Children, Schools and Families – was marginalized. This was confirmed by a report by the House of Commons Education Committee (2012a).

Cutting and refocusing children's services

While schools and the NHS were relatively protected from the most severe reductions in public services, this was not the case for local authorities who were to be subject to cutbacks of 28% over the course of the Parliament (Audit Commission, 2012b). Not only were these to be 'front-end loaded' in the first year but were greatest in the poorer areas of the north, the Midlands and some London boroughs (Ramesh, 2012). A survey of directors of children's services estimated that cuts in children's services in 2011/12 averaged 13%, ranging from 6% to 25%, with the hardest hit services being youth services, averaging 56%, and early years and Children's Centres, with average cuts of 44% (Higgs, 2011); and early years was to take a disproportionate cut in the overall reductions to the education budget (Chowdry and Sibieta, 2011). Because of the speed and size of the budget reductions, the voluntary sector, which relied on central and local government for much of its income, was particularly hard hit (Gill et al., 2011; Children England, 2011; National Children's Bureau, 2012). It was estimated that children's charities would experience a greater proportion of public sector reductions (8.2%) compared to the voluntary sector as a whole (7.7%).

The cutbacks were taking place in a context where it was clear that the impact of the economic downturn, the cuts in public expenditure more generally and the rising costs of living were greatest for the poorest sections of society, particularly for households with children – what a number of children's charities called 'the perfect storm' (Oxfam, 2012; Reed, 2012). The Family and Parenting Institute demonstrated that the median income for households with children was set to fall in real terms by 4.2% between 2010/11 and 2015/16, significantly higher than the reduction in income among all households of 0.9% (Browne, 2012); while Action for Children (2012) claimed that there had been a 13% increase of 'vulnerable families' who were struggling in 2012 compared to the previous year. UNICEF (2012) warned that the cuts in government expenditure would increase child poverty in the UK.

A report by the Office of the Children's Commissioner for England (2013) found that the funding reforms to take effect by 2015 would have a much greater impact on low-income families with children as a percentage of net income than high-income families. The cuts to the household incomes of the poorest 10% of families with children were equivalent to a one-fifth reduction in their net income, while those for the richest 10% of families with children were equivalent to a 7% net fall. On average, couples with children experienced the largest losses in cash terms of any type of household, while the largest percentage losses were felt by lone parents. In addition, the report predicted that, between 2010 and 2015, the number of children in the UK living in poverty would rise from 2.3 million to 3 million, while the number of children living below a minimum income standard would rise by 400,000 to 6.8 million.

The Chartered Institute of Public Finance and Accountancy (CIPFA, 2011) carried out research for the NSPCC, which analysed the changes in local children's social care funding during 2010/11. It found that local authority children's social care services' budgets faced reductions, on average, of over 23 per cent. While local authorities varied in where and to what degree the cuts were made, they were disproportionately directed at prevention initiatives, including Sure Start services, youth services and family support services, and included significant cuts for smaller, community-based voluntary agencies. The report concluded by highlighting:

> New lower levels of spending on early intervention and preventative services could mean that local authorities are less effective at providing early help to vulnerable children before they come to the attention of child protection services. It is possible that cuts to preventative services could result in greater demand for child protection services, which are already under considerable pressure. (CIPFA, 2011, p. 38)

Similar findings emerged from research for the Family and Parenting Institute (Hopwood et al., 2012), which sought to understand the impact of revenue spending cuts on children's services in eight different local authorities in England. The researchers analysed publicly available accounts across two budget cycles, the financial years 2011/12 and 2012/13, and carried out interviews with the officers responsible for strategy and service delivery in each authority. While there was some growth in certain areas totalling £32 million across the eight councils, this was more than outweighed by the cuts, which totalled £112 million. Services provided to schools bore the greatest burden of cuts, such as school improvements, curriculum support, education welfare, behaviour support and school transport. This partly resulted from the expansion of the academies programme, which reduced the amount of education funding held by local authorities.

The other area experiencing significant cuts was 'services designed to help and support children, young people and families below the threshold of social work and statutory intervention' (Hopwood et al., 2012, p. 8). These services included youth centres and family and parenting support, together with early years and Children's Centres as indicated by the earlier research. The universal elements of these services were particularly hit, as authorities sought to save money by targeting services at those with 'additional needs or at risk of negative outcomes'. It was 'social work services and services for children with special educational needs (SEN)' (p. 8) that were shielded from the worst of the cuts. While there had been spending reductions in these service areas, such as on independent fostering agencies, the savings were more than counterbalanced by spending growth:

> This growth was largely attributed to increased demand being placed on social work and SEN services; an early warning, perhaps, of escalating levels of need in a time of economic stagnation. This demand-led growth, of course, means that in practice more money had to be saved elsewhere. (Hopwood et al., 2012, p. 8)

Such developments were reflected in the increased demands being made on the statutory elements of children's social care. The increases, first evident in the immediate aftermath of the Baby P scandal, discussed in Chapter 5, continued. The figures in Table A1.2 in the Appendix show that, nationally, from 2009/10 to 2011/12:

- while the number of referrals to children's social care remained stable at just over 600,000, the number of initial assessments went up from 395,300 (359.0/10,000 children aged under 18 years) to 451,500 (398.1)

- the number of registered child protection plans increased from 44,300 (30.2) to 52,100 (46.0); and the number of Section 47 enquiries started during the year went up from 89,300 (81.1) to 124,600 (109.9)

- the number of children in care (Appendix, Table A1.3) increased from 64,400 (58) in 2010 to 67,050 (59) in 2012

- while the Cafcass figures (Appendix, Table A1.4) for the number of care applications showed an increase from 8.832 in 2009/10 to 10,244 in 2011/12 and 11,055 in 2012/13.

The increases were considerable and described by the Association of Directors of Children's Services as 'increases in safeguarding activity' (Brooks et al., 2012, p. 6).

When these increases in safeguarding activity are located in the context of the parallel reductions of funding for and availability of community-based family support and preventive services, it is clear that we were witnessing a significant change in the orientation and priorities of child welfare agencies and hence the nature of the relationship between state, professionals and certain families.

In addition, following the Ministry of Justice's *Family Justice Review* (MoJ, 2011), the government introduced a series of major changes to the court system in order to try and improve and speed up court processes. The changes aimed to impose a statutory six-month time limit for the completion of care cases (the average at the time for a case from start to finish was estimated at 55 weeks). The aim was to free up the court system by resolving cases via the use of pre-proceedings protocols at the earlier administrative stage so that fewer cases would come to court (MoJ, 2012). However, as Holt and Kelly (2012) have argued, while the rhetoric for the changes was laudable, there were some major tensions at their heart. In particular, it was difficult to see how parents and children were going to be able to represent their views clearly in the context of the considerable cuts to the legal aid budget. It was also difficult to see how appropriate decisions about a child's future were going to be made at the pre-proceedings stage when children's social care was itself coming under increasing pressure. In order to deliver the new strategy, more resources were needed, not less (Holt and Kelly, 2012).

The coalition government also made serious attempts to increase the use of adoption for children in care. This was something Tony Blair had been seriously interested in during the early days of the New Labour government (DH, 2000), and the Adoption and Children Act 2002 brought adoption law in line with the 1989 Children Act as well as introducing a number of important changes. These aimed to:

- widen the type of people who could adopt, including unmarried and gay couples
- speed up the process
- and, crucially, ensure that adoption became a mainstream, serious option for children in care (Kirton, 2013).

Prior to the passage of the Act, the figures for the number of adoptions were stable at around 2,000/year (DH, 2000), but then increased significantly to 3,500 in 2003 and 3,800 in 2005 before falling to 3,050 in 2011 (DfE, 2011).

Soon after coming into office, David Cameron, partly prompted by a major campaign for reform in *The Times* newspaper fronted by Martin Narey (2011), the retired chief executive of Barnardos, launched a major initiative to 'speed up adoptions and give vulnerable children loving homes' (Government Press Release, 2012). Following the appointment of Narey as the 'ministerial adviser on adoption', the government published *An Action Plan for Adoption* (DfE, 2012) and produced league tables of local authority performance. As a result:

- local authorities would be required to reduce delays in all cases and would not be able to delay adoption in order to find a suitable ethnic match
- it would be easier for children to be fostered by approved prospective adopters while the courts considered the case for adoption
- if suitable adopters had not been found within three months, the case would have to be referred to the new National Adoption Register.

It was also clear that this was one of the areas of change in relation to children's social care and child and family policy that Michael Gove, the minister of education, was committed to. On numerous occasions, he spoke positively about adoption. He himself was adopted at the age of four months and said that it had given him the stability, security and love that had allowed him to enjoy limitless opportunities – he saw it as a small, but significant route for opening up social mobility (Aitkenhead, 2012). He was determined to remove any unnecessary blockages so that children in care could be adopted.[8]

While there were clear connections with Tony Blair's initiative, there were a number of important differences. The timescales were much more stringent and local authority social workers were given much less discretion. Also, the context in which the changes were taking place was rather different. As Kirton (2013) has argued, a key difference was the coalition government's much stronger endorsement of the benefits of child removal in cases of maltreatment and especially for child neglect (DfE, 2012). While this could be partly explained as a reaction to the death of Peter Connelly and the failures of professionals to protect him, it also reflected a growing policy consensus related to the importance of early intervention and the apparent neuroscientific evidence about the impact on brain development of poor parenting. Increasingly, it seemed that early intervention was being thought about in terms of removing children into care on a statutory basis and reinforcing the authoritarian dimensions of the state. This was a rather different interpretation of the idea of early intervention and prevention that had underpinned the early New Labour approach, as exemplified by Sure Start and the *Every Child Matters: Change for Children* (DfES, 2004b) programme. Such differences become even more apparent when it is also recognized that it was felt that 'social impact bonds' could also be used to fund independent, private agencies on the basis of the money that would be saved as a result of the increased numbers of children in care going forward for adoption and as a way of addressing local authority 'failure' (Narey, 2011).

This subtle but significant shift in the way early intervention was being thought about and operationalized became explicit when the government announced that the Early Intervention Grant was being top-sliced by £150 million to establish an Adoption Reform Grant (DfE, 2013b). This was a one-year grant designed to recruit an extra 3,000 adopters for the 'backlog' of 4,600 children waiting to be adopted and to recruit more than 600 additional adopters each year to keep up with the growing number of children waiting to be adopted. It was stated that this was the last chance for local authorities to demonstrate that they could take 'convincing action' to put a long-term plan in place and recruit the adopters that children in care needed. If this failed to happen, the government would require local authorities to 'outsource' their adoption recruitment and approval services. These various changes were placed on a statutory footing with the introduction of the Children and Families Bill in February 2013.

The firming up of this much more authoritarian approach to child welfare and protection had been confirmed in a major speech by Michael Gove on 16 November 2012 at the Institute of Public Policy Research entitled 'The Failure of Child Protection and the Need for a Fresh Start' (Gove, 2012). The way he defined and characterized child protection and what he saw as its focus was particularly interesting:

I want to talk about child protection.
Specifically, how we care for the most vulnerable children – those at risk of neglect or abuse – those who come into the care of others because their families cannot care for them.
And I want to begin with an admission.
The state is currently failing in its duty to keep our children safe.
It may seem hard to believe – after the killing of Victoria Climbié, after the torture of Peter Connolly, after the cruel death of Khyra Ishaq – surely as a society, as a state, we must have got the message.
But, I fear, we haven't. (Gove, 2012)

In part, he was responding to the publication that day of the latest Ofsted (2012) inspection report on the Edlington case in Doncaster and the full SCR into the case by Lord Carlile (2012), both of which were highly critical, as well as responding to the report on child protection by the House of Commons Education Select Committee (2012b), published the previous week. However, the speech was much broader than this and made explicit the minister's thinking and set out some clear policy directions. He argued strongly that there was currently a failure of leadership in the system and that adults' interests were overriding the needs of children. More children needed to come into care, more quickly. He also said that, following the Munro Review, improving the quality of social work practice was critical to improving child protection, but he ignored any reference to the work of the Social Work Reform Board and Social Work Task Force and their recommendations to improve training. Instead, he praised a recent report from the Institute for Public Policy Research (MacAlister with Creham and Olsen, 2012), which set out a different model of training. The idea was based on an approach to teacher training that had been in operation for a number of years. The aim was to recruit 'the most talented graduates', preferably from Oxford, Cambridge and other Russell Group universities, and provide them with a 'fast track' into social work, which would be led by employers rather than universities. It was clear that Michael Gove was keen to take child protection policy and practice in a rather different direction.

Conclusion

I will return to some of these issues in Chapters 10 and 11. Here, I want to summarize some of the important developments that had taken place since the election of the coalition government in 2010 and the growing evidence that we were witnessing the emergence of, what I am calling, an 'authoritarian neoliberal state' in relation to child welfare and child protection.

Earlier in this chapter, I argued that, following Soss et al. (2009, 2011) and Wiggan (2011), the important changes in social policy made by the coalition government, particularly as these applied to welfare and housing benefits and employment services, pointed to important changes in the role of the state. The criteria for the receipt of benefits and services had become more restrictive, punitive and selective, the level of provision had been reduced and the private sector had come to play an increasingly central role.[9] These changes had significant implications for children and families. In addition to the benefit cuts already announced, the chancellor's autumn statement in late 2012 stated that the uprating for most working-age benefits and tax credits would be kept at 1 per cent per year for three years from April 2013, a figure well below the rate of inflation (HM Treasury, 2012).

Increasingly, it seemed that the coalition's economic strategy was not working in the way it had been envisaged, and there was likely to be a need for further cuts in public spending and increases in taxation in 2015 (Emmerson et al., 2013; Lanchester, 2013). In the 2013 Spending Review, announced on 26 June, the chancellor announced that there would be a further reduction of current public spending of £11.5 billion in 2015/16, including £2.6 billion from local authority budgets and £500 million from education. He presented the Spending Review as a populist crackdown on welfare and public sector pay (Wintour and Stewart, 2013).

What I am suggesting is that if we take these various changes into account along with the clear evidence of the growth in statutory child protection and safeguarding interventions with children and families, what we were witnessing was not simply the emergence of a 'paternalist neoliberal sate', as suggested by Soss et al. and Wiggan, but something that could more appropriately be characterized as an 'authoritarian neoliberal state'.

Some years ago, Loïc Wacqant (2009, 2010, 2012) argued that, in the USA, the expansion of the prison population pointed to a new form of state formation, what he called 'the penal state', which was an important appendage of the more general neoliberal state. He argued that the return of the prison to the institutional forefront of advanced society was a political response, not to rising *criminal* insecurity, but to the diffuse *social* insecurity wrought by the fragmentation of wage labour and the shake-up of ethnic hierarchy. The punitive slant of the shifts in welfare and justice policies pointed to a broader reconstruction of the state, coupling restrictive 'workfare' and expansive 'prisonfare' under a philosophy of moral behaviourism:

> The paternalist penalization of poverty aims to contain the urban disorders spawned by economic deregulation and to discipline the precarious fractions of the postindustrial working class. Diligent and belligerent programs of 'law and order' entailing the enlargement and exaltation of the police, the courts, and the penitentiary have also spread across the First world because they enable political elites to reassert the authority of the state and shore up the deficit of legitimacy officials suffer when they abandon the mission of social and economic protection established during the Fordist-Keynesian era. (Wacquant, 2010, p. 199)

Wacquant's analysis in *Punishing the Poor: The Neoliberal Government of Social Insecurity* (2009) has generated considerable heated debate (see, for example, *Theoretical Criminology*, 2010; Squires and Lea, 2012). A major critique concerns how far his analysis can be applied generally to the First World, as he claimed, or whether it was something much more specific to the USA. However, Wacquant has clearly demonstrated that changes in the state had seen the development of *both* the growth of disciplinary welfare *together with* the penalization of insecurity and that we needed to expand our understanding of the neoliberal state to include:

- economic deregulation

- welfare state devolution, retraction and recomposition

- the emergence of an expansive, intrusive and proactive penal apparatus

- the development of the cultural trope of individual responsibility, which preaches that how you fare in the world is up to you, not the state (Campbell, 2010).

Contrary to neoliberal rhetoric, Wacquant argued that what we had now was a *centaur state* – liberal at the top for the upper classes but paternalistic and authoritarian at the bottom for the lower classes. While such changes could be seen to have begun in England in the late 1970s with the governments of Margaret Thatcher and later John Major and, in a somewhat different form, the New Labour governments of Tony Blair and Gordon Brown (Harvey, 2007; Hall, 2011), it is my contention that the changes introduced by the coalition government have taken this to a new level (Rodger, 2012).

The coalition government clearly abandoned any attempt to maintain the kinds of services and principles associated with the welfare state. It developed a particular approach to the changing political economy of the country arising, in part, from the financial and economic crisis of 2007/08. The welfare reforms are best understood as attempting to achieve global economic competitiveness by offering low taxes, a deregulated marketplace, and a relatively cheap, highly motivated and disciplined workforce. Such an approach has contributed to cuts in the earned and social wage, a weakening of employment protection, and the further intrusion of private markets into new areas of state and society, leading to new levels of insecurity. The changes were a clear attempt to move towards the neoliberal model of the USA (Taylor-Gooby, 2011).

The policy changes introduced in relation to children and families were consistent with this, particularly those in relation to child welfare and child protection.

Although developments in child welfare and protection in the overall context of the scale of the changes in social policy may seem small scale, as they only directly affect a few people, in other respects they are significant. They give out clear messages to a much wider section of the population than ever become involved with children's social care. Crucially, we can identify important changes in the relationships between children, families and the state and the role of professionals in this. Not only have we seen a significant reduction, privatization and restructuring of a range of welfare benefits for children and families, we have also seen a clear shift away from the family service orientation in children's social care. There has been a greater emphasis on 'authoritative child protection', including a reframing of the idea of 'early intervention' towards taking more children into care at an earlier stage, together with an increased investment in and mainstreaming of adoption.[10]

10

Child protection and social work

While the emphasis of policy and practice over the past 40 years has been to encourage different professions and agencies to work together, it is clear that it is local authority children's social workers who have been placed at the heart of the child protection system in England and have the lead role. In this chapter, I will argue that while there is an intimate relationship between social work and child protection, this has proved a difficult relationship and had a variety of implications for all concerned.

One of the main outcomes of the high-profile, public criticisms of social work in relation to its apparent failures to protect children over the past 40 years is somewhat contradictory. On the one hand, such developments have acted to undermine the authority, legitimacy and standing of social work, while, on the other, child protection has continually been confirmed as social work's central responsibility. Although social work in England has increasingly been marginalized or excluded from numerous other areas of practice, such as probation, work with older people and adults, and a whole range of family support and community-based activities, social work is seen as *the* profession for taking the lead responsibility for child protection. Thus, the area of practice that has produced the most high-profile, fundamental critiques of the performance, authority and legitimacy of social work and social workers – child protection – has continually been reconfirmed as social work's central, overriding responsibility. As we have seen, these issues came into sharp focus in England in late 2008.

Building on a previous paper (Parton, 2012a), the purpose of this chapter is to critically reflect on this conundrum and its implications. The scandal of Baby P and the intense, rancorous and highly critical social and media reaction engendered a sense of high anxiety among politicians, government officials and children's services' managers and practitioners (Garrett, 2009b; Parton, 2011b). It was particularly notable that the Laming Report, *The Protection of Children in England* (2009), and the government's response (HM Government, 2009) were both framed in terms of 'child protection'. Whereas for the previous 10 years, policy and practice in this area in England had been framed in terms of 'safeguarding and promoting the welfare of children' (Parton, 2006a), concerns about child protection had again moved centre stage.

At the same time as rediscovering child protection, the New Labour government also rediscovered the importance of professional social work. The establishment of the Social Work Task Force, which reported in late 2009 (Social Work Task Force, 2009), and the subsequent establishment of the Social Work Reform Board to implement the changes were the clearest examples of this. The government made it clear that a major contribution to the improvement in child protection practice was crucially dependent on the rejuvenation of a well-trained, respected social work profession (HM Government, 2010d). It seemed that improvements in child protection were crucially dependent on developments and improvements in social work. Child protection and social work were intimately related.

This intimate relationship between social work and child protection became even more evident with the establishment by the coalition government in June 2010 of the independent review of child protection, chaired by Eileen Munro, which produced its final report in May 2011 (Munro, 2011b). Here, as we saw in Chapter 8, the view that improvements in child protection practice were dependent on improvements in the organization of social work and the practice of social workers was even more explicit. In many respects, however, this was simply the most recent restatement of something that had been the case since the late nineteenth century. While the language of 'safeguarding and promoting the welfare of the child' has been retained, policy and practice were now dominated by a 'child protection orientation' in which social workers continued to play the central role. What does this intimate relationship between child protection and social work tell us about the way society conceives of and responds to child abuse? More particularly, what does it tell us about the way the state attempts to regulate and govern the family, particularly in relation to the way children are brought up and protected in the family? And how might this have changed in recent years?

Revisiting *Governing the Family: Child Care, Child Protection and the State*

I considered these issues over 20 years ago in *Governing the Family: Child Care, Child Protection and the State* (Parton, 1991). The book aimed to contribute to our understanding of:

- the nature of modern social work with children and families

- the processes whereby elements of the social world become problematized and subject to social policy intervention

- the changes in the form of social regulation of the family in contemporary England.

Theoretically and methodologically, the book was informed by the work of Jacques Donzelot (1980), various writings from Michel Foucault (for example, 1977, 1979, 1980) and, more particularly, the emerging scholarship at the time that aimed to build on Foucault's ideas about governmentality (for example, Burchell et al., 1991). The approach was also informed by an important article on social work by Mark Philp (1979).

I was concerned with trying to make transparent the practical and theoretical 'space' that child protection seemed to occupy and why and how this was related to social work. In particular, I tried to address what the nature of 'the social' was, how this had emerged and for what purposes:

> In attempting to excavate forms of practice, we need to identify 'the conditions of possibility' of the discourse of child protection and demonstrate the 'space' which had to exist for this form of knowledge to develop. The space is both theoretical and practical. It is this space which can be said to provide the rules for the formation of statements and it is through this space that the discourse is related to social, economic and political factors. For the space itself arises from shifts in these structures. (Parton, 1991, p. 5)

These issues were of concern at the time because, as we saw in Chapter 2, the late 1980s was a particularly difficult period in relation to child welfare policies and practices. In the light of the Cleveland affair (Secretary of State for Social Services, 1988), it seemed that the state was intervening far too much and insensitively, as 121 children had been placed on place of safety orders on the basis of, what proved to be, highly dubious medical diagnoses. There did not seem to be sufficient possibility for either the children or the parents to withstand the interventions of the state, but, at the same time, it also seemed that the state was failing to intervene to protect children. The mid-/late 1980s were littered with a series of high-profile scandals where children had died while under the supervision of local authority social workers. The public enquiry reports into the deaths of Jasmine Beckford (London Borough of Brent, 1985), Tyra Henry (London Borough of Lambeth, 1987) and Kimberley Carlile (London Borough of Greenwich, 1987) received particularly high-profile media and political coverage. Thus, in some cases, the state seemed to be failing to intervene in the family to protect children, while in others it seemed to be intervening unnecessarily and with great insensitivity. It seemed that the law, policy and practice could not get things more wrong.

It was in this context that the Children Act 1989 was an explicit attempt to rebalance the roles, responsibilities and lines of accountability between parents, local authorities and the courts. The legislation came into force in October 1991 and made it clear that the primary place for rearing children was the private family and that parents had particular *responsibilities* in this respect. The state could only intervene to protect children with the full authority of the law behind it, on the basis of 'significant harm or the likelihood of significant harm'.

The 1989 Children Act continues to provide the statutory framework for day-to-day professional practice. In *Governing the Family* (Parton, 1991), I argued that the 1989 Act was the latest legislative attempt to address what had been a central challenge for the liberal state since its emergence in the second half of the nineteenth century. I also argued that the concept of 'child protection', which was embedded in the legislation and the official guidance, tried to combine attempts to protect children from dangerous parents and carers while also protecting the family from unwarranted interventions. This was a complex and challenging task.

I argued that three interrelated questions had lain at the heart of state child welfare practices and the law since the first major childcare legislation had been introduced in the last quarter of the nineteenth century:

1   How could child rearing be made into a matter of public concern and its qualities monitored without destroying the family as a counterweight to state power, and thus be experienced by family

members, particularly parents, as a domain of voluntary, self-regulating actions?

2   How could the state establish the rights of individual children, while promoting the family as the natural sphere for raising children and hence not intervening in all families and thus reducing their autonomy?

3   How could the state devise a *legal* basis for the power to intervene in *some* families that did not convert *all* families into clients of the state?

Such questions were posed because of the contradictory demands of, on the one hand, ensuring that the family was experienced by its members as autonomous and the primary place for rearing children, while, on the other, recognizing that there was a need for intervention in some families where they were seen as failing in this primary task, but where such laws were supposed to act as general laws applicable to all. In a liberal society, it was vital that the state was not experienced as an overinterventionist state nor as a 'nanny state'. Thus, the issue of how children could be protected from dangerous adults, particularly their parents and carers, in the context of the private family, constituted a major challenge. It was in this context that the 1989 Children Act became such an important piece of legislation, not only to try to rebalance and relegitimate professional practice and the law, but also to re-establish the role and legitimacy of the liberal state itself.

In *Governing the Family*, I argued that the late nineteenth century witnessed the emergence of what I called the sphere of 'the social' and its primary practitioners, 'social' workers (Donzelot, 1980, 1988). This was seen as a positive solution to these major challenges. Such a development provided a compromise between the extreme liberal vision of the power of the unhindered patriarchal family and the excesses of the market, and the socialist vision of the all-pervasive interventionist state, which would take responsibility for the needs and upbringing of all children and thereby undermine the privacy of the family itself. In the context of the emergence of 'the social', social workers were to play the key role in not only fulfilling these fine balances but also mediating between these challenging if not contradictory demands on a day-to-day basis.

Thus, I argued, social work developed as a *hybrid* in 'the social'. In effect, social work both occupied and was practised in an intermediary zone or space between the private sphere of the family and the public sphere of the state and the wider society in order to fulfil these major obligations (Figure 10.1).

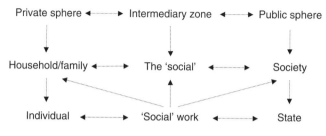

Figure 10.1　The hybridity of 'social' work

Social work evolved from the late nineteenth century onwards through a set of new relations between the law, social security, medicine and the school but could not be reduced to these other discourses or practices. I have tried to represent these new and emerging relations in Figure 10.2.

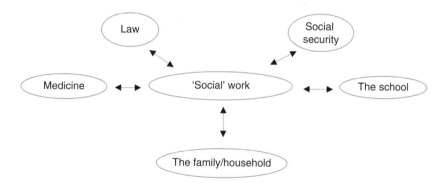

Figure 10.2　The institutional position and relations of 'social' work

As I argued in Chapter 2, the emergence of social work and child protection in particular arose in response to the rapid industrialization, urbanization and capitalist formation from the early/mid-nineteenth century and the reform of the Poor Law. The new Poor Law of 1834 was primarily a system for excluding the able-bodied from relief and defining eligibility for assistance in terms requiring personal degradation and loss of citizenship. At the same time, there was a fear that the growth in the *dangerous classes* would threaten social cohesion, security and public morals. Maintaining social order was a growing challenge (Stedman Jones, 1971). The task of classifying the poor and giving scientific assistance according to moral status complemented the narrow, exclusive focus of the Poor Law and provided a network of inclusion and distribution through voluntary agencies, which subtly reinforced the moral regime of the middle classes and also the emerging respectable working class.

From the moment of its emergence, social work has always been primarily positioned to work with those who were, or were at risk of entering, 'the residuum', the 'lumpenproletariat' or, crucially, the 'dangerous classes' (Pearson, 1975). While the vast majority of social work clients have always come from the poorest sections of society, it is not their poverty alone that makes them social work clients. They tend to have a marginal relationship with the labour market and exhibit behaviour or have characteristics that mark them out as in some way troublesome or dangerous (Jones, 1983). This is particularly the case in relation to work with children and families where social work not only has a specific class position but its work is concerned with the quality of parenting or, in most cases, mothering (Ferguson, 2004).

Thus social work occupied the space between the respectable and dangerous classes and between those with access to political influence and voice and those who, to all intents and purposes, were excluded. As Mark Philp (1979) has argued, social work provided an essentially *mediating* role between those who were excluded and the rest of society. In particular, it was concerned with trying to represent and mediate between the essential *subjectivities* of individuals and the *objectivizing* functions of the state and systems of governance more generally, including those of the legal system.

Overall, the nature of social work, and the form of knowledge it adopted from the late nineteenth century onwards, attempted to normalize the various 'deviants' with whom it worked and who had become detached from the respectable working and middle classes. In doing so, Philp made the important point that a key part of the work was thereby concerned with surveillance, which, for some, could be lengthy. Social work:

> acts as a relay, a form of surveillance, for those who are denied full discursive rights but who are not sufficiently dangerous to require the rigorous surveillance of the institution (or who have served a term there and need to be reintroduced to normal discourse). (Philp, 1979, p. 104)

Thus, the form of social work that emerged in the late nineteenth century onwards was crucially focused on trying to produce a picture of individuals that tried to emphasize their subjectivity and aimed to integrate these subjects into wider society. It also acted as a form of surveillance for those in the community who were not sufficiently dangerous to require more rigorous attention from other agencies, including closed institutions such as prisons or hospitals, or where children had been removed from their parents.

While the sphere of government from the late nineteenth century onwards was increasingly wide-ranging and complex and social work strategies formed only a small element in it, social workers provided a key part of the processes that attempted to draw individuals and families into these new spheres of government (Garland, 1985). Social work provided an important strategy to enable 'government at a distance' by indirect methods of social regulation. It was an important development if the liberal ideal of maintaining autonomous free individuals who were at the same time governed was to be realized. This was of particular significance in relation to the private family that was entrusted with the key role of bringing up children. In many respects, as the twentieth century developed, social work was to provide the humanistic dimension to the welfare state and its primary tool would be social workers' knowledge and understanding of human relationships. The work would be carried out directly with individuals and families in the community, primarily in their own homes, and 'the relationship' would be the primary tool used by social workers in their day-to-day work.

In order to fulfil these complex obligations, social work has always attempted to mediate between a number of potentially contradictory demands – care *and* control, empowerment *and* regulation, and promoting *and* safeguarding individual children's welfare. One of social work's enduring characteristics, therefore, is its ambiguous and sometimes contested nature (Martinez-Brawley and Zorita, 1998; Parton and Kirk, 2010). Crucially, this ambiguity can be seen to arise from, on the one hand, its commitment to individuals and families and their needs and, on the other, its allegiances to and legitimation by the state, in the guise of its statutory responsibilities. As Caroline Skehill (2007, 2008) has demonstrated, social work is firmly established in child protection because it is the only profession whose core is based on a socio-legal expertise, and continually attempts to mediate across the various tensions that inhabit the sphere of 'the social'. However, the way the state responds to these challenges and tensions varies over time (history) and place (across various jurisdictions).

The impact of the Maria Colwell scandal on child protection and social work

The nature of social work and its relationship with child protection was to change quickly and dramatically in the 1970s, and the public inquiry into the death of Maria Colwell (Secretary of State for Social Services, 1974), discussed in Chapter 2, was to prove key. In *Safeguarding Childhood* (Parton, 2006a), I argued that from 1973 onwards, local authority social work practice was increasingly subject to public scrutiny and public inquiries and the media took an increasingly central and pervasive role in raising the profile of issues that, for much of the twentieth century, had been hidden from view and, in the process, had a considerable impact on how the issues were framed:[1]

> The Public Inquiry into the death of Maria Colwell can be seen as a watershed in the contemporary history of social work ... Prior to this, social work practice was seen primarily as a private activity carried out between clients and professionals, the latter optimistically feeling that their skills and techniques could tackle, even solve, many social problems. The case of Maria Colwell and the numerous subsequent inquiries into cases of child abuse have quite changed all that. (Parton and Thomas, 1983, pp. 56–7)

This was explicitly stated by Jean Wall, an area director in East Sussex social services department, which was one of the departments placed under the microscope in the Maria Colwell inquiry, when she commented that the inquiry 'was beyond our experience, because, at that time nothing had been more private than social work' (Shearer, 1979, p. 14).

As Butler and Drakeford (2011, p. 8) have demonstrated, this was a 'critical moment in the history of social work in the UK', when social work was 'put on trial' and found wanting. The public inquiry and media coverage was much more about social work and its failings than it was about the nature of child abuse and the best ways of addressing it. Butler and Drakeford demonstrate, in meticulous detail, how the case linked the emergent profession of social work with the, arguably, preventable death of a child, and that, from that point, the newly established departments of social services and social work were associated in the minds of the public and, crucially, the media with failure and incompetence. From that point, the case of Maria Colwell provided the key reference point for future media coverage of child abuse cases and social work, which has, in many respects, continued ever since.

It was not simply the scale of the media reporting of the Colwell inquiry and hence of social work that was new, but the highly critical coverage and media concern to scapegoat the social worker also marked a new departure. Media reporting was heavy with disapprobation and admonition because what was alleged amounted to professional neglect. Throughout the inquiry, the media vilified the social worker concerned, who had to be protected from the public while entering and leaving the inquiry. She was questioned for 25 hours in the inquiry and eventually had to change her name to escape public and media attention (Andrews, 1974; Lees, 1979; Shearer, 1979). However, it was not just the social worker in the case but the emerging profession of social work more generally that was subject to criticism.

'Folk devils' and the nature and impact of the 'moral panics'

The media and political image of social work as being inextricably interrelated with failures in relation to children, particularly in terms of child protection, became dominant from this point. An analysis of press reporting of social work in England in national daily and Sunday news-papers 25 years later (between 1 July 1997 and 30 June 1998) is particularly instructive in this respect (Franklin and Parton, 2001). There were nearly 2,000 articles, measuring 97,932 column centimetres (ccm), of which 6,995 ccm were devoted exclusively to discussions of social work and social services. The 15 most common messages, accounting for 80 per cent of the total, were negative with regard to social work and included 'incompetent', 'negligent', 'failed', 'ineffective', 'misguided' and 'bungling'. Over 75 per cent of the stories were related to children, where the concerns were about child abuse, paedophiles, adoption and fostering. The dominant discourse was social work failure in cases of child welfare and child protection. Thus, it was not just that there was a clear and intimate relationship between social work and child protection that, as we have seen, was long established but that after 1973, this was characterized in the media in highly critical and negative terms.

In 1991, Bob Franklin and I explored the way the press portrayed cases of child abuse and the different images of social work presented in the reporting (Franklin and Parton, 1991). Our analysis was carried out at the end of the period leading up to the 1989 Children Act, when media stories were dominated by a failure to intervene and children had died, and after Cleveland (Secretary of State for Social Services, 1988), where children had been removed unwarrantedly on the basis of flimsy evidence. Two contrary stereotypes of social workers emerged. They were characterized as being 'fools and wimps' and thereby failing to intervene authoritatively to protect children, and also as 'villains and bullies', sometimes at the same time. We argued that these two stereotypes of social work were perhaps not as contradictory as may at first appear. An underlying consistency could be discerned if it was acknowledged that social workers had taken on an almost symbolic representation of the entire public sector from the mid-1970s onwards, particularly in relation to its various social and welfare functions. Thus, when the political and economic climate began to change in the 1970s, in the context of increasing criticisms of the welfare state and the growth of the New Right and ultimately the election of Margaret Thatcher in 1979, local authority social workers were always likely to be vulnerable to criticism. It was as if social workers had come to represent all that was wrong with the postwar welfare state, where the latter was presented, in many sections of the media, as being inefficient and failing to meet the various demands made of it, while also being accused of being repressive, overly interventionist and insensitive.

As I discussed earlier, the nature of social work is inherently ambiguous and has a number of significant tensions built into its fabric, particularly its attempts to mediate between the individual and the state – care and control, protection and empowerment. In addition, while state social work in social services departments was formally established as a universal service for a wide variety of client groups, in practice its priorities, as they had been since its origins in the nineteenth century, were primarily with the 'residual and dependent' sections of the working class, or what was increasingly being referred to in the 1970s and 80s as 'the underclass' (Morris, 1994; Young, 1999; Welshman, 2006b). Clients were on the margins of the labour market and excluded from the mainstream of society. Becker and Macpherson (1986) estimated that the main source of income of over 90 per cent of social service department clients was some sort of state social security benefit. Unlike the health service or education, the social class focus of the work of social services and social work was much more specific. The more this section of society was subject to vitriol, the more likely it was that social workers would be held to account for their clients' behaviour.

Two important social changes have reinforced these developments over the past 30 years – the increasing hostility towards and essentializing of 'the underclass' and, more specifically, the growing concerns about risks to children. I will say something about each. First, as Jack Young (2007) has argued, while the underclass is, in reality, an ill-defined and heterogeneous section of society, it has increasingly become the target of resentment and strong feelings of punitiveness. He argues that the processes of social exclusion have intensified, resulting in a much greater sense of social antagonism, much of which is focused on the most marginalized and deprived.[2] It seems that while the trends towards inequality, poverty and unemployment have been increasing, public opinion, media discourse and mainstream political parties have all become less sympathetic to those at the bottom, so that the poor have become increasingly stigmatized and demonized (Taylor-Gooby, 2013; Clery et al., 2013).

Second, concerns about risks to children have grown in number and depth. As David Buckingham (2000, p. 3) has argued:

> The figure of the child has always been the focus of adult fears and fantasies ... in recent years, debates about childhood have become invested with a growing sense of anxiety and panic. Traditional certainties about the meaning and status of childhood have been steadily eroded and undermined.

As traditional forms of family and community have withered and research and experts have increasingly highlighted the dangers that face children, there has been a growing sense that children are at risk, placing greater and greater expectations on the roles and responsibilities of parents, particularly mothers (Hoffman, 2010).

When I first analysed the case of Maria Colwell and its impact (Parton, 1981, 1985), I drew on the sociological concept, as originally discussed by Stanley Cohen (1972) and later by Stuart Hall et al. (1978), of a 'moral panic'.[3] A necessary requirement for such panics seemed to be that they emerge in conditions of social crisis, when traditional values and social institutions lose their credibility under threat by those designated as 'folk devils', who have a range of anxieties and fears projected on to them. The media play a central role in creating and sustaining the panic, and by identifying the group which is to serve as folk devils. Chas Critcher (2003) has concluded from his analysis of a series of moral panics in the UK in the 1970s, 80s and 90s that the central theme connecting them all was concerns about children and childhood. In the 1960s and 70s, the folk devils of British moral panics tended to be young people, specifically working-class males, for example Mods and Rockers and muggers; however, there was a clear shift in the 1980s and 90s:

> Instead of youth *as* folk devils, we have children as *the victims* of folk devils. Most transparently in the case of child abuse and paedophilia, moral panics are irresistible when they present threats to children. (Critcher, 2003, p. 155)

In 1991, Bob Franklin and I identified two particular characteristics of the moral panics about child abuse up to that point, which were unusual and rarely evident in analyses of other moral panics. Both characteristics have continued to the present time and both are important for my overall analysis here. First, media reporting of child abuse in all the cases examined identified social workers as the folk devils to be castigated, vilified and designated to be the out-group who were challenging the values of mainstream society. The wrongdoer, the person(s) actually responsible for the abuse of the child, was certainly the subject of media demonization and admonition, but this varied. A consistent theme throughout has been that the central folk devils in such cases over the past 40 years have been social workers, and in many respects the intensity of the media and political reaction and vilification of them has increased steadily during the period, to the point where Fitzgibbon (2011) has argued there is now a 'permanent moral panic'. The consistent folk devils in moral panics about child abuse in England over the past 40 years have been local authority social workers and, more recently, their managers.

The second unusual characteristic about the moral panics is that rarely do they follow the pattern suggested by moral panic theory. The theory suggests that the media and social *reaction* is disproportionate and exaggerates the size and threat of the problem being responded to. In relation to the moral panic about child abuse, rarely is this the case. In fact, in a number of cases, the media have gone out of their way to suggest that the nature and size of the *problem*, that is, child abuse, have been exaggerated. For example, in Cleveland, it was stated quite explicitly, in various sections of the media, that the problem – the sexual abuse of children – in Middlesbrough had come about because of the actions of 'fanatic' and 'overzealous' health and social work professionals. As I argue in Chapter 11, moral panics about child abuse have had the effect of deflecting attention from the nature and scale of the problem. In part, this results from the processes whereby the panics came about.

Primarily, media reporting was based on a series of public inquiries, and more recently SCRs, which investigated the practices and decision making of professionals involved with the cases. The focus of attention and hence the moral panic has not therefore primarily been about child abuse per se but about the operation, procedures and failures of what has come to be called the 'child protection system'. In the process, we have conflated concerns about the problem of child abuse and what to do about it with concerns about the operation and efficacy of the child protection system. As I have tried to demonstrate in this chapter, the child protection system in which social workers are centrally and intimately involved is primarily a system, originally established in the second half of the nineteenth century, designed to 'govern the family' and, as I will try to demonstrate in Chapter 11, can only ever have a limited impact on preventing and reducing the much more wide-ranging problems of child abuse and neglect. In many respects, child protection systems can be seen to have had the effect of actually deflecting attention from such possibilities, and in this social work can be seen, for reasons well beyond its influence, to be heavily implicated. As David Garland (2008) has argued, the folk devils of moral panics – in this case social workers as well as parents and carers of the children involved – are not randomly selected but are the 'cultural scapegoats' onto which society can project sentiments of guilt and ambivalence.

However, it is possible to identify one element of such moral panics that has acted to exaggerate the size and depth of an aspect of the problem it is responding to. As we have seen, nearly all the media stories have been based on individual public inquiries and SCRs of cases where, by definition, things have been seen to go wrong. However, on many of those occasions, the case has been seen to represent the current state of practice and, in particular, has been presented as being typical of social work rather than being seen as exceptional. While numerous efforts have been made to improve the overall image and status of social work, the continued cultural message that has been confirmed time and time again via a series of high-profile tragedies is that of blame and failure.

Writing in 1994, Marguerite Valentine tried to account for why social workers had been subjected to so much hostility, anger and hatred and had become such demons in various areas of the media.[4] Why was it that social work had become almost synonymous with failure and incompetence and why was it that social workers were subjected to so much hostility? She agreed that the origins of the widespread criticism emanated from the public inquiry into the death of Maria Colwell. Drawing on the work of Melanie Klein (Klein et al., 1971; Segal, 1979), Isabel Menzies (1988, 1989) and Robert Hinshelwood (1987), Valentine argued that social workers were the targets of many projections, and that in this there was a denial of the emotions that child abuse engenders. It was as if it belonged 'out there', preferably with the parents and the social worker, who together become represented as 'bad', while the initiators of the criticism of social workers see themselves, by implication, as 'good'. This splitting into bad and good 'part objects' was observed by Klein in her clinical work with infants and she developed the view that such splitting was one of the earliest defences against the unbearable and unmanageable experience of anxiety, which the infant is unable to understand or contain. Drawing on this theoretical perspective, Valentine provided a framework for understanding how the phenomenon of child abuse engenders anxiety, and how its denial becomes projected onto others – particularly individual social workers and, more recently, their managers, and the profession of social work more generally.

Valentine (1994) argued that social workers act as the primary 'containers' for society's anxieties and expectations about children's welfare. They are not simply held accountable when things go wrong but have projected onto them a whole range of anger and hostility. As our expectations and anxieties about children have increased over the past 40 years, so has the potential depth of anger and hostility projected and the media have played a key role in this. In this respect, the idea of 'moral panic' does not perhaps capture the force and depth of feelings that have been generated and projected at social workers in more recent years. With each childcare tragedy and scandal that has been evident over the past 40 years, the intensity of the reaction has increased, in the context of 'why don't the professionals learn from previous mistakes?'[5] The depth of emotion and anger projected onto social work and social workers has the effect of increasing the social denial of the level of suffering and harm involved for many children (Cohen, 2001; Warner, 2013a, 2013b).

Such psychodynamic analysis clearly connects with Jock Young's sociological analysis (2007) of the increasing evidence of 'othering' in contemporary society and the growing hostility towards the underclass. As the more traditional boundaries associated with class, status, family, community, gender and ethnicity become more permeable and liquid (Bauman, 2007), new barriers and boundaries are constructed in order to establish individual and social identities. In the process, the self is granted a superior and more secure ontology, which projects negative attributes onto the other and thereby grants positive attributes to oneself. What Young calls the 'vertigo of modernity' generates a level of insecurity and uncertainty that provides the social and emotional raw material for a strength of othering not seen in the postwar period up to the 1970s. As Harry Ferguson (2004, p. 121) has argued:

> Because of its closeness to and structurally ambiguous relationship with those dirty, dangerous Others who abuse children, social work itself represents a threat to ontological security and becomes a focus of the blaming system. Now it is not only 'abusing' families but social workers too who are subjected to purity and pollution rituals by the community.[6]

Conclusion

In this chapter, I have explored how and why social work and social workers have come to play such a central role in child protection in England. From the late nineteenth century onwards, social work played the key role in protecting children in the family, in the context of the operation of the liberal state, which also needed to maintain the idea that the family was *the* private sphere with the prime responsibility for rearing children. Social work played the key role in 'governing the family'.

However, from the early 1970s onwards, society began to change in important ways and the role of social work was subject to high-profile political and media scrutiny and criticism. In the process, child protection systems and social work were increasingly characterized in terms of incompetence and failure. As a result, while the authority, legitimacy and standing of social work has been undermined, child protection has continued to be its central responsibility. In the process, child maltreatment and what to do about it has been marginalized from mainstream public and political debates. Political outrage and concern has been so focused on the problems and 'failures' of the child protection system that there has been a failure to seriously address the problem of child maltreatment, and it is to this that I turn in Chapter 11.

11

Moving beyond individualized child protection systems

The purpose of this final chapter is to bring the various threads of my argument together and provide the foundations for thinking about 'the politics of child protection' differently, thereby opening up new ways of taking policy and practice forward. Throughout, I have argued that a number of high-profile scandals have proved key in the way policy and practice have developed in England since the early 1970s. The cases of Maria Colwell, the Cleveland affair, Victoria Climbié and Baby Peter Connelly have all been crucial in providing the catalysts for ensuring that concerns about child protection have received major public and professional attention. The politics of child protection over the past 40 years can be characterized as being punctuated by periods of high-profile scandals, where the intensity of anger and anxiety expressed by senior politicians and certain sections of the media, particularly the popular press, has steadily grown, resulting in increasingly dramatic professional and managerial fallout. Such moments have also witnessed significant shifts in policy direction.

Drawing on the policy framework developed by Gilbert et al. (2011b) (see Table 1.2), I have argued that the period from the public inquiry into the death of Maria Colwell (Secretary of State for Social Services, 1974) to the mid-1990s can be characterized as being consistent with an overall child protection orientation, where the primary focus was a narrow forensic and legalistic concern with the protection of children from actual and potential significant harm, while ensuring that the privacy of the family and the rights and responsibilities of parents were not undermined (Parton, 1991; Berridge, 1997). However, from the second half of the 1990s, particularly following the election of the New Labour government in May 1997, there were clear attempts to move towards a family service orientation, where the focus was the much broader idea of 'safeguarding and promoting the welfare of the child'. This was taken further with the passage of the Children Act 2004 and the introduction of the *Every Child Matters: Change for Children* programme (DfES, 2004b) from late 2004 onwards, where the focus was the integration of services in order to improve outcomes for all children in terms of being healthy, staying safe, enjoying and achieving, making a positive contribution and achieving economic wellbeing. The aim was to improve the wellbeing of all children, while reducing the gap between the best and worst off (Parton and Berridge, 2011).

However, following the huge critical media and political reaction to the death of Baby Peter Connelly in late 2008, concerns about child protection again moved centre stage. Such a development was reinforced with the election of the Conservative-led coalition government in May 2010, which aimed to reduce the role of the state and cut back public expenditure. In the process, we witnessed attempts to significantly shift the relationships between parents, children and the state and thereby the roles and responsibilities of professionals. While I have previously characterized the changes introduced by New Labour as indicative of a move towards a 'preventive surveillance state' (Parton, 2008), I have argued here that changes in recent years can be more appropriately characterized as a move towards an 'authoritarian neoliberal state'. While a number of the key policies and characteristics of this development had been evident during the period of the New Labour government, particularly in its latter years, changes under the Conservative-led coalition government made the realization of such a state formation far more concrete.

The emergence of an authoritarian neoliberal state approach to services for children and families has a number of key interlinking characteristics:

- a reduction in the range and level of universal benefits and secondary prevention services

- an increasing willingness to intervene in some families with statutory interventions, including increasing the numbers of children taken into care

- a much higher priority given to adoption as a mainstream alternative for children in care

- a much greater use of private and third sector providers of services previously provided by the state.

Not only has the state become more residualized, marketized and commercialized, it has also become more authoritarian for certain sections of the population.

In this context, it is important to consider how far and in what ways high-profile scandals have acted as the main drivers of policy change and influenced the direction that such change has taken, or whether they act primarily as helpful vehicles for bringing about changes that were already planned. Butler and Drakeford (2005, p. 240), in their analysis of the relationship between scandal and social welfare more generally in the British context, argue that 'although scandal can accelerate a rising policy tide, it cannot, of itself, originate a change in the policy direction, or alter the course of a policy which is already well-established', a view supported by Ray Jones (2009). While scandals may influence the priority or timing of a policy change, invariably they are used by governments for bringing about changes they had already planned. As I argued in Chapter 4, this was what happened with the public inquiry into the death of Victoria Climbié, which New Labour used for bringing about the fundamental organizational and policy changes related to the *ECM: Change for Children* programme (DfES, 2004b). Scandal provides opportunities for policy change that might otherwise be difficult to bring about and might come up against significant political, professional and community resistance. However, for such change to be introduced, it is important that the scandal is seen to arise because of institutional as well as individual failures, thus warranting major change; this was certainly the case in relation to Victoria Climbié. Juliet Gainsborough (2009, 2010) has come to similar conclusions in her analysis of the impact of scandal on child welfare policy in the US context. (See also Jacobsson and Löfmark (2008) in relation to Sweden.)

However, the dynamics in relation to the death of Baby Peter Connelly were rather different. As I argued in Chapter 5, the New Labour government initially seemed unprepared for the strength of anger unleashed by the scandal when it erupted in all sections of the media in November 2008. The campaign run by *The Sun* was particularly significant. In a period of major economic and political turmoil, the case provided an opportunity for the Conservative Party and other critical commentators to argue that it provided evidence that many of the changes introduced by New Labour had failed – not only in relation to the *ECM: Change for*

Children programme but its social policy reforms more generally. The case was seen to exemplify all that was wrong with the 'broken society' and the inadequacies of a range of professional and managerial practices that had failed to address it. The fact that the period from late 2008 to early 2010 was littered with similar high-profile scandals and failures only reinforced the criticisms. Not only did the scandals seem to demonstrate the fundamental problems with the New Labour project, particularly in relation to children and families, which had been so central to its attempts to modernize Britain, but they also provided clear evidence that change was required. In many respects, the scandals provided fertile ground for the Conservative Party to differentiate itself from New Labour and develop a number of key themes in its approach to policies for children and families and welfare more generally.

While New Labour had responded in late 2008 and 2009 with a series of initiatives in an attempt to gain the political and policy initiative, it was to prove a major challenge for it to regain control of the situation. In this respect, the Baby P scandal cannot be understood simply as providing the government of the day with an opportunity to introduce policies and initiatives that it was already planning, as, in many respects, the scandal seemed to undermine much of what had been introduced following the death of Victoria Climbié. What we witnessed was the re-emergence of child protection as a major policy priority, the growing political significance of SCRs in child protection policy and practice, and the rediscovery of the importance of professional social work as a way of bringing about positive change. These themes continued in the first two years of the Conservative-led coalition government.

Evidence of the failure of the New Labour government to control the situation was even clearer at the level of practice. In the two years following the Baby Peter Connelly scandal:

- the number of children placed on child protection plans increased from 34,000 in 2007/08 to 44,300 in 2009/10

- the number of applications to court increased from 6,241 in 2007/08 to 8,832 in 2009/10

- the number of children looked after in the care system increased from 59,360 in 2008 to 64,400 in 2010 (see Appendix, Tables A1.2–A1.4).

None of this was planned, and, as we have seen in Chapter 9, these trends increased after the 2010 election. A major difference, however, was that the Conservative-led coalition government made clear statements that it supported such trends and they should increase further. This was a significant departure from the New Labour approach and from government policy for many years before 1997.

I have argued that, despite periods of relative calm, the overriding policy narrative in relation to child protection in England from 1973 onwards has been one of blame and failure and that the profession of social work has been intimately implicated. Yet, while it seems that social work has been subject to almost continual criticism because of child protection failures, it also seems that child protection policy and practice, although subjected to increased proceduralization and bureaucratization, cannot do without social work. In Chapter 10, I explained how this had come about and with what implications. Partly as a result, the coalition government established an independent review of the child protection system as the basis for introducing a number of significant reforms to the child protection system in England (Munro, 2010b, 2011a, 2011b).

However, as I argued in Chapter 8 (see also Parton, 2012b), the Munro Review took a narrow view of child protection and, in particular, what causes harm to children. While it aimed to give professionals, particularly social workers, much greater discretion and authority when making judgements and planning interventions, and wanted to shift the balance towards a more family service-oriented system that prioritized early help, the focus of the review was only on the way the state protected children from 'poor or dangerous *parental* care' (Munro, 2011b, p. 69, emphasis added) – what I described in Chapter 10 as systems for 'governing the family' under the auspices of the liberal state.

However, as I demonstrated in Chapter 8, the nature and size of the problem the review claimed to be addressing was not based on any estimates about the prevalence of child abuse in society and the amount of harm experienced by children but by the increasing referrals being made to local authority children's social care departments, which had risen from 547,000 children in 2008/09 to 603,500 in 2009/10, with even greater percentage increases in the number of initial and core assessments being completed (see Appendix, Table A1.2). An overall aim of the Munro Review was therefore to try and improve the way children's social care responded to the demands made of it so that it could 'govern the family' more efficiently. With the publication of the revised Working Together in 2013 (HM Government, 2013, p. 22), it became clear that one of the government's aims was to ensure that child protection became more 'authoritative' and should not be afraid of 'rescuing children from chaotic, neglectful and abusive homes'. But again, the starting point for the revised Working Together was that in 2011/12, over 600,000 children in England were referred to local authority children's social care services by individuals who had concerns about their welfare (HM Government, 2013, p. 7).

However, as I argue in the next section, the number of referrals to children's social care gives us little realistic idea about the prevalence and nature of maltreatment experienced by children and young people. One would have thought that the overriding aim of any child protection system would be to identify and reduce the incidence and prevalence of child maltreatment in society. This is what it appeared would be the prime focus of the Munro Review, because the opening sentence of its first report stated that 'protecting children from abuse and neglect has been high on the political agenda for many decades' (Munro, 2010b, p. 5). It also claimed that its first principle – hence the title of the final report (Munro, 2011b) – *A Child-Centred System* – was based on the United Nations Convention on the Rights of the Child:

> The United Nations Convention on the Rights of the Child (UNCRC) provides a child-centred framework that spells out the basic human rights that children everywhere have: the right to survival; to develop to the fullest; to protection from harmful influences, abuse and exploitation; and to participate fully in family, cultural and social life. (Munro, 2011a, p. 14)

However, the implications of this perspective, as expressed in the interim report, were never seriously followed through to the review's final report.

While child protection systems have been extended, revised and updated on many occasions since the early 1970s – as I discussed in Chapter 6 and summarized in Table A1.1 in the Appendix – there have been two major problems with such systems from the outset. As Gary Melton (2005) has argued, the original designers of modern child protection systems made two interconnected and fundamental errors, and both could be seen to emanate from assumptions that underpinned the notion of 'the battered child syndrome' (Kempe et al., 1962). Both the *scope* and the *complexity* of the problem of child abuse and neglect were underestimated:

> The assumption early in the history of the modern child protection system was that the problem of child maltreatment was reducible to

'syndromes' – in effect, that abusive and neglectful parents were either very sick or very evil and that they could thus be appropriately character-ised as 'those people' who were fundamentally different from ourselves ... Although such cases do occur, they are relatively rare. Most cases involve neglect ... further, searches for distinctive behavioural syndromes have proven elusive. (Melton, 2005, p. 11)

The idea that child maltreatment is an individual problem caused by particularly malevolent parents is one projected strongly in the media and by many politicians; such ideas are reinforced when most of the public and political discussion of the problem takes place in a context of a scandal. Although such scandals have increasingly been seen as evidence of systemic failure, and not just individual failure on the part of particular workers and managers, the scandal-driven politics of child protection still encourage a narrow view of what is at stake in policy making. The failures of child protection are seen to result from problems in the design and operation of the systems and the decisions of certain professionals, particularly social workers.

Through the lens of scandal, discussions about child protection are largely disconnected from any wider appreciation of what harms children, how their welfare might be improved, and how such issues are related to wider social and economic forces. This appreciation should begin by focusing on what we know about the prevalence of child maltreatment and what some of the prime causes might be. Once we are clearer about that, we would then be in a much better position to develop and implement appropriate policies, systems and practices.

The prevalence of child maltreatment

An authoritative review of research on the prevalence of child maltreat-ment in 'high-income countries' published in *The Lancet* in 2009 (Gilbert et al., 2009b) concluded that, every year, between 4 and 16% of children were physically abused and 1 in 10 were neglected or psycho-logically abused. During childhood, between 5 and 10% of girls and up to 5% of boys were exposed to penetrative sexual abuse and up to three times that number were exposed to some form of sexual abuse. The review also concluded that the numbers of cases of substantiated child maltreatment known to official agencies only accounted for a tenth of this total. In addition, exposure to multiple types and repeated episodes of maltreatment was also associated with increased risks of severe maltreatment and psychological consequences. Child maltreatment was found to substantially contribute to child mortality and morbidity and had long-lasting effects on mental health, drug and alcohol misuse (especially in girls), risky sexual behaviour, obesity and criminal behaviour, which persisted into adulthood. The review suggested that neglect was at least as damaging as physical or sexual abuse.

Two years later, Carol-Ann Hooper (2011) provided a helpful summary of what was known about the nature and size of the problem of child maltreatment in the UK and how this might have changed over time. She demonstrated that research had consistently shown that only a small number of incidents were ever reported to any agency (Cawson et al., 2000; Sidebotham and the ACSPAC Study Team, 2000) and these cases were often described as 'the tip of the iceberg' (Creighton, 2004). Crucially, there was little evidence to suggest that those children who were harmed and injured would tell anyone and even less likely they would tell an official agency (see, for example, Wattam and Woodward, 1996a). The problem was less to do with overreporting – as implied by the Munro Review – and more to do with underreporting and the type of response that children and young people receive (Tucker, 2011).

The most comprehensive research on the prevalence of child abuse in the UK was funded by the NSPCC and published in 2000 and 2011. The first study, *Child Maltreatment in the UK* (Cawson et al., 2000), was based on a sample of 2,689 18- to 24-year-olds who were interviewed in 1998 about their childhood experiences in the late 1970s, 80s and 90s. The second study, carried out 11 years later (Radford et al., 2011), involved randomly selected households across the UK. While the focus was children and young people under 17, the sample also included 1,761 young adults aged 18–24 to allow for comparison with the findings of the earlier survey by Cawson et al. (2000). For the 2,160 children under 11, parents or carers were interviewed as proxy reporters, and 2,275 children and young people aged 11–17 were interviewed directly, together with a primary carer. The interviews were carried out in 2009. Because the 2000 and 2011 studies excluded young people living in residential care, hostels or in custody, and parental consent was required for all those interviewed under 18, the findings almost certainly underestimated the amount of child abuse and neglect experienced. Even so, severe child maltreatment was reported as an experience for a substantial minority – amounting to 25.3% of all children, young people and young adults at some point in their lives (Radford et al., 2011) – and included:

- *Physical assault by an adult carer:* 1.2% of under 11s, 6.9% of 11–17s, 11.5% of 18–24s
- *Neglect:* 5% of under 11s, 13.3% of 11–17s, 16% of 18–24s
- *Contact sexual abuse (as defined by criminal law):* 0.5% of under 11s, 4.8% of 11–17s, 11.3% of 18–24s
- *Sexual abuse (including non-contact offences):* 1.2% of under 11s, 16.5% of 11–17s, 24.1% of 18–24s
- Under the broad category of *emotional abuse:*
  - *Exposure to domestic violence:* 12% of under 11s, 17.5% of 11–17s, 23.7% of 18–24s
  - *Other aspects of emotional abuse:* 3.6% of under 11s, 6.8% of 11–17s, 6.9% of 18–24s.

Radford et al. (2011, p. 118) concluded that:

> There is still a substantial minority of children and young people today who are severely maltreated and are experiencing abuse at home, in school and in the community, from adults and from peers. Almost 1 in 5 11–17s (18.6 per cent), 1 in 4 18–24s (25.3 per cent) and 1 in 17 (5.9 per cent) under 11s had experienced severe maltreatment during childhood.

These figures compare with a total number 42,850 who were the subject of a child protection plan on 31 March 2012 (see Appendix, Table A1.2) or 0.42% of the child population under the age of 18. The number of referrals to children's social care in 2011/12 was 605,000, or about 6% of the total population of children and young people in England, and a number of these would have been re-referrals.

The research by Radford et al. (2011) confirms what Gilbert et al. (2009b) established in their review of research that only a small proportion of abuse ever becomes known to official agencies and is therefore included in official statistics.[1] The research also established that in 22.9% of cases where a young person aged 11–17 was physically hurt by a parent or guardian, nobody else knew about it, as with 34% of cases of sexual assault by an adult and 82.7% of cases of sexual assault by a peer.

Another important finding from the research was that it was clear that child abuse did not only arise because of 'poor or dangerous parental care'

(Munro, 2011b, p. 69). In particular, sexual abuse was perpetrated in a wide range of relationships and in a variety of different contexts, but was typically perpetrated by those, usually men, who were known to the child or young person – 65.9 per cent of the contact sexual abuse reported by children and young people aged up to 17 was perpetrated by other children and young people under the age of 18. In fact, it became clear, as was first demonstrated in the earlier research by Cawson et al. (2000), that victimization by peers was a significant problem and was experienced by 28% of the children aged under 11, 59.5% of 11–17s and 63.2% of 18–24s. It seems that a high proportion of both physical assault and sexually harmful behaviour was being carried out by peers and siblings and may be seen in terms of bullying. Since children identify relationships with peers as equally as important as those with their families, bullying can have similar consequences to child maltreatment and is widespread (James, 2010).

The study by Radford et al. (2011) also underlined the important links between child maltreatment and certain social divisions, particularly in relation to gender and social class. While mothers/mother figures were responsible for marginally more abuse to under 11s and slightly less abuse of 11–17s than were fathers/father figures, males were the vast majority of perpetrators of domestic violence against another parent. Gender differences were also evident for severely maltreated young adults. Female 18–24s reported significantly higher rates of severe maltreatment by a parent or guardian, with 17.5% having experienced this in childhood, compared to 11.6% of male 18–24s. For specific types of maltreatment, males were the most frequently reported perpetrators and this was most evident for severe physical and contact sexual abuse. For those who reported severe physical violence by a parent or guardian, males were perpetrators in 86.4% of cases reported for the under 11s, in 72.9% for 11–17s, and 64.7% for 18–24s. For those who reported having experienced contact sexual abuse by a parent or guardian, around two-thirds of respondents reported a male as being the perpetrator. Gender clearly had a significant but far from straightforward relationship with child maltreatment.

Similarly, social class was a complex but important factor in child maltreatment. For example:

- 8.1% of those in social classes A–C2 reported neglect compared to 16% in social classes D–E

- 5.2% in A–C2 reported regular verbal aggression compared to 8.6% in D–E

- 9% in A–C2 reported any physical violence compared to 13.1% in D–E
- 4.3% in A–C2 reported coercive sexual acts compared to 7.2% in D–E.

While the prevalence of all forms of abuse seemed significantly greater in the lower social classes, the picture was complex. The 2000 prevalence study (Cawson et al., 2000) suggested there was a clear relationship between social group and physical discipline and abuse, with absence of care and the more serious absence of supervision being evident, particularly being out all night at a young age. Absence of supervision at the less serious levels, however, was not particularly linked with socioeconomic status and appeared to be an equal issue for all social groups. Sexual abuse and emotional abuse showed little differentiation between socioeconomic groups.

However, while there was a link between social class and child abuse, the picture that emerged was rather different to that portrayed in the media and reflected in much public and political debate – particularly where these were prompted by high-profile scandals:

> This study clearly shows that each type of abuse was experienced across social classes to varying degrees. Levels of prevalence in social classes AB shown by this survey are not reflected in official statistics which predominantly include parents in low paid employment or who are unemployed. This confirms that one of the most under reported aspects of child maltreatment is that experienced by upper or middle class children. Much further analysis remains to be done to explore the links between social class and abuse and also with poverty and health problems which may be connected. (Cawson et al., 2000, p. 95)

Finally, while the prevalence of child abuse is much greater than ever becomes known to official agencies, a comparison of the two prevalence studies suggested there might have been an overall reduction, something confirmed by Harker et al. (2013). The findings from the two representative samples of young adults aged 18–24 showed a decrease in reports of certain types of physical abuse (from 13.1% in 1998 to 9.8% in 2009), sexual abuse (6.8% to 5%), and verbal abuse (14.5% to 6%). No significant changes were found in the prevalence of neglect (Radford et al., 2011, Ch. 6).

Radford et al. (2011) conclude that the overall findings paint an optimistic picture, with a general decline between 1998 and 2009 in reported experiences of harsh and physical punishment by parents and carers, and in the experiences of physical violence. Furthermore, improvements for socially disadvantaged children had matched those for the rest of the population. They suggest that the improvements had arisen because of a number of factors, including:

- the impact of positive economic changes
- public health measures, such as early intervention policies
- and, more generally, changes in parental attitudes and behaviour, including a decline in the use of physical punishment of children and young people (Nuffield Foundation, 2009).

However, child maltreatment was still experienced by a sizeable minority of children and these improvements had taken place in the 11 years prior to the economic crisis of 2008 and the major cutbacks in public expenditure from 2010 onwards.

Prevalence studies have provided considerable insights into the nature and characteristics of child abuse and neglect, as well as an important demographic picture of who in the population might be most at risk of both experiencing and perpetrating the problem. At the same time, there is an appreciation that we have neither the knowledge nor the expertise to predict and identify such cases in an individualized way and with any great success. In this context, there have been a number of moves to develop a public health approach to child maltreatment, some of which are informed by a recognition of emphasizing the importance of the rights of the child.

A public health approach

Gilbert et al. (2009b, p. 68) explicitly located their review of research in a public health approach:

> Maltreatment of children by their parents or other caregivers is a major public-health and social-welfare problem in high-income countries. It is common and can cause death, serious injury and long-term consequences that affect the child's life into adulthood, their family and society in general.

The researchers were highly sceptical of the child protection orientation's ability to overcome child maltreatment, but were also of the view that a family service orientation had limitations that a public health approach could address.[2] As with the study by Radford et al. (2011), Gilbert et al. based their approach on the 2006 World Health Organization report on the prevention of child maltreatment (Butchart et al., 2006, p. 9), which defined child maltreatment as:

> All forms of physical and/or emotional ill-treatment, sexual abuse, neglect or negligent treatment or commercial or other exploitation, resulting in actual or potential harm to the child's health, survival, development or dignity in the context of a relationship of responsibility, trust or power.

A number of key assumptions inform a public health approach:

1   Epidemiology is seen as crucial as attempts to collect and analyse data on prevalence are seen as central to identify the factors that might differentiate geographical areas, social classes, ethnic groups, age groups, and other social divisions.

2   It is important to identify some of the key indicators and proxies for children's wellbeing so that these can be monitored and measured over time.

3   There is an emphasis on primary prevention and 'minimally sufficient' interventions that need to be available to all members of the community, in order to reduce risk and optimize the wellbeing of the total population of children and young people. It is assumed that a substantial percentage of the population will show signs of risk at some level and at some point in their life – there is a continuum of risk, along which a child's position may change over time.

4   The provision of universal primary prevention services potentially available to everyone is key, but these can be topped up for those in greater need as required.

5   There is an important role for research and evaluation to identify patterns, including risk and protective factors, measure effectiveness, and aid the process of implementation.

The approach has received considerable international support in recent years (Theodore and Runyon, 1999; WHO, 2000; Kydd, 2003; Garrison, 2005; Whitaker et al., 2005; Scott, 2007; Bromfield and Arney, 2008; Putnam-Hornstein et al., 2011; Segal and Dalziel, 2011) and has increasingly come to inform policy and practice strategies in different countries.

It is only more recently that attempts to apply the model to child protection and safeguarding in England have been made (Macmillan et al., 2009; Barlow and Scott, 2010; Barlow and Calam, 2011; Peckover and Smith, 2011; Davies and Ward, 2012; Radford, 2012; Gilbert et al., 2012a). The approach clearly aims to build on many of the principles and practices that lay at the core of the *ECM: Change for Children* programme (DfES, 2004b) and *The Children's Plan* (DCSF, 2007b), in terms of emphasizing the importance of responding to problems early, the integration of services, and the importance of multidisciplinary teams. Barlow and Calam (2011) comment favourably on the way services had been developed in Nordic countries and, drawing on the work of Boddy and Statham (2009), argue for the importance of social workers playing a central role in the delivery and integration of services right across the spectrum and not just in terms of investigating and intervening at the tertiary and highly targeted level. Because of the breadth and potentially complex nature of the work, Barlow and Calam (2011) emphasize the importance of communication.

The importance of communication and the sharing of information between professionals has been one of the central messages and practice priorities in relation to child protection work in England since the early 1970s, and surveillance of the population is clearly central to any public health approach. However, as we saw in Chapters 4 and 8, a major criticism of the *ECM: Change for Children* programme was its potential challenge to civil liberties, the privacy of the family, and the unintended consequences that might arise as a result of the amount and type of information in circulation (Parton, 2008). The rights of parents and children were both seen as at risk (Penna, 2005; Roche, 2008). The introduction of the ContactPoint database came in for particular criticism (Munro and Parton, 2007) and was withdrawn by the incoming Conservative-led coalition government soon after it came to power in 2010.

Recognizing rights, social harms and structural inequalities

Recognizing the importance of such issues, Reading et al. (2009) have attempted to apply a children's rights perspective to a public health approach. They argue that the way child maltreatment is defined is central to the way it is recognized, managed and prevented, and that most approaches are defined in terms of the physical, emotional and sexual violence or neglect perpetrated by individual adults, usually parents or those in a position of trust. Professional and societal responses are framed in terms of the protection of the child from adult perpetrators. In the process, such approaches do not permit any recognition of the collective harm and exploitation that can be caused by institutions, harmful policies and laws, conflicts, failure of governance and social disruption.

Reading et al. (2009) are sympathetic to the much broader definition developed over 40 years ago by David Gil (1970) in the light of his comprehensive demographic research carried out in 1967/68 of over 12,000 cases of US children who had been physically abused and their parents. A subsample of 1,380 of the parents was analysed for more detailed socioeconomic data. Not only did the research demonstrate an overrepresentation of those from a low socioeconomic background, particularly from non-white families, but there were clear links between individual cases and wider socioeconomic structures. Gil (1975, p. 349) defined child maltreatment as:

> The inflicted gaps or deficits between the circumstances of living which would facilitate the optimum development of children, to which they should be entitled, and to their actual circumstances, irrespective of the sources or agents of the deficit.

Following Gil (1975, 1978), I argued in *The Politics of Child Abuse* (Parton, 1985, pp. 167–8):

> Any act of commission or omission by individuals, institutions or the whole society or the state, together with their resultant conditions, which deprive children of equal rights and liberties, and/or interfere with their optimal development, constitute, by definition, abuse or neglectful acts or conditions.

Child abuse can therefore be manifested at the institutional or societal levels, as well as within families and with individuals. The activities of certain institutions, such as schools and the church, the processes of racial discrimination, social class exploitation, gender violence, and the role of government and global corporations are all potentially implicated.

A similarly wide and inclusive definition was adopted by Wattam and Woodward (1996b, para. 1.4):

> Child abuse consists of anything which individuals, institutions, or processes do or fail to do which directly or indirectly harms children or damages their prospects of safe and healthy development into adulthood.

UNICEF (2005) has promoted a children's rights approach to protecting children from 'all forms of violence', and the definition chosen for the UN's study of violence against children (Pinheiro, 2006) follows Article 19 of the UNCRC that includes 'all forms of physical or mental violence, injury and abuse, neglect or negligent treatment, maltreatment or exploitation, including sexual abuse'. It bases its understanding of physical violence on the definition in the *World Report on Violence and Health* (Krug et al., 2002, p. 5):

> The intentional use of physical force or power, threatened or actual, against a child, by an individual or group, that either results in or has a high likelihood of resulting in actual or potential harm to the child's health, survival, development or dignity.

Such approaches are clearly consistent with a view that violations of basic human rights constitute 'social harms'. These can be made up of physical, financial/economic, emotional, psychological and sexual harms. It includes the idea of 'cultural safety', which encompasses notions of autonomy, development and growth, and access to cultural, intellectual and information resources generally available in any given society (Hillyard et al., 2004; Dorling et al., 2008; Roberts, 2009). A *social harm* perspective takes into account corporate and collective responsibility, together with the activities and inactivities of the state and focuses on structures of inequality and vulnerability (Pemberton et al., 2012). It has a particular concern with trying to produce greater social justice. For example, Wild (2013) has argued that corporate exploitation of children and childhood – in terms of a variety of unhealthy mass-produced and massively advertised products, such as unhealthy foods, material goods and pornography – has created new forms of child abuse.

A good example of a social harm approach is the research carried out by Danny Dorling (2004), who analysed the 13,000 murders committed in Britain between January 1981 and December 2000. He treated murder as a Durkheimian social fact, rather than a series of individual acts, and related the data to social structures and social change. He demonstrated that the majority of murders were concentrated in the poor parts of Britain. He showed that in the five years 1981–85, people living in the poorest 10% of wards in Britain were four and a half times more likely to be murdered than those living in the least poor 10%. This differential increased further in each successive five-year period, as poverty and, crucially, inequality increased. As a consequence, despite the national doubling of the murder rate by 1996–2000, people living in the least poor 20% of the country saw their already low rate of murder fall further. The increase in murder was concentrated almost exclusively in the poorer parts of Britain and most strongly in the poorest tenth of wards – and knives, broken glass/bottles and fights were most important.

It was among men born in 1965 and after where the murder rate increased the most with age. As Dorling pointed out, most of these men left school in the summer of 1981, which was the first summer for over 40 years that a young man living in a poor area would find work or training scarce. The situation got steadily worse as the then Conservative government pursued a neoliberal economic agenda, which decimated the manufacturing sector in Britain. Dorling (2004, p. 191) argues that 'murders are placed at the tip of this pyramid of social harm and their changing numbers and distributions provide one of the key clues as to where harm is most and least distributed'.

As I argued in Chapter 4, the work of Richard Wilkinson (1996, 2005) and his writing with Kate Pickett (Pickett and Wikinson, 2007; Wilkinson and Pickett, 2009) is particularly important in helping us understand the impact of inequality on health and violence in society, and why societies that have become more unequal also have the poorest relative levels of child wellbeing (UNICEF, 2007; Mapp, 2011). There is evidence of a cultural shift towards an emphasis on competitive individualism in such societies, which contributes to a poor sense of wellbeing among children and young people (Layard and Dunn, 2009; Utting, 2009), and social inequality and its negative impact has increased over the past 30 years (OECD, 2011; Lansley, 2012a, 2012b).

There is considerable evidence that while there is a clear relationship between inequality and the levels of violence in society, the issue of how inequality is generated is important (Ray, 2011). For example, Savolainen (2000) and Messner et al. (2008) argue that the effect of economic inequality on the level of lethal violence is limited to nations characterized by relatively weak collective institutions of social protection such as welfare states. It is argued that in societies where the economic market is dominant, there is a loss of social bonds and interpersonal empathy and an increase in social marginalization, egoistic individualism and high risk taking – all of which are conducive to higher levels of violence. This is the direction of change evident in England over the past 30 years and the period since 2008 in particular (Dorling, 2012). For example, it is now well established that intergenerational social mobility is much reduced by greater levels of inequality (Krueger, 2012).

However, we cannot assume that such an approach is appropriate for all dimensions of child maltreatment – particularly sexual abuse. Keith Pringle (2005, 2010) has argued that while Nordic welfare systems may have a positive impact on forms of child maltreatment associated with poverty and class inequality, via their more collectivist/solidaristic approach, this is not necessarily appropriate for other forms of maltreatment. They are much less concerned with what Pringle (2005, 2010) calls 'bodily integrity or citizenship', where issues associated with sexual violence are central. As Ferguson (2004, p. 131) has argued, the increased individualization evident in Britain over the past 40 years has 'both created the social conditions that make it more possible to gain more protection and for public outcry when they do not'. In this context, an emphasis on the importance of children's rights is key.

As we saw in Chapter 1, Gilbert et al. (2011a) identified the emergence of a child focus orientation in addition to the child protection and family service orientations identified by Gilbert in 1997. However, they also argued that while it was inspired in part by the UN Convention on the Rights of the Child, its emergence was also influenced by the increasing emphasis in some countries of the idea of the 'social investment state' in the 1990s, which was promoted by both the Organisation for Economic Co-operation and Development and the European Union. According to this view, investment in children should take on a strategic significance to equip citizens to respond and adapt to global economic change in order to enhance individual and national competitiveness. In this respect, trying to ensure that all children maximize their developmental opportunities, educational attainment and overall health and wellbeing became a key priority for social and economic policy. Here, childhood is seen as a preparation for a productive adulthood and it was this approach that influenced the New Labour government's *ECM: Change for Children* (DfES, 2004b) programme rather than a serious commitment to enhancing children's rights. As Cornock and Montgomery (2014) and the Children's Rights Alliance for England (2012) have demonstrated, not only have the application and development of children's rights approaches in England been uneven over the past 25 years, there has been increasing scepticism and uncertainty about such an approach among a growing number of politicians, particularly in the Conservative Party. So, for example, while it is claimed that the 2013 Working Together (HM Government, 2013, para. 8) is based on a 'child-centred and coordinated approach to safeguarding', as I argued in Chapter 8, the guidance is premised on a clear child protection orientation where notions of child rescue are dominant. Thus, while many current policy and practice developments claim to be 'child centred' or 'child focused', it is also clear that these terms have become highly contested and open to a variety of interpretations. It cannot be assumed that the use of such terms means that policies and practices are premised on a children's rights perspective.

Conclusion

What I am arguing is that combining a children's rights orientation with one that takes a broad public health approach to child maltreatment provides the most positive framework for developing policy and practice in the future. In doing so, we need to recognize that child maltreatment has cultural, institutional and structural dimensions as well as individual ones and that these must be taken seriously and addressed.

In some respects, LSCBs, which were established under the Children Act 2004 and have been in operation since April 2006, have the seeds for what is required to take these ideas forward. A major problem is that because they are 'local', being coterminous with the boundaries of local authorities, they are not in a good position to address the wider cultural, institutional and structural issues on their own. Nor do they have the resources available to them to seriously take this forward even at the local level. Even so, the statutory functions of LCSBs open up some important possibilities. They have the statutory responsibility for coordinating and ensuring the effectiveness of the work of partner bodies to 'safeguard and promote the welfare of children' (Children Act 2004, Section 14).[3]

It is clear that LSCBs have not been able to take on such a wide role; the research that evaluated their operation in their early years showed that most LSCBs had been quite conservative about what they were able to achieve and had focused on the core business of ensuring that work to protect children was properly coordinated and effective, so that they had not been able to develop their preventive work (France et al., 2010b). Much of the time was taken up with detailed administrative and managerial issues, including the important responsibility of overseeing the operation of SCRs. As Brandon et al. (2012) have demonstrated, the vast majority of the recommendations of SCRs are concerned with procedures and compliance with procedures rather than reflecting on and developing action plans in relation to wider issues, for example the relationship between social deprivation and child maltreatment. Yet, if LSCBs have a duty to safeguard and promote the welfare of children in their area, issues concerned with poverty, increased vulnerability and social deprivation are central (Hooper et al., 2007). Taking such issues forward in a local context would require working closely with the new local authority Public Health and Wellbeing Boards, which would emphasize the importance of early intervention.

Similarly, it is also vital that approaches informed by a public health model are not simply imposed from above. If we are serious about making child abuse 'everybody's business', it is important to recognize the key role of a variety of community-based and user-led groups and initiatives (see, for example, Colclough et al., 1999; Pasura et al., 2013), and that local communities are actively involved in the development of policies and services (Jack, 2006; Jack and Gill, 2010) in the way promoted by Freymond and Cameron (2006) (see note 1, Chapter 1).

Clearly, such initiatives cannot be left to LSCBs alone. If the central structural issues are to be addressed, a whole range of policies concerned with taxation, welfare benefits, health and crime are important and addressing social inequalities and the distribution of income and wealth are key. While children's social care and social work are important, their role should not be exaggerated. One of the problems of attempts to reform child protection in recent years has been a tendency to overstate the contribution that social work can make, such that we have been deflected from making serious attempts to address the problem of child maltreatment. An important first step would be to ensure that reliable and up-to-date research is carried out, along the lines of that carried out by Radford et al. (2011) on the prevalence of child maltreatment, to ensure that we understand the size and nature of the problem and how it is changing. While child maltreatment may be a 'socially constructed phenomenon' (Parton, 1985; DH, 1995a), which varies according to time and place, this is no excuse for not gathering data in this *place* – England – at this *time* – the twenty-first century – as a basis for policy and practice. To do this requires careful thought as to what the definition and nature of the problem is – child maltreatment – that we are wanting to measure and overcome.

Appendix

Table A1.1 The changing structure, contents and focus of central government child protection guidance in England, 1974–2013

Document	Number of pages	Number of footnotes	Reading lists, references and internet sites	Other directly related documents	Other
1974 *Non-Accidental Injury to Children*, LASSL(74)(13) (DHSS Circular)	7	1	The footnote included four references, three of which were previous DHSS circulars	None	–
1988 *Working Together: A Guide to Arrangements for Inter-Agency Cooperation for the Protection of Children from Abuse* (DHSS/the Welsh Office)	72, made up of 48 pages of guidance and nine appendices of 24 pages	None	11	None	Part 5 'Working together in individual cases' is 13 pages long. For the first time, in Part 9, a system of senior management 'case reviews' was introduced in cases of child death or serious harm where child abuse was confirmed or suspected (4 pages long)
1991 *Working Together under the Children Act 1989: A Guide to Arrangements for Inter-Agency Cooperation for the Protection of Children from Abuse* (Home Office/Department of Health/Department of Education and Science/the Welsh Office)	126, made up of 60 pages of guidance and nine appendices of 66 pages	None	39, of which 35 were HMSO or a government department	None	Part 5 'Working together in individual cases' is 15 pages long. Part 8 'Case reviews' is 4 pages long

1999 *Working Together to Safeguard Children: A Guide to Inter-Agency Working to Safeguard and Promote the Welfare of Children* (Department of Health/ Home Office/ Department for Education and Employment)	119, made up of 102 pages of guidance and six appendices of 17 pages	12	Reading list (Appendix 6) of 50 references, of which 31 are HMSO/TSO or government departments. No internet links/web addresses	Published at the same time as: Department of Health, Department of Education and Employment, and the Home Office (2000) *Framework for the Assessment of Children in Need and their Families*. Also issued under Section 7 of the LASS Act 1970 and was incorporated into *Working Together to Safeguard Children*	The *Assessment Framework* is 109 pages long, including 7 appendices of 20 pages and a bibliography of 140 references, of which 83 were HMSO/ TSO or government departments. No internet links/web addresses
2006 *Working Together to Safeguard Children: A Guide to Inter-Agency Working to Safeguard and Promote the Welfare of Children* (HM Government)	231 pages, including 155 pages of statutory guidance, 30 pages of non-statutory guidance, and six appendices of 28 pages	43	78 references and internet links, including 69 internet links/web addresses, of which 60 are gov.uk	*Assessment Framework* (2000) as in *Working Together* (1999) above, primarily through the Integrated Children System	
2010 *Working Together to Safeguard Children: A Guide to Inter-Agency Working to Safeguard and Promote the Welfare of Children* (HM Government)	399 pages, which include: executive summary 15 pages; statutory guidance 228 pages; non-statutory guidance 51 pages; six appendices of 34 pages	273	200 references and internet links, including 124 with internet links/web addresses, of which 78 are gov.uk	*Assessment Framework* (2000) as in *Working Together* (1999) and (2006) above. Chapter 6 'Supplementary guidance on safeguarding and promoting the welfare of children' makes direct links to other supplementary statutory guidance: • Sexually exploited children (2009) 96 pages • Children affected by gang activity (2010) 52 pages • Fabricated or induced illness (FII) (2008) 88 pages • Investigating complex (organised or multiple) abuse (2002)	

(continued)

Table A1.1 Continued

Document	Number of pages	Number of footnotes	Reading lists, references and internet sites	Other directly related documents	Other
				• Female genital mutilation LA circular 2004 • Forced marriage and honour-based violence (2009) 26 pages • Allegations of abuse made against a person who works with children, plus Appendix 5, 10 pages • Abuse of disabled children (2009) 84 pages • Child abuse linked to belief in 'spirit possession' (2007) 23 pages • Child victims of trafficking (2007) 55 pages	Chapter 1 'Assessing need and providing help in individual cases' is 36 pages long; Chapter 4 'Learning and improvement framework', including SCRs, is 8 pages long; and Chapter 5 'Child death reviews, including LSCBs, is 7 pages long
2013 *Working Together to Safeguard Children: A Guide to Inter-Agency Working to Safeguard and Promote the Welfare of Children* (HM Government)	95 pages, which includes half-page summary, 85 pages of guidance and three appendices of 10 pages	43	Of the 43 footnotes, 23 have web addresses/links, and 22 of these are to a range of government department web pages. Of the 20 footnotes without web addresses/links, 18 provide a reference to a particular statute, section of statute or another formal definition. There are just two references to research: one (note 28) on 'inter-agency training' (Carpenter et al., 2009) and the other (note 38) on 'sudden unexpected death in infancy' (Fleming et al, 2000)	• Appendix A 'Glossary' of key terms and definitions • Appendix B 'Statutory framework' briefly summarizes the legislation seen as relevant (seven statutes) to 'safeguarding and promoting the welfare of children' • Appendix C 'Further sources of information' provides links to 'Supplementary guidance on particular safeguarding issues'. Has 45 links to guidance, totalling over 3,500 pages; the Ministry of Justice *Public Protection Manual* alone is nearly 700 pages long	

Table A1.2 Children in each stage of the referral and assessment process

	Numbers per year to 31 March										
	2001/02	2002/03	2003/04	2004/05	2005/06	2006/07	2007/08	2008/09	2009/10	2010/11	2011/12
Referrals of children to children's social care	569,400	570,200	572,700	552,000	569,300	545,000	538,500	547,000	603,700	615,000	605,100
(Rate/10,000 children under 18 years)									(548.2)	(556.8)	(533.5)
Initial assessments completed	261,500	263,900	290,800	290,300	300,200	305,000	319,900	349,000	395,300	439,800	451,500
									(359.0)	(398.2)	(398.1)
Core assessments completed	56,100	55,700	63,700	74,100	84,800	93,400	105,100	120,600	142,100	185,400	220,700
									(129.0)	(167.8)	(194.6)
Registered child protection plans during the year	27,800 (25/10,000)	30,200	31,000	30,700	31,500	33,300	34,000	37,900	44,300 (40.2)	49,000 (44.3)	52,100 (46.0)
Section 47 enquiries started during the year	69,900 (62/10,000)				71,800	73,800 (67/10,000)		84,100 (76/10,000)	89,300 (81.1)	111,700 (101.1)	124,600 (109.9)

Note: These figures are derived from the annual national statistics: 'Referrals, Assessments and Children and Young People on Child Protection Registers Year Ending 31 March', published annually since 2002, most recently by the Department for Education. It is important to be cautious when comparing the figures between 2009/10 and 2010/11 because of concerns about quality of data in 2009/10.

Table A1.3 Children in care/looked after at 31 March, 1994–2012[1]

	1994	1996	1998	2000	2001	2003	2005	2007	2008	2009	2010	2011	2012
All children	49,100	50,600	53,300	58,100	58,900	61,200	61,000	59,970	59,360	60,890	64,400	65,520	67,050
Rate/10,000 children under 18	45	45	47	51	53	55	55	55	54	55	58	59	59
Number (%) in care because of abuse or neglect		6,500	7,700	8,600[2]		38,800	38,200	37,270	36,750	37,160	39,290	40,410	41,790
		(20%)	(26%)	(31%)		(63%)	(63%)	(62%)	(62%)	(61%)	(61%)	(62%)	(62%)
Placement type													
Foster	31,300	33,100	35,000	37,900	38,300	41,000	41,300	42,030	41,930	43,870	46,840	48,530	50,260
	(64%)	(65%)	(66%)	(65%)	(65%)	(67%)	(68%)	(70%)	(71%)	(72%)	(73%)	(74%)	(75%)
Placed for adoption	2,200	2,200	2,400	3,100	3,400	3,800	3,400	2,720	2,860	2,690	2,500	2,450	2,680
	(4%)	(4%)	(5%)	(5%)	(6%)	(6%)	(6%)	(5%)	(5%)	(4%)	(4%)	(4%)	(4%)
With parents	4,400	4,700	5,700	6,500	6,900	6,300	5,800	5,110	4,580	4,170	4,230	3,970	3,600
	(9%)	(9%)	(11%)	(11%)	(12%)	(10%)	(9%)	(9%)	(8%)	(7%)	(7%)	(6%)	(5%)
Residential	7,890	7,370	7,100	7,400	6,800	8,700	8,660	8,140	7,870	7,870	8,200	7,910	7,950
	(16%)	(15%)	(13%)	(13%)	(11%)	(14%)	(14%)	(14%)	(13%)	(13%)	(14%)	(12%)	(12%)
Voluntary agreement S20 A 1989	18,800	19,900	19,100	19,300	19,100	18,400	18,400	17,200	17,260	19,270	20,630	19,730	19,370
	(38%)	(39%)	(36%)	(33%)	(32%)	(30%)	(30%)	(29%)	(29%)	(32%)	(32%)	(31%)	(29%)

Notes: 1 Figures for years 2007–11 from DfE Children looked after in England year ending 31 March 2011 (SFR21/2011), Table A1. Figures for years 2003 and 2005 from DCSF Children looked after in England year ending 31 March 2007 (SFR27/2007), Table A1.
2 These figures are based on children who started to be looked after during the year, not those accommodated at 31 March. Figures are from Children looked after by LAs year ending 31 March 2000, Table E.

Table A1.4   Cafcass figures for care applications

Month	05/06	06/07	07/08	08/09	09/10	10/11	11/12	12/13
April	546	507	497	380	682	692	679	756
May	532	595	569	399	648	686	835	983
June	547	613	514	369	798	773	860	809
July	564	569	590	485	793	848	873	993
August	559	614	542	492	687	777	891	982
September	565	546	504	483	722	759	842	878
October	521	606	511	496	726	731	861	949
November	581	595	539	592	769	827	879	954
December	501	480	422	719	746	689	812	861
January	563	558	514	666	670	698	921	967
February	504	525	502	659	736	826	889	967
March	630	578	537	748	855	897	900	925
TOTAL	6,613	6,786	6,241	6,488	8,832	9,203	10,244	11,055

Notes

1 The politics of child protection: an introduction

1 Freymond and Cameron (2006, p. 6) also identified what they called 'community care systems', which I will return to in Chapter 11, taking their inspiration from many Aboriginal communities around the world:

> Ties to extended family, community, place, history, and spirit are considered integral to healthy individual identities: ideally, community caring relies on consultations with parents, extended family, and the local community about the protection and care of children. Because of the devastating effects on Indigenous Peoples of colonialism, residential care and child protection, a strong connection is made between caring for children and fostering a healthy process for whole communities. A strong value is given to keeping children within their families and communities. Respect for traditional Aboriginal values and procedures is integral to community care processes.

2 The three orientations outlined in *Child Protection Systems* (Gilbert et al., 2011a) were derived from comparing policies and practices in different jurisdictions. However, they have a number of similarities to other models for analysing childcare policies in a particular country often over a historical period. For example, Frost and Stein's (1989) discussion of the politics of child welfare drew on 'child saving', 'child welfare' and 'child liberation' perspectives, and Roger Smith (1991) talked in terms of 'protection', 'welfare' and 'rights'. Perhaps the most detailed and sophisticated analysis was by Lorraine Fox Harding, who outlined different value perspectives in childcare. While originally based on her identification of two value positions in childcare law in England and Wales (Fox, 1982), she subsequently developed this into a fourfold classification (Fox Harding, 1997): laissez-faire and patriarchy; state paternalism and child protection; the modern defence of the birth family and parents' rights; and children's rights and child liberation. Roger Smith (2005) later revised this classification in terms of: laissez-faire and minimal state intervention; child protection and the authoritative state; working in partnership; the state and family support; and children's rights and child liberation.

2   Children's services in the postwar period

1   The Cleveland 'affair' broke in the early summer of 1987 and was focused
    on the activities of two paediatricians and social workers in a general hospi-
    tal in Middlesbrough, a declining chemical and industrial town in northeast
    England. During a period of a few weeks, 121 children were removed from
    their families to an emergency place of safety (the hospital) on the basis of
    what was seen by the media and two local MPs as questionable diagnoses
    of child sexual abuse. As a result, a number of techniques for diagnosing
    and identifying sexual abuse developed by paediatricians and psychiatrists,
    particularly the anal dilation test, the use of anatomically correct dolls, and
    'disclosure' work, were subjected to close scrutiny.

5   The tragedy of Baby Peter Connelly and its effects

1   However, at the time of Baby P's death, the postmortem was not conclusive
    about this and it was only confirmed subsequently.
2   Jo Warner (2013b) has demonstrated that during the three-week period from
    11 November to 2 December 2008, there were 2,054 articles about Baby P
    in local and national newspapers. Of these, 1,002 were in the national press,
    630 of them in tabloids. Of this 630, a third (216) were published in *The Sun*,
    the UK newspaper with the highest national circulation (3.2 million in 2008).
        The influence of *The Sun* at this time became very evident three and a
    half years later, when Rebekah Brooks, who was editor of *The Sun* at the
    time, was giving evidence to the Leveson Inquiry (2012) into the culture,
    practice and ethics of the press following the exposure of newspaper's
    practice of accessing private telephone and email accounts. On 11 May
    2012, she was asked directly by council to the inquiry: 'Did you telephone
    Mr Balls during the week commencing 17 November 2008 telling him to
    get rid of Sharon Shoesmith or they would "turn this thing on him"?' (p. 46).
    She was, effectively, asked the same question three times and on each
    occasion Rebekah Brooks said 'No'. She admitted speaking to Ed Balls at
    the time but that at no point did she ask him to sack Sharon Shoesmith and
    that her main purpose in speaking to him was to find out the contents of the
    unpublished SCR and the 'whitewash that I felt Haringey council had done
    on their own review' (p. 50). However, she said that she did not directly ask
    Ed Balls to sack Sharon Shoesmith, because 'it was very clear that that was
    the Sun's editorial line on it, Mr Balls was under no illusion that that was
    the point of our campaign' (p. 45).
3   Subsequently, evidence to the Leveson Inquiry (2012) also demonstrated
    that, during the period leading up to the death of Baby P, relationships
    between the Metropolitan Police and journalists at *The Sun* were very close.

Evidence to the inquiry also demonstrated that not only were Rebekah Brooks and David Cameron neighbours but they saw much of each other socially and mixed in the same circles.

4 At the time, it was suggested by the Association of Directors of Children's Services and Cafcass that the rise in care applications occurred as a result of the review by local authorities of cases that were on the threshold of care applications, as a response to the publicity generated by the circumstances surrounding Peter Connelly's death – 'the Baby P' effect. A study carried out by Cafcass at the time (2009b) appeared to support the theory. It also found that:

- A substantial proportion of the increase could be attributed to local authorities re-evaluating their involvement with families where they were already providing a service.

- There was an increase in the percentage of children aged 5–10 years being made the subject of care proceedings in the period 11–30 November 2008 compared to the same three weeks in 2007. There was also a higher incidence of long-term involvement with children's services, with chronic neglect being a primary factor in the decision to bring an application to court.

- Most guardians who responded to the survey did not believe that local authorities had lowered the legal threshold at which applications were made but had been triggered to act in cases already past the threshold.

- Guardians viewed the increase in care applications from late 2008 as being mainly a corrective action, in that proceedings were being initiated sooner after it had been identified that the legal threshold was met, and that this was to the benefit of the individual children concerned.

Cafcass (2012) produced a follow-up report three years later where guardians' responses suggested that they believed applications were more appropriately timed than in the 2009 study.

5 While Sharon Shoesmith lost an appeal against her dismissal from Haringey Council in January 2009, in February she returned to the offensive in determined fashion. On 7 February, on BBC Radio 4's *Weekend Woman's Hour*, she blamed party politics and the media for her dismissal and was scathing about the behaviour of Ed Balls, the secretary of state, claiming that his actions had encouraged a defensive 'blame culture' to take hold in local authorities. The same day, *The Guardian* published an extensive interview with her where, again, she set out to tell her side of the story. While she was heavily criticized in many parts of the media for her apparent failure to apologize for her (in)actions (for example, the *Mail on Sunday* headline for its extensive, two-page report of the

interview was 'No sorry from Baby P chief'), the interviews had the effect of keeping both the story and the high emotions attached to it very much in the public eye.

Throughout 2009 and early 2010, solicitors acting on behalf of Sharon Shoesmith produced a number of documents as part of her application for a judicial review of her dismissal from Haringey Council. These came to a head in April 2010. Her solicitors produced key court documents, which alleged that key information about the police handling of the case were edited out of successive drafts of the key Ofsted inspection report in November/December 2008, and her solicitors claimed that it was 'beyond dispute' that the minister had 'interfered' with the report, which was denied by the Department for Children, Schools and Families (*The Guardian*, 10 April 2010, p. 4 and p. 32).

However, on 23 April, Sharon Shoesmith lost her claim that she was unlawfully dismissed. The judge also ruled that Ofsted did not act unfairly in the way it produced the damning report. However, the judge, Mr Justice Foskett, did criticize Haringey Council and Ed Balls for the manner of his press conference in December 2008, when he demanded Shoesmith's removal. The judge also had strong words to say about Ofsted's late disclosure of thousands of pages of evidence that it had previously said did not exist. He also said that the manner of Sharon Shoesmith's dismissal would hardly inspire feelings of security among directors of children's services. He said that:

> The prospect of summary dismissal with no compensation and a good deal of public opprobrium is hardly likely to be an inducement for someone thinking of taking the job or, perhaps, in some circumstances, continuing in it. (quoted in Butler, 2010, p. 4)

6 In fact, this dynamic continued well after the election and on 28 May 2011, the Appeal Court ruled that Sharon Shoesmith's dismissal by the former children's secretary was 'intrinsically unfair and unlawful', and she was subsequently awarded financial compensation. While *The Guardian* included a sympathetic interview with her in its coverage of the ruling on 29 May, she received much less sympathy on the front pages of other newspapers. *The Sun* headline ran 'Baby P chief in "job win"', with its main editorial headed 'No shame', and the *Daily Mail* (with a photograph) 'The £1m smirk: Shoesmith set for huge payout – but still won't say sorry for Baby P'. Among other things, it is notable that while it had been known for nearly two years that the young child's name was Peter Connelly, he – and the case/scandal – continued to be referred to as 'Baby P'.

7 In fact, this was an old photograph downloaded from a family Facebook page.

6 Central government guidance and child protection: 1974–2010

1 The first part of the chapter, together with much of Table A1.1 in the Appendix, is based on my evidence to the Munro Review of Child Protection, available at http://eprints.hud.ac.uk/9906.

8 Reforming child protection: a child-centred system?

1 This came in a written statement to a parliamentary question on 27 February 2012:

> We have engaged the partners in ADCS, health, police and education and have concluded that we do not need a new statutory duty to deliver early help and that there is sufficient existing legislation to realise Professor Munro's recommendation. (www.publications.parliament.uk/pa/cm201212/cmhansrd/cm120227/text/120227w0006.htm)

2 The three consultative documents were:

- *Working Together to Safeguard Children:* draft guidance on what was expected of organizations, individually and jointly, to safeguard and promote the welfare of children.

- *Managing Individual Cases: the Framework for the Assessment of Children in Need and their Families:* draft guidance on undertaking assessments of children in need.

- *Statutory Guidance on Learning and Improvement:* proposed new arrangements for SCRs, reviews of child deaths and other learning processes led by LSCBs.

3 For example, the statutory guidance on training, development and supervision for interagency working was reduced from a 19-page chapter to a checklist of employers' responsibilities; while the chapter on the statutory roles and responsibilities of organizations was reduced from a 46 to an 11-page chapter made up of a checklist that set out the legislative requirements for each organization.

4 The LSCB threshold document should include:

- the process for the early help assessment and the type and level of early help services to be provided

- the criteria, including the level of need, for when a case should be referred to local authority children's social care for assessment and for statutory services under:
  - Section 17 of the Children Act 1989 (children in need)
  - Section 47 of the Children Act 1989 (reasonable cause to suspect children suffering or likely to suffer significant harm)
  - Section 20 (duty to accommodate a child) of the Children Act 1989.

5 On 16 July 2013, following receipt of the report by Julian Le Grand, Alan Wood and Dame Moira Gibb (Le Grand et al., 2013), Michael Gove announced that he was taking children's services in Doncaster out of the control of the local authority, and that from April 2014 it would be 'spun out' into a staff-owned, not-for-profit trust independent of the council and strategic oversight for the service would be provided by a commissioner appointed by the secretary of state. It was interesting that Doncaster was the parliamentary constituency for Ed Miliband, leader of the Labour Party, the government opposition.

6 When the four members of the independent panel were announced on 10 June 2013, none had direct experience of child protection management or practice and none were social workers. Peter Wanless had just been appointed chief executive of the NSPCC and had previously been chief executive of the Big Lottery Fund for five years. Nicholas Dann was head of international development at the Air Accidents Investigation Branch. Elizabeth Clarke was a practising solicitor and Jenni Russell was a columnist with the *Sunday Times*.

7 In September and early October 2012, almost a year after his death, allegations that the high-profile disc jockey and long-standing BBC children's TV presenter Jimmy Savile (1926–2011) had sexually abused under-age adolescent and prepubescent girls and boys and adults was widely publicized. This came to a head with the broadcast on 3 October of an ITV documentary, *Exposure: The Other Side of Jimmy Savile*. In it, several women said that as teenagers they had been sexually abused by Savile, who obtained access to them through TV programmes such as *Top of the Pops*, *Jim'll Fix It* and *Clunk, Click* and his extensive charity work. Following the broadcast, many people came forward to 13 British police forces to make allegations about Savile's conduct. Some abuse was said to have taken place on BBC and NHS premises, and it was suggested that members of the BBC had been aware of the allegations for many years and there had been a 'cover-up'. Inquiries were established into practices at the BBC, headed by Dame Janet Smith and Nick Pollard, which reported in December 2012 (Pollard, 2012), and the NHS. The original NHS investigation was launched into Savile's activities at Broadmoor, Stoke Mandeville and Leeds General

Infirmary hospitals along with 10 other health trusts. On 14 October 2013, Jeremy Hunt, secretary of state for health, announced that more hospitals may be investigated as part of the inquiries; however, as of December 2013, no report had been published.

On 19 October 2012, the Metropolitan Police launched Operation Yewtree, a criminal investigation into historic allegations of child sexual abuse by Savile and others, some of whom were still living. On 6 November 2012, Theresa May, the home secretary, announced that Her Majesty's Inspectorate of Constabulary (HMIC) would carry out an assessment of all the investigations relating to Savile undertaken by police forces around the country to establish whether allegations were properly investigated. On 12 November 2012, the Metropolitan Police described the alleged abuse as being 'on an unprecedented scale' and that the number of alleged victims was 589, of whom 450 alleged abuse by Savile. On 12 March 2013, the report showed that mistakes had been made and included material showing that the police had received intelligence about Savile's sexual conduct dating back to 1964 (HMIC, 2013).

A joint report by the NSPCC and the Metropolitan Police (Gray and Watt, 2013), published in January 2013, reported on allegations covering 50 years. The allegations involved people from the age of 8–47 at the time of the alleged assaults and included 28 children under 10, 10 boys as young as 8, 63 girls between 13 and 16; three-quarters were under 18. Two hundred and fourteen possible criminal offences were recorded, including 34 rapes reported across 28 police forces. In its 2013 annual report, the BBC stated that it had spent over £5 million on Savile-related inquiries in the year up to 31 March 2013.

9   Child welfare reform and the authoritarian neoliberal state

1   By the spring of 2012, the coalition was making hardly any mention of 'the big society'. Significantly, a series of reports were published indicating that not only was the idea dead but that nearly all the policy changes closely associated with it, in terms of empowering communities, encouraging more social action and developing the third sector, had either failed to develop or had never really started in the first place. More fundamentally, the shift in power from the centralized state and large private corporations in favour of the growth of civil society had never been seriously addressed and, in many respects, had gone in the opposite direction. The reports came from a variety of quarters inside Parliament (House of Commons Public Administration Select Committee, 2012) and parts of the voluntary sector and influential think tanks that had previously been supportive (Evans,

2011; Fisher and Gruescu, 2011; Centre for Social Justice, 2012; Civil Exchange, 2012; Hetherington, 2013). Phillip Blond (2012, p. 34), one of the main architects of 'the big society' initiative, went as far as to say that, as a consequence, David Cameron had lost any hope of redefining the Conservative Party and had 'abandoned the vision of one-nation conservatism that so inspired me, and retoxified his party'.

2   The reduction in benefits for families with children included cuts in working tax credit (WTC) and child tax credit payments and revised eligibility criteria so that at least one parent in a couple-headed family household had to work a minimum of 24 hours a week (instead of 16 hours a week as previously) for a household to qualify for WTC. The percentage of childcare costs that parents could claim through the childcare element of the WTC was reduced to 70 per cent of costs for one child and less for other children. The 2010 emergency budget announced that child benefit payments were to be withdrawn completely from households where one parent was earning over £50,000 from January 2013 (originally this had been set at £43,875). Other benefit cutbacks included the abolition of the health in pregnancy grant (worth £190) from April 2011 and more restricted Sure Start maternity grant payments (worth £500 per child), so that eligible mothers would only receive payment for the first child. Changes to housing benefit were introduced in April 2011, together with the introduction of housing benefit caps in April 2013, thus making it difficult for private rents to be covered in full, particularly in London and the southeast. Much stricter eligibility and medical assessments for disability benefits were also introduced from 2013/14, which meant that children living in families where the adults were in receipt of disability or sickness benefits could suffer increased hardship as a result of the family's reduced income.

3   The idea of a universal credit was first outlined in a report by the Centre for Social Justice (2009) and originally planned an even 55 per cent withdrawal rate and would reduce penalties for couples, mortgage holders and low income savers so that people would be better off and the total cost would be more costly than the current benefit budget in the early years. In the event, universal credit was to be introduced at a withdrawal rate of 65 per cent. More significantly, the enforcement of work conditions was strengthened ahead of the introduction of the scheme and at a time of shrinking employment opportunities. According to Jordan and Drakeford (2012, p. 21):

> as a result the universal credit scheme could become a rationale for forcing claimants into low-paid jobs in which they get stuck or a succession of precarious short-term contracts where the prime beneficiaries become the employers at the bottom of the hollowed-out labour market.

4   The brain science on which the reports by Graham Allen were based (Allen and Smith, 2008; Allen, 2011a, 2011b) has come in for considerable

critique (see Bruer, 1999, 2011; Wastell and White, 2012; Gillies, 2014). Bruer (2011) has demonstrated that the so-called 'new brain science' was in fact rather 'old science' and was not nearly as clear-cut in its policy and practice implications as Allen and others were claiming. Wastell and White (2012, p. 399) contended that it was 're-presenting an older ideological argument about the role of the state and family in terms of a biologically privileged world view'.

5 On 5 February 2013, the Department for Education and the Early Years Foundation Consortium signed a contract to create an independent Early Intervention Foundation (EIF). The consortium (consisting of 4Children, the Local Government Association and Achievement for All 3As) would initially support the EIF before handing over responsibility to the EIF trustees and management once it was established as a charity in its own right. The EIF would:

- *Assess* what programmes work – to determine the best early intervention available and their relative value for money

- Translate this into practical evidence-based *advice* to local commissioners, service providers and potential investors to enable them to make the best choices

- *Advocate* for early intervention as a serious alternative to expensive and ineffective late intervention.

The EIF was formally launched at 10 Downing Street on 15 April 2013.

6 In early 2012, A4e and Emma Harrison came in for enormous criticism and were subject to allegations of fraud and police investigations. In March 2012, the Department of Work and Pensions announced that it was carrying out an independent audit of all commercial relationships with A4e, and in May 2012 terminated all contracts with the company. Emma Harrison resigned as the 'family champion' and chair of A4e in February 2012.

7 The Troubled Families programme was allocated £448 million over three years, drawn down from other government departments and programmes. It was estimated that intervention for each family would cost, on average, £10,000, with government providing 40 per cent and local authorities required to fund the remainder. Local authorities could only access the government contribution on a 'payments by results' basis, the requirement being that for any 'troubled family', there needed to be clear evidence of:

- More than 85% attendance in school and fewer than three exclusions from school

- A 60% reduction in antisocial behaviour across the whole family; and a 33% reduction in youth offending.

Plus:

- Progress towards work such as a referral and attachment to the Work Programme or the European Social Fund provision for troubled families

Or:

- One adult in family moving off benefits and into continuous work (DCLG, 2012).

In the Spending Review on 26 June 2013, the chancellor announced a further investment of £200 million to extend the Troubled Families programme to cover a further 400,000 families.

8 This commitment to focusing on adoption was further strengthened when Tim Loughton, who had been central to much of the Conservative Party support for bringing about changes to social work and child protection, and who had been shadow children's minister for seven years up to coming into government and the key political architect of the Munro Review, was sacked as minister for children and families in September 2012. He was replaced by Edward Timpson, whose major brief was to see through the changes to adoption and fostering and was known to have a long-standing personal and professional interest in the issue.

9 It was estimated that the value of government contracts for the outsourcing of public services had increased from £9.6 billion in 2008 to £20.4 billion in 2012 and was due to increase to £101 billion by 2014/15 (Williams, 2013).

10 The developments evident under the coalition government could also be seen to be consistent with the value perspective characterized by Fox Harding (1997) and Smith (2005) (see note 2, Chapter 1) as 'child protection and the authoritative state'. They argue that the perspective was associated with the growth of state intervention in welfare from the late nineteenth century onwards. Here, extensive state intervention to protect and care for children was legitimated and intervention may be authoritative, such that family bonds and the blood tie were not seen as sacrosanct. Good quality substitute care, preferably adoption, was favoured when the care of the biological parents was felt to be inadequate.

10 Child protection and social work

1 In *Safeguarding Childhood* (Parton, 2006a), I argued that, following Hobsbawm (1994), the year 1973, when Maria died and when the public inquiry was established, was to prove crucial in opening up a series of major

social and economic changes related to the growing impact of globalization. The changes were particularly evident in relation to the family and the community and the increasingly individualized nature of social relationships and identity (see, in particular, Parton 2006a, Ch. 3).

2   For example, the 2012 *British Social Attitudes Survey 29* (www.bsa-29. natcen.ac.uk) found that neither redistribution in general nor welfare benefits in particular were as popular as they once were. These changes predated the 2007/08 recession and reflected a change in public attitudes during the New Labour government years of 1997–2010. The findings pointed to an increased sense of 'them' and 'us', with the most vulnerable in the labour market being viewed far less sympathetically than before.

3   The period since 2002 has seen a resurgence of interest in moral panic theory and research in the social sciences, particularly in sociology, media and cultural studies and criminology. A third edition of Stan Cohen's *Folk Devils and Moral Panics* was published in 2002, 30 years after the original, with an extended new introduction entitled 'Moral panics as cultural politics' (Cohen, 2002). Chas Critcher's book *Moral Panics and the Media* was published in 2003 followed by his edited collection in 2006 (Critcher, 2006). *The British Journal of Criminology* had a whole special issue 'Moral Panics – 36 Years on' (Ben-Yehuda, 2009), while *Crime, Media, Culture* had a special issue on 'Moral Panics in the Contemporary World' in 2011 (Rohloff et al, 2011); see also the edited book by Sean Hier (2011a). The period was also littered with a number of one-off articles on the concept (see, for example, Hier, 2002, 2011b; Garland, 2008) and in 2013 there were two articles on moral panics, child protection and social work (Clapton et al., 2013a, 2013b).

4   Many thanks to Mark Furlong for reminding me of the article by Marguerite Valentine.

5   This is a continual theme in the reaction of the media and senior politicians. There is almost a disbelief that social workers can be so naive and miss such apparently obvious signs of abuse and not simply remove children. This was evident in the response of Gordon Brown and David Cameron to the case of Peter Connelly in November 2008 (see Chapter 5). It was also evident in the attempts to reform social work following the publication of the report from the Institute of Public Policy Research in late 2012, and the introduction of the Frontline fast-track training for young graduates from elite universities (MacAllister with Crehan and Olsen, 2012). It seemed to assume that the challenges arose primarily because of a lack of common sense and commitment on behalf of practitioners and their managers. What was required was a twenty-first-century version of the nineteenth-century middle-class 'child-savers' (see also Holmes et al., 2013). The highly complex emotional, relational, organizational and social factors involved were barely recognized. However, it was also clear that

anxiety levels among child protection social workers had become very high and morale was very low and that staffing levels and resources, particularly in the context of government cutbacks and austerity measures, were not adequate (BASW, 2012).

6 As I demonstrated in Chapter 5, this was evident in late 2008, in relation to the Baby P and Shannon Matthews scandals, which Cameron used as explicit examples of the depth of 'social breakdown' in 'breakdown Britain'. In many respects, it was these scandals that crystallized key elements of such an analysis and helped frame much of the overall approach to social policy and welfare reform of the Conservative Party and the coalition government. Clearly, social work was seen as highly culpable in both cases and hence as symptomatic of many of the problems of British society and welfare policy and practice.

11 Moving beyond individualized child protection systems

1 In 2013, Harker et al. (2013) used the research by Radford et al. (2011) as a basis for measuring the extent of abuse in the UK but also drew on a range of other statistics: child homicides; child mortality; child suicides; the number of recorded sexual offences and cruelty and neglect offences against children; contacts with ChildLine (the telephone helpline for children and young people); contacts with the NSPCC adult helpline; survey data on online harm; violent incidents experienced by 10- to 15-year-olds; as well as all the local authority children's social care statistics I have summarized in Tables A1.2–1.4 in the Appendix. They concluded that although there had been an increase in the number of children being made subject to child protection plans, there were likely to be eight other children who had suffered maltreatment for every child on a child protection plan.

2 In another article, Gilbert et al. (2012b) explored trends in child maltreatment in six developed countries – Sweden, England, New Zealand, Western Australia, Manitoba (Canada) and the USA – over a 30-year period. They found that there was no consistent evidence of a decrease or an increase in all types of indicators of child maltreatment across the six jurisdictions. While there were large differences between the countries in the rate of contacts with child protection agencies, there was little variation in rates of maltreatment-related injury or violent death. Lower levels of maltreatment indices in Sweden than in the USA were consistent with lower rates of child poverty and parental risk factors, and policies providing higher levels of universal support for parenting in Sweden. While high and rising rates of out-of-home care affected a substantial minority of children, particularly those of non-white or Aboriginal origin, there was little evidence of its effectiveness.

3 Under the Local Safeguarding Children Boards Regulations (2006, Section 5), the functions are:

(a) developing policies and procedures for safeguarding and promoting the welfare of children in the area of the authority;

(b) communicating to persons and bodies in the area of the authority the need to safeguard and promote the welfare of children, raising their awareness of how this can be done, and encouraging them to do so;

(c) monitoring and evaluating the effectiveness of what is done by the authority and their Board partners individually and collectively to safeguard and promote the welfare of children, and advising them on ways to improve;

(d) participating in the planning of services for children in the area of the authority;

(e) undertaking reviews of serious cases and advising the authority and their Board partners on lessons to be learned.

References

6, Perri (2000) *The Politics of Moral Character: Cultural Change and Public Policy*. London: Demos.

Action for Children (2012) *The Red Book 2012: The Annual Review of the Impact of Spending Decisions on Vulnerable Children and Families*. London: Action for Children.

Aitkenhead, D. (2012) 'Michael Gove: the next Tory leader', *The Guardian Weekend*, 6 October, 35–42.

Allen, G. (2011a) *Early Intervention: The Next Steps: An Independent Report to Her Majesty's Government*. London: Cabinet Office.

Allen, G. (2011b) *Early Intervention: Smart Investment, Massive Savings*. London: Cabinet Office.

Allen, G. (2012) 'Early Interveners: "Leave your Comfort Zone!"', *Journal of Children's Services*, 7(1), 73–7.

Allen, G. and Smith, I.D. (2008) *Early Intervention: Good Parents, Great Kids, Better Citizens*. London: Centre for Social Justice/Smith Institute.

Anderson, R., Brown, I., Clayton, R. et al. (2006) *Children's Databases – Safety and Privacy: A Report for the Information Commissioner*. Cambridge: Foundation for Information Policy Research.

Andrews, C. (1974) 'The Maria Colwell Inquiry', *Social Work Today*, 4, 637–44.

Association of Directors of Children's Services (2010) *Safeguarding Pressures Project: Results of Data Collection*. Manchester: ADCS.

Audit Commission (1994) *Seen But Not Heard: Coordinating Community Health and Social Services for Children in Need*. London: HMSO.

Audit Commission (2012a) *Local Payment by Results: Briefing: Payment by Results for Local Services*. London: Audit Commission.

Audit Commission (2012b) *Tough Times: Councils' Financial Health in Challenging Times*. London: Audit Commission.

Ayre, P. and Preston-Shoot, M. (eds) (2010) *Children's Services at the Crossroads: A Critical Evaluation of Contemporary Policy and Practice*. Lyme Regis: Russell House.

Baistow, K. and Wilford, G. (2000) 'Helping Parents, Protecting Children: Ideas from Germany', *Children and Society*, 14(5), 343–54.

Ball, S.J. (2007) '"Going Further?" Tony Blair and New Labour Education Policies', in K. Clarke, T. Maltby and P. Kennett (eds) *Social Policy Review 19: Analysis and Debate in Social Policy*. Bristol: Policy Press.

Barclay, P.M. (1982) *Social Workers: Their Role and Tasks*. London: Bedford Square Press.

Barlow, J. and Calam, R. (2011) 'A Public Health Approach to Safeguarding in the 21st Century', *Child Abuse Review*, 20(4), 238–55.

Barlow, J. and Scott, J. (2010) *Safeguarding in the 21st Century: Where To Now?* Dartington: Research in Practice.

Barry, A., Osborne, T. and Rose, N. (eds) (1996) *Foucault and Political Reasons: Liberalism, Neoliberalism and the Rationalities of Government*. London: University College Press.

BASW (British Association of Social Workers) (2012) *The State of Social Work 2012: What Social Workers Think about the State of their Profession in 2012*. Birmingham: BASW.

Bauman, Z. (2007) *Liquid Times: Living in an Age of Uncertainty*. Cambridge: Polity Press.

Becker, S. and Macpherson, S. (1986) *Poor Clients: The Extent and Nature of Financial Poverty amongst Consumers of Social Work Services*. Nottingham: University of Nottingham, Benefits Research Unit.

Behlmer, G.K. (1982) *Child Abuse and Moral Reform in England, 1870–1908*. Stanford: Stanford University Press.

Bell, V. (1994) 'Dreaming and Time in Foucault's Philosophy', *Theory, Culture and Society*, 11(2), 151–63.

Bellamy, C., Perri, 6 and Raab, C. (2005) 'Joined-up Government and Privacy in the United Kingdom: Managing Tensions Between Data Protection and Social Policy, Part II, *Public Administration*, 83(2), 393–415.

Belsky, J., Melhuish, E., Barnes, J. et al. (2006) 'Effects of Sure Start Local Programmes on Children and Families: Early Findings from a Quasi-experimental, Cross Sectional Study', *British Medical Journal*, 332(7556), 1476–8.

Bennett, F. (2012) 'Universal Credit: Overview and Gender Implications', in M. Kilkey, G. Ramia and K. Farnsworth (eds) *Social Policy Review 24: Analysis and Debate in Social Policy, 2012*. Bristol: Policy Press.

Ben-Yahuda, B. (2009) 'Moral Panics: 36 Years On' (guest editor), *British Journal of Criminology*, Special Issue, 49(1).

Berridge, D. (1997) 'England: Child Abuse Reports, Responses and Reforms', in N. Gilbert (ed.) *Combatting Child Abuse: International Perspectives and Trends*. New York: OUP.

Blair, T. (1993) 'Why Crime is a Socialist Issue', *New Statesman*, 29(12), 27–8.

Blair, T. (1998) *The Third Way: New Politics for the New Century*, Fabian Pamphlet 588. London: The Fabian Society.

Blair, T. (1999) 'Beveridge Revisited: Welfare State for the 21st Century', in R. Walker (ed.) *Ending Child Poverty: Popular Welfare for the 21st Century*. Bristol: Policy Press.

Blond, P. (2009) 'The new Conservatism can create a capitalism that works for the poor', *The Guardian*, 3 July, 3.

Blond, P. (2010) *Red Tory: How Left and Right have Broken Britain, and How We Can Fix It*. London: Faber and Faber.

Blond, P. (2012) 'Cameron has lost any hope of redefining the Tories', *The Guardian*, 4 October, 34.

Boddy, J. and Statham, J. (2009) *European Perspectives on Social Work: Models of Education and Professional Roles*. London: Thomas Coram Research Unit, Institute of Education.

Brandon, M., Bailey, S. and Belderson, P. (2010) *Building on the Learning from Serious Case Reviews: A Two-year Analysis of Child Protection Database Notifications 2007-2009*. London: DfE.

Brandon, M., Sidebotham, P., Bailey, S. et al. (2012) *New Learning from Serious Case Reviews: A Two Year Report for 2009–2011*, RR226. London: DfE.

Brewer, M., Browne, J. and Joyce, R. (2011) *Child and Working-Age Poverty from 2010-2020*. London: IFS.

Brewer, M., Sibieta, L. and Wren-Lewis, L. (2008) *Racing Away? Income Inequality and the Evolution of High Incomes*. London: IFS.

Brewer, M., Goodman, A., Myck, M. et al. (2004) *Poverty and Inequality in Britain*. London: IFS.

Brighenti, A. (2007) 'Visibility: A Category of Social Sciences', *Current Sociology*, 55(3), 323–42.

Broadhurst, K., Grover, C. and Jamieson, J. (eds) (2009) *Critical Perspectives on Safeguarding Children*. Chichester: Wiley-Blackwell.

Broadhurst, K., Hall, C., Wastell, D. et al. (2010a) 'Risk, Instrumentalism and the Humane Project in Social Work: Identifying the Informal Logics of Risk Assessment in Children's Statutory Services', *British Journal of Social Work*, 40(5), 1046–65.

Broadhurst, K., Wastell, D., White, S. et al. (2010b) 'Performing Initial Assessment: Identifying the Latent Conditions for Error at the Front-door of Local Authority Children's Services', *British Journal of Social Work*, 40(2), 352–70.

Bromfield, L. and Arney, F. (2008) *Developing a Road Map for Research: Identifying the Priorities for a National Child Protection Research Agenda*. Melbourne: Australian Institute of Family Studies.

Bromfield, L. and Holzer, P. (2007) *A National Approach for Child Protection Project Report*. Melbourne: Australian Institute of Family Studies.

Brooks, C., Brocklehurst, P. and Freeman, S. (2012) *Safeguarding Pressures: Phase 3*. Manchester: ADCS.

Brown, W. (2006) 'American Nightmare: Neoliberalism, Neoconservatism and De-Democratization', *Political Theory*, 34(6), 690–714.

Browne, J. (2012) *The Impact of Austerity Measures on Households with Children*. London: Family and Parenting Institute.

Bruer, J. (1999) *The Myth of the First Three Years: A New Understanding of Early Brain Development and Lifelong Learning*. New York: Free Press.

Bruer, J. (2011) 'Revisiting "The Myth of the First Three Years"', http://blogs. kent.ac.uk/parentingculturestudies/files/2011/09/soecuak-briefing.on-The-Myth.pdf (accessed 15/11/13).

Buckingham, D. (2000) *After the Death of Childhood: Growing Up in the Age of Electronic Media*. Cambridge: Polity Press.

Burchell, G., Gordon, C. and Miller, P. (1991) *The Foucault Effect: Studies in Governmentality*. London: Harvester Wheatsheaf.

Burgess, A. (2010) 'Media Risk Campaigning in the UK: From Mobile Phones to "Baby P"', *Journal of Risk Research*, 13(1), 59–72.

Butchart, A., Kahane, T., Phinney Harvey, A. et al. (2006) *Preventing Child Maltreatment: A Guide to Taking Action and Generating Evidence*. Geneva: WHO/International Society for the Prevention of Child Abuse and Neglect.

Butler, I. and Drakeford, M. (2005) *Scandal, Social Policy and Social Welfare* (2nd edn). Bristol: Policy Press.

Butler, I. and Drakeford, M. (2011) *Social Work on Trial: The Colwell Inquiry and the State of Welfare*. Bristol: Policy Press.

Butler, P. (2009) 'Sharon Shoesmith emails reveal extent of media and political storm', *The Guardian*, 8 October, 6.

Butler, P. (2010) 'Analysis: a crisis in child protection', *The Guardian*, 24 April, 4.

Butler, P. (2011) 'Munro Report: child protection workers need freedom to do jobs', *The Guardian*, 10 May, 5.

Byrne, D. (2005) *Social Exclusion* (2nd edn). Buckingham: Open University Press.

Cabinet Office (1999) *Modernising Government*. London: TSO.

Cable, V. (2004) 'Liberal Economics and Social Justice', in P. Marshall and D. Laws (eds) *The Orange Book: Reclaiming Liberalism*. London: Profile Books.

Cafcass (Children and Family Court Advisory and Support Service) (2009a) *Cafcass Care Demand: Latest Quarterly Figures*. London: Cafcass.

Cafcass (2009b) *The Baby Peter Effect and the Increase in S31 Care Order Applications*. London: Cafcass.

Cafcass (2012) *Three Weeks in November ... Three Years On ... Cafcass Care Application Study 2012*. London: Cafcass.

Cameron, D. (2007) 'A Liberal Conservative Consensus to Restore Trust in Politics', Bath, 22 March, www.conservatives.com/News/Speeches/2007/03/Cameron_A_liberal_conservative_consensus_to_restore_trust_in_politics.aspx (accessed 16/11/2013).

Cameron, D. (2009) 'The Big Society', Hugo Young lecture, 10 November, www.conservatives.com/News/Speeches/2009/11/David_Cameron_The BigSociety.aspx (accessed 16/11/2013).

Cameron, D. (2010) 'Speech on Families and Relationships', 10 December, www.number10.gov.uk/news/speech-on-families-and-relationsips (accessed 16/11/2013).

Cameron, D. (2011a) 'Modern Public Services', speech to the Royal Society of Arts, 17 January, www.gov.uk/government/speeches/prime-ministers-speech-on-modern-public-service (accessed 16/11/2013).

Cameron, D. (2011b) 'PM's Speech on Big Society', 15 February, www.gov.uk/government/speeches/pms-speech-on-big-society (accessed 16/11/2013).

Cameron, D. (2011c) 'PM's Speech on the Fightback after the Riots', 15 August, www.gov.uk/government/speeches/pms-speech-on-the-fightback-after-the-riots (accessed 16/11/2013).

Cameron, G., Coady, N. and Adams, G.R. (2007) *Moving Towards Positive Systems of Child and Family Welfare: Current Issues and Future Directions.* Waterloo, Canada: Wilfrid Laurier University Press.

Campbell, D. (2008) 'Sacked head of council children's services receives death threats', *The Guardian*, 2 December, 5.

Campbell, J.L. (2010) 'Neoliberalism's Penal and Debtor States: A Rejoinder to Loic Wacquant', *Theoretical Criminology*, 14(1), 59–73.

Carlile, Lord (2012) *The Edlington Case: A Review by Lord Carlile of Berriew CBE QC.* London: DfE.

Carrabine, E. (2012) 'Just Images: Aesthetics, Ethics and Visual Criminology', *British Journal of Criminology*, 52(3), 463–89.

Castells, M. (2009) *Communication Power.* Oxford: OUP.

Cawson, P., Wattam, C., Brooker, S. and Kelly, G. (2000) *Child Maltreatment in the UK: A Study of the Prevalence of Child Abuse and Neglect.* London: NSPCC.

Centre for Social Justice (2009) *Dynamic Benefits: Towards Welfare that Works.* London: Centre for Social Justice.

Centre for Social Justice (2012) *Building a Social Recovery? A Second Year Report Card on the Coalition Government.* London: Centre for Social Justice.

Children England (2011) *Counting the Cuts: The Impact of Public Spending Cuts on Children's Charities.* London: Children England.

Children's Rights Alliance for England (2012) *Why Incorporate? Making Rights a Reality for Every Child.* London: CRAE.

Chouliaraki, L. (2008) 'The Symbolic Power of Transnational Media: Managing the Visibility of Suffering', *Global Media Communication*, 4(3), 329–51.

Chowdry, H. and Sibieta, L. (2011) *Trends in Education and School Spending. IFS Briefing Note*. London: IFS.

Churchill, H. (2011) *Parental Rights and Responsibilities: Analysing Social Policy and Lived Experience*. Bristol: Policy Press.

Churchill, H. (2012) 'Family Support and the Coalition: Retrenchment, Refocusing and Restructuring', in M. Kilkey, G. Ramia and K. Farnsworth (eds) *Social Policy Review 24: Analysis and Debate in Social Policy 2012*. Bristol: Policy Press.

CIPFA (Chartered Institute of Public Finance and Accountancy) (2011) *Smart Cuts? Public Spending on Children's Social Care*. London: NSPCC.

Civil Exchange (2012) *The Big Society Audit, 2012*. London: Civil Exchange.

Clapton, G., Cree, V.E. and Smith, M. (2013a) 'Moral Panics and Social Work: Towards a Sceptical View of UK Child Protection', *Critical Social Policy*, 33(2), 197–217.

Clapton, G., Cree, V.E. and Smith, M. (2013b) 'Critical Commentary: Moral Panics, Claims-Making and Child Protection in the UK', *British Journal of Social Work*, 43(4), 803–12.

Clarke, G. and Mather, J. (eds) (2003) *Total Politics: Labour's Command State*. London: Conservative Policy Unit.

Clarke, J. (1980) 'Social Democrat Delinquents and Fabian Families: A Background to the 1969 Children and Young Persons Act', in National Deviancy Conference (eds) *Permissiveness and Control: The Fate of the Sixties Legislation*. London: Macmillan.

Clarke, J. and Glendinning, C. (2002) 'Partnership and the Remaking of Welfare Governance', in C. Glendinning, M. Powell and K. Rummer (eds) *Partnerships, New Labour and the Governance of Welfare*. Bristol: Policy Press.

Clarke, J. and Newman, J. (2012) 'The Alchemy of Austerity', *Critical Social Policy*, 32(3), 299–319.

Clarke, J., Gewitz, S. and McLaughlin, E. (eds) (2000) *New Managerialism: New Welfare*. London: Sage.

Clarke, J., Smith, N. and Vidler, E. (2006) 'The Indeterminacy of Choice: Political, Policy and Organisation Implications', *Social Policy and Society*, 5(3), 327–36.

Clarke, K. (2011) 'Punish the feral rioters, but address the social deficit too', *The Guardian*, 6 September, 34.

Cleaver, H., Unell, I. and Aldgate, J. (1999) *Children's Needs – Parenting Capacity: The Impact of Parental Illness, Problem Alcohol and Dug Use, and Domestic Violence on Children's Development*. London: TSO.

Cleaver, H., Walker, S., Scott, J. et al. (2008) *The Integrated Children's System: Enhancing Social Work and Inter-Agency Practice*. London: Jessica Kingsley.

Clery, E., Lee, L. and Kunz, S. (2013) *Public Attitudes to Poverty and Welfare, 1983–2011*. London: National Centre for Social Research.

Cohen, S. (1972) *Folk Devils and Moral Panics*. St Albans: Paladin.

Cohen, S. (2001) *States of Denial: Knowing about Atrocities and Suffering*. Cambridge: Polity Press.

Cohen, S. (2002) *Folk Devils and Moral Panics* (3rd edn). London: Routledge.

Colclough, L., Parton, N. and Anslow, M. (1999) 'Family Support', in N. Parton and C. Wattam (eds) *Child Sexual Abuse: Responding to the Experiences of Children*. Chichester: Wiley/NSPCC.

Connolly, M. and Morris, K. (2012) *Understanding Child and Family Welfare: Statutory Responses to Children at Risk*. Basingstoke: Palgrave Macmillan.

Conservative Party (2010) *Invitation to Join the Government of Britain: The Conservative Manifesto 2010*. London: Conservative Party.

Conservative Party Commission on Social Workers (2009) *Response to Lord Laming's Inquiry*, chair T. Loughton. London: Conservative Party.

Conservatives/Liberal Democrats (2010) *Conservative Liberal Democrat Coalition Negotiations: Agreement Reached 11 May 2010*. London: Conservative Party/Liberal Democrat Party.

Cooper, A. (1992a) 'Anxiety and Child Protection Work in Two National Systems', *Journal of Social Work Practice*, 6(2), 117–28.

Cooper, A. (1992b) *Methodological and Epistemological Considerations in Cross-National Comparative Research*. London: CCSWS.

Cooper, A., Freund, V., Grevot, A. et al. (1992) *The Social Work Role in Child Protection: An Anglo-French Comparison*. London: CCSWS.

Cooper, A., Hetherington, R., Baistow, K. et al. (1995) *Positive Child Protection: A View from Abroad*. Lyme Regis: Russell House.

Cooper, J. (1983) *The Creation of the British Personal Social Services 1962–74*. London: Heinemann.

Corbett, S. and Walker, A. (2013) 'The Big Society: Rediscovery of "the Social" or Rhetorical Fig-leaf for Neo-liberalism?', *Critical Social Policy*, 33(3), 451–72.

Corby, B. (2006) 'Book Review of Safeguarding Childhood', *Social Work Education*, 25(2), 199–201.

Corby, B., Doig, A. and Roberts, V. (1998) 'Inquiries into Child Abuse', *Journal of Social Welfare and Family Law*, 20(4), 377–95.

Corby, B., Doig, A. and Roberts, V. (2001) *Public Inquiries into Abuse of Children in Residential Care*. London: Jessica Kingsley.

Cornock, M. and Montgomery, H. (2014) 'Children's Rights Since Margaret Thatcher', in S. Wagg and J. Pilcher (eds) *Thatcher's Grandchildren? Politics, Childhood and Society Since 2000*. Basingstoke: Palgrave Macmillan.

Crawford, R. (2010) *Where Did the Axe Fall?* London: IFS.

Creighton, S. (2004) *Prevalence and Incidence of Child Abuse: International Comparisons.* London: NSPCC.

Critcher, C. (2003) *Moral Panics and the Media.* Buckingham: Open University Press.

Critcher, C. (ed.) (2006) *Critical Readings: Moral Panics and the Media.* Maidenhead: Open University Press.

Critcher, C. (2009) 'Widening the Focus: Moral Panics as Moral Regulation', *British Journal of Criminology*, 49(1), 17–34.

Cunningham, H. (1995) *Children and Childhood in Western Society since 1500.* London: Longman.

Curtice, J. (1999) *Was it the Sun Wot Won it Again? The Influence of Newspapers in the 1997 Election Campaign,* CREST Working Paper No.75. University of Oxford.

Curtis, P. and Ward, L. (2007) 'Fitter, happier and better educated: the hope for 2020', *The Guardian*, 12 December, 6–7.

Curtis Report (1946) *Report of the Care of Children Committee,* Cmd 6922. London: HMSO.

Davies, C. and Ward, H. (2012) *Safeguarding Children Across Services: Messages from Research.* London: Jessica Kingsley.

DCLG (Department of Communities and Local Government) (2012) *The Troubled Families Programmes: Financial Framework for the Troubled Families Programme's Payment-by-results Scheme for Local Authorities.* London: DCLG.

DCSF (Department for Children, Schools and Families) (2007a) *ContactPoint: Policy Statement,* June. London: TSO.

DCSF (2007b) *The Children's Plan: Building Brighter Futures.* London: TSO.

DCSF (2007c) *Staying Safe: A Consultation Document.* London: TSO.

Devo, J. (2007) 'Deaths Spark Media Storm', *Professional Social Work*, September, 5.

DfE (Department for Education) (2010) 'More Freedom and Flexibility: A New Approach for Children's Trust Boards, Children and Young People's Plans, and the Duty to Cooperate', News Release, 2 November, DfE.

DfE (2011) *Children Looked After by Local Authorities in England (Including Adoption and Care Leavers) Year ending 31 March 2011.* London: DfE.

DfE (2012) *An Action Plan for Adoption: Tackling Delay.* London: DfE.

DfE (2013a) *The Government's Response to Lord Carlile's Report on the Edlington Case.* London: DfE.

DfE (2013b) *Further Action on Adoption: Finding More Loving Homes.* London: DfE.

DfES (Department for Education and Skills) (2004a) *Every Child Matters: Next Steps.* London: DfES.

DfES (2004b) *Every Child Matters: Change for Children*. London: DfES.

DfES (2005a) *Youth Matters: Next Steps. Something to Do, Somewhere to Go, Someone to Talk to*. London: DfES.

DfES (2005b) *The Common Core of Skills and Knowledge for the Children's Workforce*. London: DfES.

DfES (2005c) *Higher Standards, Better Schools for All: More Choice for Parents and Pupils*, Cm 6677. London: TSO.

DfES (2006a) *Children's Workforce Strategy: Building a World-class Workforce for Children, Young People and Families: The Government's Response to the Consultation*. London: DfES.

DfES (2006b) *The Lead Professional: Managers' Guide. Integrated Working to Improve Outcomes for Children and Young People*. London: DfES.

DfES (2006c) *The Lead Professional: Practitioners' Guide. Integrated Working to Improve Outcomes for Children and Young People*. London: DfES.

DfES (2006d) *The Common Assessment Framework for Children and Young People: Practitioners' Guide. Integrated Working to Improve Outcomes for Children and Young People*. London: DfES.

DfES (2006e) *Common Assessment Framework for Children and Young People: Managers' Guide. Integrated Working to Improve the Outcomes for Children and Young People*. London: DfES.

DH (Department of Health) (1988) *Protecting Children: A Guide for Social Workers Undertaking a Comprehensive Assessment in Cases of Child Protection*. London: HMSO.

DH (1994) *Children Act Report 1993*, Cm 2584. London: HMSO.

DH (1995a) *Child Protection: Messages from Research*. London: HMSO.

DH (1995b) *Looking After Children: Good Parenting, Good Outcomes Training Guide*. London: HMSO.

DH (1998a) *Modernising Social Services: Promoting Independence, Improving Protection, Raising Standards*, Cm 4169. London: TSO.

DH (1998b) *The Quality Protects Programme: Transforming Children's Services*, LAC(98)28. London: DH.

DH (2000) *The Prime Minister's Review of Adoption*. London: TSO.

DH (2001) *The Children Act Now: Messages from Research*. London: TSO.

DH (2002) *Safeguarding Children: A Joint Inspectors' Report on Arrangements to Safeguard Children*. London: DH.

DH (2003) *About the Integrated Children's System*. London: DH.

DH (2004) *National Service Framework for Children, Young People and Maternity Services*. London: DH.

DH/Department of Education and Employment/Home Office (2000) *Framework for the Assessment of Children in Need and their Families*. London: TSO.

DH/Home Office/Department of Education and Employment (1999) *Working Together to Safeguard Children: A Guide to Inter-Agency Working to Safeguard and Promote the Welfare of Children*. London: TSO.

DHSS (Department of Health and Social Security) (1970) *The Battered Baby*, Cm 02/70. London: DHSS.

DHSS (1972) *Battered Babies*, LASSC, 26/72. London: DHSS.

DHSS (1974) *Non-Accidental Injury to Children*, LASSL(74)(13). London: DHSS.

DHSS (1976a) *Non-Accidental Injury to Children: Area Review Committees*, LASSL(76)(2). London: DHSS.

DHSS (1976b) *Non-Accidental Injury to Children: The Police and Case Conferences*, LASSL(76)(26). London: DHSS.

DHSS (1978) *Child Abuse: The Register System*, LA/C396/23D. London: DHSS.

DHSS (1980) *Child Abuse: Central Register Systems*, LASSL(80)4, HN(80). London: DHSS.

DHSS (1982) *Child Abuse: A Study of Inquiry Reports 1973-1981*. London: HMSO.

DHSS (1985) *Review of Child Care Law: Report to Ministers of an Interdepartmental Working Party*. London: HMSO.

DHSS (1986) *Child Abuse: Working Together. A Draft Guide to Arrangements for Inter-Agency Cooperation for the Protection of Children*. London: DHSS.

DHSS (1988) *Working Together: A Guide to Inter-Agency Co-operation for the Protection of Children from Abuse*. London: HMSO.

Dobrowolsky, A. and Jenson, J. (2005) 'Social Investment Perspectives and Practices: A Decade in British Politics', in M. Powell, L. Bauld and K. Clarke (eds) *Social Policy Review 17: Analysis and Debate in Social Policy, 2005*. Bristol: Policy Press.

Donzelot, J. (1980) *The Policing of Families: Welfare versus the State*. London: Hutchinson.

Donzelot, J. (1988) 'The Promotion of the Social', *Economy and Society*, 17(3), 395–427.

Dorling, D. (2004) 'Prime Suspect: Murder in Britain', in P. Hillyard, C. Pantazis, S. Tombs and D. Gordon (eds) *Beyond Criminology: Taking Harm Seriously*. London: Pluto Press.

Dorling, D. (2012) *The Case for Austerity Amongst the Rich*. London: Institute for Public Policy Research.

Dorling, D. (2014) '"What Have the Romans Ever Done for Us?": Child Poverty and the Legacy of "New" Labour', in S. Wagg and J. Pilcher (eds) *Thatcher's Grandchildren? Politics, Childhood and Society Since 2000*. Basingstoke: Palgrave Macmillan.

Dorling, D., Gordon, D., Hillyard, P. et al. (2008) *Criminal Obsessions: Why Harm Matters More than Crime*. London: Centre for Crime and Justice Studies, King's College.

Driver, S. and Martell, L. (1997) 'New Labour's Communitarianisms', *Critical Social Policy*, 17(3), 27–46.

Dryfoos, J.G. (1990) *Adolescents at Risk: Prevalence and Prevention*. Oxford: OUP.

Eisenstadt, N. (2011) *Providing a Sure Start: How Government Discovered Early Childhood*. Bristol: Policy Press.

Ellison, N. (2011) 'The Conservative Party and the "Big Society"', in C. Holden, M. Kilkey and G. Ramia (eds) *Social Policy Review 23: Analysis and Debate in Social Policy, 2011*. Bristol: Policy Press.

Emmerson, C., Johnson, P. and Miller, H. (eds) (2013) *The IFS Green Budget February 2013*. London: IFS.

Esping-Andersen, G. (1990) *The Three Worlds of Welfare Capitalism*, Princeton, NJ: Princeton University Press.

Esping-Andersen, G. with Gallie, D., Hemerijck, A. and Myles, J. (2002) *Why We Need a New Welfare State*. Oxford: OUP.

Etzioni, A. (1993) *The Spirit of Community: Rights, Responsibilities and the Communitarian Agenda*. New York: Simon & Schuster.

Etzioni, A. (1997) *The New Golden Rule: Community and Morality in a Democratic Society*. New York: HarperCollins.

Evans, K. (2011) '"Big Society" in the UK: A Policy Review', *Children & Society*, 25(2), 164–71.

Fairclough, N. (2000) *New Labour, New Language?* London: Routledge.

Farrington, D. (1996) *Understanding and Preventing Youth Crime*. York: Joseph Rowntree Foundation.

Farrington, D. (2000) 'Explaining and Preventing Crime: The Globalisation of Knowledge', *Criminology*, 38(1), 1–24.

Fawcett, B., Featherstone, B. and Goddard, J. (2004) *Contemporary Child Care Policy and Practice*. Basingstoke: Palgrave Macmillan.

Ferguson, H. (1990) 'Rethinking Child Protection Practices', in The Violence Against Children Study Group (eds) *Taking Child Abuse Seriously: Contemporary Issues in Child Protection Theory and Practice*. London: Unwin Hyman.

Ferguson, H. (1996) 'The Protection of Children in Time', *Child and Family Social Work*, 1(4), 205–18.

Ferguson, H. (1997) 'Protecting Children in New Times: Child Protection and the Risk Society', *Child and Family Social Work*, 2(4), 221–34.

Ferguson, H. (2004) *Protecting Children in Time: Child Abuse, Child Protection and the Consequences of Modernity*. Basingstoke: Palgrave Macmillan.

Field, F. (2010) *The Foundation Years: Preventing Poor Children Becoming Poor Adults. Report of the Independent Review on Poverty and Life Chances*. London: Cabinet Office.

Finch, J. and Groves, D. (eds) (1983) *A Labour of Love*. London: Routledge & Kegan Paul.

Finn, D. (2011) 'Welfare to Work after the Recession: From the New Deals to the Work Programme', in C. Holden, M. Kilkey and G. Ramia (eds) *Social Policy Review 23: Analysis and Debate in Social Policy, 2011*. Bristol: Policy Press.

Fisher, D. and Gruescu, S. (2011) *Children and the Big Society: Backing Communities to Keep the Next Generation Safe and Happy*. London: ResPublica/Action for Children.

Fitzgibbon, W. (2011) *Probation and Social Work on Trial: Violent Offenders and Child Abusers*. Basingstoke: Palgrave Macmillan.

Flegel, M. (2009) *Conceptualizing Cruelty to Children in Nineteenth-Century England: Literature, Representations and the NSPCC*. Farnham: Ashgate.

Foucault, M. (1977) *Discipline and Punish*. London: Allen Lane.

Foucault, M. (1979) *The History of Sexuality*, vol. 1: *An Introduction*. London: Allen Lane.

Foucault, M. (1980) 'Space, Knowledge and Power', in P. Rabinow (ed.) *The Foucault Reader*. Harmondsworth: Penguin.

Fox, L.M. (1982) 'Two Value Positions in Recent Child Care Law and Practice', *British Journal of Social Work*, 12(2), 265–90.

Fox Harding, L. (1997) *Perspectives in Child Care Policy* (2nd edn). London: Prentice Hall.

France, A. and Utting, D. (2005) 'The Paradigm of "Risk and Protection-Focused Prevention" and its Impact on Services for Children and Families', *Children & Society*, 19(2), 77–90.

France, A., Freiburg, K. and Homel, R. (2010a) 'Beyond Risk Factors: Towards a Holistic Prevention Paradigm for Children and Families', *British Journal of Social Work*, 40(4), 1192–210.

France, A., Munro, E. and Waring, A. (2010b) *The Evaluation of Arrangements for Effective Operation of the New Local Safeguarding Children Boards in England: Final Report*, RR027. London: DfE.

Franklin, B. (ed.) (1986) *The Rights of Children*. Oxford: Basil Blackwell.

Franklin, B. (ed.) (1995) *A Comparative Handbook of Children's Rights*. London: Routledge.

Franklin, B. (2003) 'The Hand of History: New Labour, News Management and Governance', in A. Chadwick and R. Heffernan (eds) *The New Labour Reader*. Oxford: Polity Press.

Franklin, B. and Parton, N. (eds) (1991) *Social Work, the Media and Public Relations*. London: Routledge.

Franklin, B. and Parton, N. (2001) 'Press-ganged! Media Reporting of Social Work and Child Abuse', in M. May, R. Payne and E. Brunsdon (eds) *Understanding Social Problems: Issues in Social Policy*. Oxford: Blackwell.

Fraser, D. (2009) *The Evolution of the British Welfare State: A History of Social Policy since the Industrial Revolution* (4th edn). Basingstoke: Palgrave Macmillan.

Freeman, M.D.A. (1983) *The Rights and Wrongs of Children*. London: Frances Pinter.

Freeman, R. (1992) 'The Idea of Prevention: A Critical Review', in S. Scott, G. Williams, S. Platt and H. Thomas (eds) *Private Risk and Public Dangers*. Aldershot: Avebury.

Freeman, R. (1999) 'Recursive Politics: Prevention, Modernity and Social Systems', *Children & Society*, 13(4), 232–41.

Freeman, R. (2009) 'Comparing Health Systems', in R. Mullner (ed.) *Encyclopaedia of Health Services Research*. Thousand Oak, CA: Sage.

Freymond, N. and Cameron, C. (eds) (2006) *Towards Positive Systems of Child and Family Welfare: International Comparisons of Child Protection, Family Service and Community Caring*. Toronto: University of Toronto Press.

Frost, N. (1992) 'Implementing the Children Act 1989 in a Hostile Climate', in P. Carter, T. Jeffs and M.K. Smith (eds) *Changing Social Work and Welfare*. Buckingham: Open University Press.

Frost, N. and Parton, N. (2009) *Understanding Children's Social Care: Politics, Policy and Practice*. London: Sage.

Frost, N. and Stein, M. (1989) *The Politics of Child Welfare: Inequality, Power and Change*. London: Harvester Wheatsheaf.

Gainsborough, J.F. (2009) 'Scandals, Lawsuits and Politics: Child Welfare Policy in the US States', *State Politics and Policy Quarterly*, 9(3), 325–55.

Gainsborough, J.F. (2010) *Scandalous Politics: Child Welfare Politics in the States*. Washington DC: Georgetown University Press.

Gamble, A. (1988) *The Free Economy and the Strong State: The Politics of Thatcherism*. Basingstoke: Macmillan.

Gamble, A. (2012) 'Economic Policy', in T. Heppell and D. Seawright (eds) *Cameron and the Conservatives: The Transition to Coalition Government*. Basingstoke: Palgrave Macmillan.

Garland, D. (1985) *Punishment and Welfare: A History of Penal Strategies*. Aldershot: Gower.

Garland, D. (2008) 'On the Concept of Moral Panic', *Crime, Media, Culture*, 4(1), 9–30.

Garrett, P.M. (2009a) *Transforming Children's Services? Social Work, Neoliberalism and the 'Modern' World*. Maidenhead: Open University Press.

Garrett, P.M. (2009b) 'The Case of 'Baby P': Opening up Spaces for Debate on the Transformation of Children's Services', *Critical Social Policy*, 29(3), 533–47.

Garrison, M. (2005) 'Reforming Child Protection: A Public Health Perspective', *Virginia Journal of Social Policy and Law*, 12(3), 590–637.

Geach, H. and Szwed, E. (eds) (1983) *Providing Civil Justice for Children*. London: Arnold.

Giddens, A. (1994) *Beyond Left and Right: The Future of Radical Politics*. Cambridge: Polity Press.

Giddens, A. (1998) *The Third Way: The Renewal of Social Democracy*. Cambridge: Polity Press.

Giddens, A. (2000) *The Third Way and its Critics*. Cambridge: Polity Press.

Gil, D. (1970) *Violence Against Children*. Cambridge: Harvard University Press.

Gil, D. (1975) 'Unravelling Child Abuse', *American Journal of Orthopsychiatry*, 45(3), 346–56.

Gil, D. (1978) 'Societal Violence and Violence in Families', in J.M. Eekelaar and S.N. Katz (eds) *Family Violence: An International and Interdisciplinary Study*. London: Butterworths.

Gilbert, N. (ed.) (1997) *Combatting Child Abuse: International Perspectives and Trends*. New York: OUP.

Gilbert, N., Parton, N. and Skivenes, M. (eds) (2011a) *Child Protection Systems: International Trends and Orientations*. New York: OUP.

Gilbert, N., Parton, N. and Skivenes, M. (2011b) 'Changing Patterns of Response and Emerging Orientations', in N. Gilbert, N. Parton and M. Skivenes (eds) *Child Protection Systems: International Trends and Orientations*. New York: OUP.

Gilbert, R., Kemp, A., Thoburn, J. et al. (2009a) 'Recognising and Responding to Child Maltreatment', *The Lancet*, 373(9658), 167–80.

Gilbert, R., Widom, C.P., Browne, K. et al. (2009b) 'Burden and Consequences of Child Maltreatment in High-income Countries', *The Lancet*, 373(9657), 68–81.

Gilbert, R., Woodman, J. and Logan, S. (2012a) 'Developing Services for a Public Health Approach to Child Maltreatment', *International Journal of Children's Rights*, 20(3), 323–42.

Gilbert, R., Fluke, J., O'Donnell, M. et al. (2012b) 'Child Maltreatment: Variation in Trends and Policies in Six Developed Countries', *The Lancet*, 379(9817), 758–72.

Gill, C., La Ville, I. and Brady, M.L. (2011) *The Ripple Effect: The Nature and Impact of the Cuts on the Children and Young People's Voluntary Sector*. London: NCB.

Gillies, V. (2008) 'Perspectives on Parenting Responsibility: Contextualising Values and Practices', *Journal of Law and Society*, 35(1), 95–112.

Gillies, V. (2014) 'Troubling Families: Parenting and the Politics of Early Intervention', in S. Wagg and J. Pilcher (eds) *Thatcher's Grandchildren? Politics, Childhood and Society Since 2000*. Basingstoke: Palgrave Macmillan.

Glendinning, C., Powell, M. and Rummery, K. (eds) (2002) *Partnerships, New Labour and the Governance of Welfare*. Bristol: Polity Press.

Goldblatt, P. and Lewis, C. (eds) (1998) *Reducing Offending. Home Office Research Study No 187*. London: HMSO.

Golding, P. (1986) *Excluding the Poor*. London: CPAG.

Goodwin, R.E. (1996) 'Inclusion and Exclusion', *European Journal of Sociology*, 37(2), 343–71.

Gordon, L. (1989) *Heroes of their Own Lives: The Politics and History of Family Violence*. London: Virago.

Gove, M. (2010) 'Munro Review of Child Protection: Better Frontline Services to Protect Children', letter to Professor Eileen Munro, 10 June, www.hillingdonconnected.org.uk/sites/hillingdonconnected.org.uk/files/Michael%20Gove%20to%20Eileen%20Munro%2010.06.10.pdf (accessed 16/11/2013).

Gove, M. (2012) 'The Failure of Child Protection and the Need for a Fresh Start', speech, 16 November, Institute of Public Policy Research, www.gov.uk/government/speeches/the-failure-of-child-protection-and-the-need-for-a-fresh-start (accessed 16/11/2013).

Government Press Release (2012) *Government Sets Out Measures to Speed up Adoptions and Give Vulnerable Children Loving Homes*, 9 March, www.gov.uk/government/news/government-sets-out-measures-to-speed-up-adoptions-and-give-vulnerable-children-loving-homes (accessed 13/03/2013).

Gray, D. and Watt, P. (2013) *Giving Victims a Voice: Joint Report into Sexual Allegations Made against Jimmy Savile*. London: NSPCC/Metropolitan Police.

Gray, J. (2002) 'National Policy on the Assessment of Children in Need and their Families', in H. Ward and W. Rose (eds) *Approaches to Needs Assessment in Children's Services*. London: Jessica Kingsley.

Greer, C. and McLaughlin, E. (2010) 'We Predict a Riot? Public Order Policing, New Media Environments and the Rise of the Citizen Journalist', *British Journal of Criminology*, 50(6), 1041–59.

Greer, C. and McLaughlin, E. (2011) '"Trial by Media": Policing the 24–7 Mediasphere and the "Politics of Outrage"', *Theoretical Criminology*, 15(1), 23–46.

Greer, C. and McLaughlin, E. (2012a) '"This is not Justice": Ian Tomlinson, Institutional Failure and the Press Politics of Outrage', *British Journal of Criminology*, 52(2), 274–93.

Greer, C. and McLaughlin, E. (2012b) '"Media Justice": Madeleine McCann, Intermediatization and "Trial by Media" in the British Press', *Theoretical Criminology*, 16(4), 395–416.

Hall, C., Parton, N., Peckover, S. and White, S. (2010) 'Child-centric Information and Communication Technology (ICT) and the Fragmentation of Child Welfare Practice in England', *Journal of Social Policy*, 39(3), 393–413.

Hall, P. (1976) *Reforming the Welfare*. London: Heinemann.

Hall, S. (2011) 'The Neoliberal Revolution', *Soundings*, 48, 9–27.

Hall, S., Critcher, C., Jefferson, T. et al. (1978) *Policing the Crisis*. London: Macmillan.

Hannon, C., Wood, C. and Bazalgette, L. (2010) *In Loco Parentis*. London: Demos.

Harder, M. and Pringle, K. (eds) (1997) *Protecting Children in Europe: Towards a New Millennium*. Aalborg: Aalborg University Press.

Haringey LSCB (2008) *Serious Case Review 'Child A', Executive Summary*, November.

Haringey LSCB (2009) *Serious Case Review: Baby Peter, Executive Summary*, February.

Harker, L., Jutte, S., Murphy, T. et al. (2013) *How Safe are Our Children?* London: NSPCC.

Harvey, D. (2007) *A Brief History of Neoliberalism*. Oxford: OUP.

Hayton, R. (2012) 'Fixing Broken Britain', in T. Heppell and D. Seawright (eds) *Cameron and the Conservatives: The Transition to Coalition Government*. Basingstoke: Palgrave Macmillan.

Hayward, K. and Yar, M. (2006) 'The "Chav" Phenomenon: Consumption, Media and the Construction of a New Underclass', *Crime, Media, Culture*, 2(1), 9–28.

Hawker, D. (2006) 'Joined up Working: the Development of Childhood Services', in G. Pugh and B. Duffy (eds) *Contemporary Issues in Early Years*. London: Sage.

Hendrick, H. (2003) *Child Welfare: Historical Dimensions, Contemporary Debates*. Bristol: Policy Press.

Hetherington, P. (2013) 'Is this the end of Cameron's big idea?', *The Guardian*, 6 March, 34.

Hetherington, R. (2006) 'Learning from Difference: Comparing Child Welfare systems', in N. Freymond and C. Cameron (eds) *Towards Positive Systems of Child and Family Welfare*. Toronto: Toronto University Press.

Hetherington, R., Cooper, A., Smith, P. and Wilford, G. (1997) *Protecting Children: Messages from Europe*. Lyme Regis: Russell House.

Hier, S.P. (2002) 'Conceptualizing moral panic through a moral economy of harm', *Critical Sociology*, 28(3), 311–34.

Hier, S.P. (2011a) *Moral Panic and the Politics of Anxiety*. London: Routledge.

Hier, S.P. (2011b) 'Tightening the Focus: Moral Panic, Moral Regulations, and Liberal Government', *British Journal of Sociology*, 62(3), 523–41.

Higgs, L. (2011) 'Exclusive Survey: Youth Services and Children's Centres Worst Hit as Cuts Average 13 Per Cent', *Children and Young People Now*, 24 January, 6–7.

Hillyard, P., Pantazis, C., Tombs, S. and Gordon, D. (eds) (2004) *Beyond Criminology: Taking Harm Seriously*. London: Pluto Press.

Hilton, Z. and Mills, C. (2007) 'Ask the Children', *Criminal Justice*, 16, 16–18.

Hinshelwood, R.D. (1987) *What Happens in Groups*. London: Free Association.

HM Government (2006a) *Reaching Out: An Action Plan on Social Exclusion*. London: Cabinet Office.

HM Government (2006b) *Working Together to Safeguard Children: A Guide to Inter-Agency Working to Safeguard and Promote the Welfare of Children*. London: TSO.

HM Government (2006c) *Care Matters: Transforming the Lives of Children and Young People in Care*. London: TSO.

HM Government (2008) *Youth Action Plan*. London: TSO.

HM Government (2009) *The Protection of Children in England: Action Plan. The Government Response to Lord Laming*, Cm 758. London: DCSF.

HM Government (2010a) *Working Together to Safeguard Children: A Guide to Inter-Agency Working to Safeguard and Promote the Welfare of Children*. London: DCSF.

HM Government (2010b) *Working Together to Safeguard Children: Government Response to Public Consultation*. London: DCSF.

HM Government (2010c) *The Coalition: Our Programme for Government*. London: Cabinet Office.

HM Government (2010d) *Building a Safe and Confident Future: Implementing the Recommendations of the Social Work Task Force*. London: DCSF/DH/Department for Business, Innovation and Skills.

HM Government (2011a) *Open Public Services*, White Paper, Cm 8145. London: TSO.

HM Government (2011b) *A New Approach to Child Poverty: Tackling the Causes of Disadvantage and Transforming Family Lives*, Cm 7942. London: TSO.

HM Government (2012a) *Open Public Services 2012*. London: Cabinet Office.

HM Government (2012b) *Social Justice: Transforming Lives*, Cm 8314. London: TSO.

HM Government (2013) *Working Together to Safeguard Children: A Guide to Inter-Agency Working to Safeguard and Promote the Welfare of Children*. London: DfE.

HMIC (Her Majesty's Inspectorate of Constabulary) (2013) *"Mistakes Were Made": HMIC Review into Allegations and Intelligence Material Concerning Jimmy Savile between 1964 and 2012*. London: HMIC.

HM Treasury (2002) *2002 Spending Review: Opportunity and Security for All, Investing in an Enterprising Society: New Public Spending Plans 2003–2006*. London: TSO.

HM Treasury (2003) *Every Child Matters*, Cm 5860. London: TSO.

HM Treasury (2010a) *Budget 2010*, HC61. London: TSO.

HM Treasury (2010b) *Spending Review 2010*, Cm 7942. London: TSO.

HM Treasury (2012) *Autumn Statement 2012*, Cm 8480. London: TSO.

HM Treasury/Department for Education and Skills/Department for Work and Pensions/Department of Trade and Industry (2004) *Choice for Parents, the Best Start for Children: A Ten Year Strategy for Childcare*. London: HM Treasury.

Hobsbawm, E. (1994) *The Age of Extremes: The Short Twentieth Century, 1914-1991*. London: Michael Joseph.

Hoffman, D.M. (2010) 'Risky Investments: Parenting and the Production of the "Resilient Child"', *Health, Risk and Society*, 12(4), 385–94.

Holman, B. (1998) *Child Care Revisited: The Children's Departments 1948–1971*. London: Institute of Childcare and Social Education.

Holmes, E., Miscampbell, G. and Robin, B. (2013) *Reforming Social Work: Improving Social Worker Recruitment, Training and Retention*. London: Policy Exchange.

Holt, K. and Kelly, N. (2012) 'Rhetoric and Reality Surrounding Care Proceedings: Family Justice under Strain', *Journal of Social Welfare and Family Law*, 34(2), 155–66.

Home Office/Department of Health/Department of Education and Science/Welsh Office (1991) *Working Together under the Children Act 1989: A Guide to Arrangements for Inter-Agency Co-operation for the Protection of Children from Abuse*. London: HMSO.

Hooper, C.A. (2011) 'Child Maltreatment', in J. Bradshaw (ed.) *The Well-Being of Children in the UK* (3rd edn). Bristol: Policy Press.

Hooper, C.A., Gorin, S., Cabral, C. and Dyson, C. (2007) *Living with Hardship 24/7: The Diverse Experiences of Families in Poverty in England*. London: Frank Buttle Trust/NSPCC.

Hopwood, O., Pharoah, R. and Hannon, C. (2012) *Families on the Front Line? Local Spending on Children's Services in Austerity*. London: Family and Parenting Institute.

Horton, S. and Farnham, D. (1999) *Public Management in Britain*. Basingstoke: Macmillan – now Palgrave Macmillan.

House of Commons Children, Schools and Families Committee (2009) *Looked-After Children*, www.publications.parliament.uk/pa/cm200809/cmselect/cmchilsch/111/11102.htm (accessed 06/08/13).

House of Commons Education Committee (2012a) *Governance and Leadership of the Department for Education: Third Report of Session 2012–13*, HC700. London: TSO.

House of Commons Education Committee (2012b) *Children First: The Child Protection System in England: Fourth Report of Session 2012–13*, vols 1, 2 and 3, HC137. London: TSO.

House of Commons Education and Skills Committee (2005) *Every Child Matters: Ninth Report of Session 2004-05*, HC40-1. London: TSO.

House of Commons Public Administration Select Committee (2012) *The Big Society: Further Report*, HC98. London: TSO.

Hudson, B. (2005a) 'Partnership Working and the Children's Services Agenda: Is it Feasible?', *Journal of Integrated Care*, 13(2), 7–17.

Hudson, B. (2005b) 'User Outcomes and Children's Services Reform: Ambiguity and Conflict in the Policy Implementation Process', *Social Policy and Society*, 5(2), 227–36.

Hudson, B. (2005c) '"Not a Cigarette Paper Between Us": Integrated Inspection of Children's Services in England', *Social Policy and Administration*, 139(5), 513–27.

Hudson, J. (2002) 'Digitising the Structures of Government: The UK's Information Age Government Agenda', *Policy and Politics*, 30(4), 515–31.

Hudson, J. (2003) 'E-galitarianism? The Information Society and New Labour's Repositioning of Welfare', *Critical Social Policy*, 23(2), 268–90.

Information Commissioner's Office (2005) *Memorandum to the Education and Skills Committee in Respect of the Committee's Enquiry into Every Child Matters*, www.ico.org.uk/upload/documents/library/corporate/notices/memo_to_the_education_and_skills_select_committee_-_every_child_matters.pdf (accessed 21/02/13).

Information Policy Unit Social Care (2003) *Defining the Electronic Social Care Record*, http://webarchive.nationalarchives.gov.uk/+/www.dh.gov.uk/en/Publicationsandstatistics/Publications/PublicationsPolicyAndGuidance/DH_4006371 (accessed 10/01/13).

Jack, G. (2006) 'The Area and Community Components of Children's Well-being', *Children & Society*, 20(5), 334–47.

Jack, G. and Gill, O. (2010) 'The Role of Communities in Safeguarding Children and Young People', *Child Abuse Review*, 19(2), 82–96.

Jackson, S. and Kilroe, S. (eds) (1996) *Looking After Children: Good Parenting, Good Outcome Reader*. London: HMSO.

Jacobsson, K. and Löfmark, E. (2008) 'A Sociology of Scandal and Moral Transgression: The Swedish "Nannygate" Scandal', *Acta Sociologica*, 51(3), 203–16.

James, A. (2010) *School Bullying: Research Briefing*. London: NSPCC.

Jones, C. (1983) *State Social Work and the Working Class*. Basingstoke: Macmillan.

Jones, E. (2011) *Chavs: The Demonization of the Working Class*. London: Verso.

Jones, R. (2009) 'Children Acts 1948-2008: The Drivers for Legislative Change in England over 60 Years', *Journal of Children's Services*, 4(4), 39–52.

Jones, R. (2012) 'Child Protection, Social Work and the Media: Doing As Well As Being Done To', *Research, Policy and Planning*, 29(2), 83–94.

Jordan, B. (1996) *A Theory of Poverty and Social Exclusion*. Cambridge: Polity Press.

Jordan, B. (2005) 'New Labour: Choice and Values', *Critical Social Policy*, 25(4), 427–46.

Jordan, B. (2006a) *Social Policy for the Twenty-First Century*. Cambridge: Polity Press.

Jordan, B. (2006b) 'Public Services and the Service Economy: Individualism and the Choice Agenda, *Journal of Social Policy*, 35(1), 143–62.

Jordan, B. (2010a) *What's Wrong with Social Policy and How to Fix it*. Cambridge: Polity Press.

Jordan, B. (2010b) *Why the Third Way Failed: Economics, Morality and the Origins of the 'Big Society'*. Bristol: Policy Press.

Jordan, B. and Drakeford, M. (2012) *Social Work and Social Policy under Austerity*. Basingstoke: Palgrave Macmillan.

Jordan, B. with Jordan, C. (2000) *Social Work and the Third Way: Tough Love as Social Policy*. London: Sage.

Kempe, C.H., Silverman, F.N., Steel, B.F. et al. (1962) 'The Battered Child Syndrome', *Journal of the American Medical Association*, 181, 17–24.

Kemshall, H. (2010) 'Community Protection and Multi-Agency Public Protection Arrangements', in M. Nash and A. Williams (eds) *The Handbook of Public Protection*. Cullompton: Willan.

Khoo, E.G., Hyvönen, U. and Nygren, I. (2002) 'Child Welfare Protection: Uncovering Swedish and Canadian Orientations to Social Intervention in Child Maltreatment', *Qualitative Social Work*, 1(4), 451–71.

Kirton, D. (2013) 'Kinship by Design in England: Reconfiguring Adoption from Blair to the Coalition', *Child and Family Social Work*, 18(1), 97–106.

Kisby, B. (2010) 'The Big Society: Power to the People?', *The Political Quarterly*, 81(4), 484–91.

Klein, M., Heimann, P. and Money-Kyrle, R. (eds) (1971) *New Directions in Psycho-analysis*. London: Tavistock.

Krueger, A. (2012) *The Economic Report of the President and the Annual Report of Economic Advisors*. Washington DC: US Government Printing Office.

Krug, E.J., Dahlberg, L.L., Mercy, J.A. et al. (2002) *World Report on Violence and Health*. Geneva: WHO.

Kruger, D. (1997) 'Access Denied', *Demos Collection*, 12, 20–1.

Kydd, J.W. (2003) 'Preventing Child Maltreatment: An Integrated Multisectoral Approach', *Health and Human Rights*, 6(2), 34–63.

Laming Report (2003) *The Victoria Climbié Inquiry: Report of an Inquiry by Lord Laming*, Cm 5730. London: TSO.

Laming Report (2009) *The Protection of Children in England: A Progress Report*. London: TSO.

Lanchester, J. (2013) 'Let's Call it Failure', *London Review of Books*, 35(1), 3–6.

Langan, M. (2010) 'Children's Social Care Under New Labour', in I. Greener, C. Holden and M. Kilkey (eds) *Social Policy Review 22: Analysis and Debate in Social Policy*. Bristol: Policy.

Lansley, S. (2012a) *The Cost of Inequality: Why Equality is Essential*. London: Gibson Square.

Lansley, S. (2012b) 'Inequality, the Crash and the Ongoing Crisis', *Political Quarterly*, 83(4), 754–61.

Lasch, C. (1977) *Haven in a Heartless World*. New York: Basic Books.

Laws, D. (2004) 'Reclaiming Liberalism: A Liberal Agenda for the Liberal Democrats', in P. Marshall and D. Laws (eds) *The Orange Book: Reclaiming Liberalism*. London: Profile Books.

Layard, R. and Dunn, J. (2009) *A Good Childhood: Searching for Values in a Competitive Age*. London: Children's Society/Penguin.

Lee, S. (2011) 'No Plan B: The Coalition Agenda for Cutting the Deficit and Rebalancing the Economy', in S. Lee and M. Beech (eds) *The Cameron-Clegg Government: Coalition Politics in an Age of Uncertainty*. Basingstoke: Palgrave Macmillan.

Lees, D. (1979) 'As the Hurt Fades', *Social Work Today*, 10, 15.

Le Grand, J., Wood, A. and Gibb, M. (2013) *Report to the Secretary of State for Education on Ways Forward for Children's Services in Doncaster*. London: DfE.

Leveson Inquiry (2012) *An Inquiry into the Culture, Practices and Ethics of the Press*. London: TSO.

Levitas, R. (ed.) (1986) *The Ideology of the New Right*. Cambridge: Polity Press.

Levitas, R. (1996) 'The Concept of Social Exclusion and the New Durkheimian Hegemony', *Critical Social Policy*, 16(1), 5–20.

Levitas, R. (2005) *The Inclusive Society? Social Exclusion and New Labour* (2nd edn). Basingstoke: Palgrave Macmillan.

Levitas, R. (2012) 'The Just Umbrella: Austerity and the Big Society in Coalition Policy and Beyond', *Critical Social Policy*, 32(3), 320–42.

Lewis, J. (2001) *The End of Marriage? Individualism and Intimate Relations*. Cheltenham: Edward Elgar.

LGA (Local Government Association) (2009) *Councils Struggling to Recruit Social Workers in Wake of Baby P*. London: LGA.

Liberal Democrats (2010) *Liberal Democrat Manifesto, 2010*. London: Liberal Democrat Party.

Lister, R. (1990) *The Exclusive Society: Citizenship and the Poor*. London: CPAG.

Lister, R. (2011) 'The Age of Responsibility: Social Policy and Citizenship in the Early 21st Century', in C. Holden, M. Kilkey and G. Ramia (eds) *Social Policy Review 21: Analysis and Debate in Social Policy, 2011*. Bristol: Policy Press.

London Borough of Brent (1985) *A Child in Trust: Report of the Panel of Inquiry Investigating the Circumstances Surrounding the Death of Jasmine Beckford*. London Borough of Brent.

London Borough of Greenwich (1987) *A Child in Mind: Protection in a Responsible Society; Report of the Commission of Inquiry into the Circumstances Surrounding the Death of Kimberley Carlile*. London Borough of Greenwich.

London Borough of Lambeth (1987) *Whose Child? The Report of the Panel Appointed to Inquire into the Death of Tyra Henry*. London Borough of Lambeth.

Lonne, B., Parton, N., Thomson, J. and Harries, M. (2009) *Reforming Child Protection*. London: Routledge.

Luckock, B. (2007) 'Safeguarding Children and Integrated Children's Services', in K. Wilson and A. James (eds) *The Child Protection Handbook* (3rd edn). London: Baillière Tindall.

Mabbett, D. (2013) 'The Second Time as Tragedy? Welfare Reform under Thatcher and the Coalition', *The Political Quarterly*, 84(1), 43–52.

MacAlister, J. with Crehan, L. and Olsen, A. (2012) *Frontline: Improving the Children's Social Work Profession*. London: IPPR.

McAnulla, B. (2007) 'New Labour, Old Epistemology? Reflections on Political Science, New Institutionalism and the Blair Government', *Parliamentary Affairs*, 60(2), 313–31.

McDonald, C. (2006) 'Institutional Transformation. The Impact of Performance Measurement on Professional Practice in Social Work', *Social Work and Society*, 4(1), 25–37.

McDonald, R. (2006) 'Creating a Patient-led NHS: Empowering "Consumers" or Shrinking the State?', in L. Bauld, K. Clarke and T. Maltby (eds) *Social Policy Review 18: Analysis and Debate in Social Policy*. Bristol: Policy Press.

Macmillan, H.L., Wathen, C.N., Barlow, J. et al. (2009) 'Interventions to Prevent Child Maltreatment and Associated Impairment', *The Lancet*, 373(9659), 250–66.

Mapp, S.C. (2011) *Global Child Welfare and Well-Being*. New York: OUP.

Marshall, P. and Laws, D. (eds) (2004) *The Orange Book: Reclaiming Liberalism*. London: Profile Books.

Martin, S. (2005) 'Speeches and Addresses: Evaluation, Inspection and the Improvement Agenda: Contrasting Fortunes in an Era of Evidence-based Policy-Making', *Evaluation*, 11, 496–504.

Martinez-Brawley, E.E. and Zorita, P.M. (1998) 'At the Edge of the Frame: Beyond Science and Art in Social Work', *British Journal of Social Work*, 28(2), 5–27.

May-Chahal, C. and Herezog, M. (eds) (2003) *Child Sexual Abuse in Europe*. Strasburg: Council of Europe Publishing.

Mead, L. (ed.) (1997) *The New Paternalism: Supervisory Approaches to Welfare*. Washington DC: Brooking Institution Press.

Mead, L. (2007) 'Towards a Mandatory Work Policy for Men', *The Future of Children*, 17(2), 43–72.

Melton, G. (2005) 'Mandated Reporting: A Policy Without Reason', *Child Abuse and Neglect*, 25(1), 9–18.

Menzies, I. (1988) *Containing Anxiety in Institutions*. London: Free Association.

Menzies, I. (1989) *The Dynamics of the Social*. London: Free Association.

Messner, S.F., Thome, H. and Rosenfeld, R. (2008) 'Institutions, Anomie and Violent Crime: Clarifying and Elaborating Institutional-Anomie Theory', *International Journal of Conflict and Violence*, 2(2), 163–81.

Millar, J. and Ridge, T. (2002) 'Parents, Children and Families and New Labour: Developing Family Policy?', in M. Powell (ed.) *Evaluating New Labour's Welfare Reforms*. Bristol: Policy Press.

MoJ (Ministry of Justice) (2011) *Family Justice Review: Final Report*. London: MoJ.

MoJ (2012) *The Government Response to the Family Justice Review: A System with Children and Families at its Heart*. London: MoJ.

Moeller, S.D. (2002) 'A Hierarchy of Innocence: The Media's Use of Children in the Telling of International News', *Harvard International Journal of Press/Politics*, 7(1), 35–56.

Monckton Inquiry (1946) *Report by Sir Walter Monckton on the Circumstances which led to the Boarding out of Dennis and Terence O'Neill at Bank Farm, Minsterley, and the Steps Taken to Supervise their Welfare*, Cm 6636. London: HMSO.

Morris, A., Giller, H., Szwed, E. and Geach, H. (1980) *Justice for Children*. London: Macmillan.

Morris, L. (1994) *Dangerous Classes: The Underclass and Social Citizenship*. London: Routledge.

Mrazek, P.J. and Haggerty, R.J. (eds) (1994) *Reducing Risks for Mental Disorders: Frontiers for Preventive Intervention Research*. Washington DC: Institute of Medicine/National Academy Press.

Munro, E. (1998) 'Improving Social Workers' Knowledge Base in Child Protection Work', *British Journal of Social Work*, 28(1), 89–105.

Munro, E. (2004a) 'The Impact of Audit on Social Work Practice', *British Journal of Social Work*, 34(8), 1079–95.

Munro, E. (2004b) 'State Regulation of Parenting', *Political Quarterly*, 75(2), 180–5.

Munro, E. (2005) 'Improving Practice: Child Protection as a Systems Problem', *Children and Youth Services Review*, 27(4), 375–91.

Munro, E. (2007a) *Child Protection*. London: Sage.

Munro, E. (2007b) 'Confidentiality in a Preventive Child Welfare System', *Ethics and Social Welfare*, 1(1), 41–55.

Munro, E. (2008) *Effective Child Protection* (2nd edn). London: Sage.

Munro, E. (2009) 'Managing Societal and Institutional Risk in Child Protection', *Risk Analysis*, 29(7), 1015–23.

Munro, E. (2010a) 'Learning to Reduce Risk in Child Protection', *British Journal of Social Work*, 40(4), 1135–51.

Munro, E. (2010b) *The Munro Review of Child Protection, Part One: A System's Analysis*. London: DfE.

Munro, E. (2010c) 'Conflating Risks: Implications for Accurate Risk Prediction in Child Welfare Services', *Health, Risk and Society*, 12(2), 119–30.

Munro, E. (2011a) *The Munro Review of Child Protection: Interim Report. The Child's Journey*. London: DfE.

Munro, E. (2011b) *The Munro Review of Child Protection: Final Report. A Child-Centred System*, Cm 8062. London: DfE.

Munro, E. (2012) *The Munro Review of Child Protection: Progress Report: Moving Towards a Child-Centred System*. London: DfE.

Munro, E. and Calder, M. (2005) 'Where has Child Protection Gone?', *Political Quarterly*, 76(3), 439–45.

Munro, E. and Parton, N. (2007) 'How Far is England in the Process of Introducing a Mandatory Reporting System?', *Child Abuse Review*, 16(1), 5–16.

Murray, C. (1990) *The Emerging British Underclass*. London: IEA.

Murray, C. (1994) *The Underclass: The Crisis Deepens*. London: IEA.

Narey, M. (2011) *Narey Report on Adoption*, special supplement of *The Times*, 5 July.

National Children's Bureau (2012) *Beyond the Cuts: Children's Charities Adapting to Austerity*. London: NCB.

Nelson, S. (1987) *Incest: Fact and Myth*. Edinburgh: Stamullion.

Newman, J. (2001) *Modernising Governance: New Labour, Policy and Society*. London: Sage.

Norgrove, D. (2011) *Family Justice Review*. London: MoJ/DfE/Welsh Government.

Norman, A. (2013) 'Working Together 2013 Ignores Human Rights and We Must Act on This', *Community Care*, http://www.communitycare.co.uk/articles/25/04/2013/119131 (accessed 29/04/2013).

NSPCC (National Society for the Prevention of Cruelty to Children) (2011) *Payments by Results: Opportunities and Challenges for Improving Outcomes for Children*. London: NSPCC.

Nuffield Foundation (2009) *Time Trends in Parenting and Outcomes for Young People*. London: Nuffield Foundation.

OECD (2011) *Divided We Stand: Why Inequality Keeps Rising*. Paris. OECD.

Office of the Children's Commissioner (2013) *A Child Rights Impact Assessment of Budget Decisions*. London: Office of the Children's Commissioner.

Ofsted (2008a) *The Annual Report of Her Majesty's Chief Inspector of Education, Children's Services and Skills 2007/08*. London: TSO.

Ofsted (2008b) *Learning Lessons, Taking Action: Ofsted's Evaluations of Serious Case Reviews, 1 April 2007 to 31 March 2008*. London: Ofsted.

Ofsted (2012) *Inspection of Local Authority Arrangements for the Protection of Children*. Doncaster Metropolitan Borough Council: Ofsted.

Ormerod, P. (2005) 'The Impact of Sure Start', *Political Quarterly*, 76(4), 565–7.

Orton, M. and Rowlinson, K. (2007) 'A Problem of Riches: Towards a New Social Policy Research Agenda on the Distribution of Economic Resources', *Journal of Social Policy*, 36(1), 59–77.

Ost, D. (2004) 'Politics as the Mobilization of Anger', *European Journal of Social Theory*, 7(2), 229–44.

Oxfam (2012) *The Perfect Storm: Economic Stagnation, The Rising Cost of Living, Public Expenditure Cuts, and the Impact on UK Poverty*. Oxford: Oxfam.

Packman, J. (1981) *The Child's Generation*. 2nd edn. Oxford: Basil Blackwell/Martin Robertson.

Packman, J. (1993) 'From Prevention to Partnership: Child Welfare Services Across Three Decades', *Children & Society*, 7(2), 183–95.

Parker, R. (1983) 'The Gestation of Reform: The Children Act 1948', in P. Bean and S. MacPherson (eds) *Approaches to Welfare*. London: Routledge & Kegan Paul.

Parker, R. (1995) 'A Brief History of Child Protection', in E. Farmer and M. Owen (eds) *Child Protection Practice: Private Risks and Public Remedies*. London: HMSO.

Parker, R., Ward, H., Jackson, S. et al. (eds) (1991) *Looking After Children: Assessing Outcomes in Child Care. The Report of an Independent Working Party Established by the Department of Health*. London: HMSO.

Parton, N. (1981) 'Child Abuse, Social Anxiety and Welfare', *British Journal of Social Work*, 11(4), 394–414.

Parton, N. (1985) *The Politics of Child Abuse*. Basingstoke: Macmillan.

Parton, N. (1991) *Governing the Family: Child Care, Child Protection and the State*. Basingstoke: Macmillan.

Parton, N. (ed.) (1997) *Child Protection and Family Support: Tensions, Contradictions and Possibilities.* London: Routledge.

Parton, N. (1998) 'Risk, Advanced Liberalism and Child Welfare: The Need to Rediscover Uncertainty and Ambiguity', *British Journal of Social Work,* 28(1), 5–27.

Parton, N. (2004) 'From Maria Colwell to Victoria Climbié: Reflections on Public Inquiries into Child Abuse a Generation Apart', *Child Abuse Review,* 13(2), 80–94.

Parton, N. (2006a) *Safeguarding Childhood: Early Intervention and Surveillance in a Late Modern Society.* Basingstoke: Palgrave Macmillan.

Parton, N. (2006b) '"Every Child Matters": The Shift to Prevention whilst Strengthening Protection in Children's Services in England', *Children and Youth Services Review,* 28(8), 976–92.

Parton, N. (2008) 'The "Change for Children" Programme in England: Towards the "Preventive-Surveillance State"', *Journal of Law and Society,* 35(1), 166–87.

Parton, N. (2011a) 'The Increasing Length and Complexity of Central Government Guidance about Child Abuse in England: 1974-2010. Evidence to the Munro Review', University of Huddersfield, available at http://eprints.hud.ac.uk/9006.

Parton, N. (2011b) 'Child Protection and Safeguarding in England: Changing and Competing Conceptions of Risk and their Implications for Social Work', *British Journal of Social Work,* 41(5), 854–75.

Parton, N. (2012a) 'Reflections on "Governing the Family": The Close Relationship Between Child Protection and Social Work in Advanced Western Societies – the Example of England', *Families, Relationships and Societies,* 1(1), 87–100.

Parton, N. (2012b) 'The Munro Review of Child Protection: An Appraisal', *Children & Society,* 26(2), 150–62.

Parton, N. and Berridge, D. (2011) 'Child Protection in England', in N. Gilbert, N. Parton and M. Skivenes (eds) *Child Protection Systems: International Trends and Orientations.* New York: OUP.

Parton, N. and Kirk. S. (2010) 'The Nature and Purposes of Social Work', in I. Shaw, B. Briar-Lawson, J. Orme and R. Ruckdeschel (eds) *Sage Handbook of Social Work Research.* London: Sage.

Parton, N. and Thomas, T. (1983) 'Child Abuse and Citizenship', in B. Jordan and N. Parton (eds) *The Political Dimensions of Social Work.* Oxford: Basil Blackwell.

Pascall, G. (1987) *Social Policy: A New Feminist Analysis.* London: Routledge.

Pasura, D., Jones, A. and Da Breo, H. (2013) 'IMPACT: Interventions and Mitigations to Prevent the Abuse of Children – it's Time. A Public Health Oriented Systems Model for Change', in A. Jones (ed.) *Understanding*

Child Sexual Abuse: Perspectives from the Caribbean. Basingstoke: Palgrave Macmillan.

Pearson, G. (1975) *The Deviant Imagination: Psychiatry, Social Work and Social Change.* Basingstoke: Macmillan.

Peckover, S. and Smith, S. (2011) 'Public Health Approaches to Safeguarding Children', *Child Abuse Review*, 20(4), 231–7.

Peckover, S., White, S. and Hall, C. (2008) 'Making and Managing Electronic Children: E-assessment in Child Welfare', *Information, Communication and Society*, 11(3), 375–94.

Pemberton, S., Gordon, D. and Nandy, S. (2012) 'Child Rights, Child Survival and Child Poverty: The Debate', in A. Minu and S. Nandy (eds) *Global Child Poverty and Well-Being: Measurement, Concepts, Policy and Action.* Bristol: Policy Press.

Penna, S. (2005) 'The Children Act 2004: Child Protection and Social Surveillance', *Journal of Social Welfare and Family Law*, 27(2), 143–57.

Perry, B. (1995) 'Incubated in Terror: 20 Neurodevelopmental Factors in the Cycle of Violence', in J.D. Osofsky (ed.) *Children, Youth and Violence: Searching for Solutions.* New York: Guilford Press.

Philp, A.F. and Timms, N. (1962) *The Problem of the Problem Family.* London: Family Service Units.

Philp, M. (1979) 'Notes on the Form of Knowledge in Social Work', *Sociological Review*, 27(1), 83–111.

Pickett, K. and Wilkinson, R. (2007) 'Child Wellbeing and Income Inequality in Rich Societies: Ecological Cross Sectional Study', *British Medical Journal*, 335(7629), 1080–7.

Pickles, E. (2012) 'Eric Pickles hails 100% Troubled Families Take Up', www.gov.uk/government/news/eric-pickles-hails-100-troubled-families-take-up (accessed 27/11/2013).

Pinheiro, P.S. (2006) *World Report on Violence Against Children.* Geneva: UN.

Pollard, N. (2012) *The Pollard Review Report.* London: BBC.

Power, M. (1997) *The Audit Society: Rituals of Verification.* Oxford: OUP.

Prabhakar, R. (2011) 'What is the Legacy of New Labour?', in S. Lee and M. Beech (eds) *The Cameron-Clegg Government: Coalition Politics in an Age of Uncertainty.* Basingstoke: Palgrave Macmillan.

Pringle, K. (1998) *Children and Social Welfare in Europe.* Buckingham: Open University Press.

Pringle, K. (2005) 'Neglected Issues in Swedish Child Protection Policy and Practice: Age, Ethnicity and Gender', in M. Erikson, M. Hester, S. Keskinen and K. Pringle (eds) *Tackling Men's Violence in Families: Nordic Issues and Dilemmas.* Bristol: Policy Press.

Pringle, K. (2010) 'Epilogue: On Developing Empowering Child Welfare Systems and the Welfare Research Needed to Create Them', in H. Forsberg and T. Kroger (eds) *Social Work and Child Welfare Politics: Through Nordic Lenses*. Bristol: Policy Press.

Pritchard, C. and Williams, R. (2010) 'Comparing Possible "Child-abuse-related Deaths" in England and Wales with the Major Developed Countries 1974–2006: Signs of Progress', *British Journal of Social Work*, 40(6), 1700–18.

Pugh, G. and Parton, N. (eds) (2003) 'New Labour Policy and its Outcomes for Children', *Children and Society*, Special Issue, 17(3).

Puttnam-Hornstein, E., Webster, D., Needell, B. and Magruder, J. (2011) 'A Public Health Approach to Child Maltreatment Surveillance: Evidence from a Data Linkage Project in the United States', *Child Abuse Review*, 20(4), 256–73.

Radford, J. (2010) *Serious Case Review in Respect of a Child: Case Number 14*. Birmingham: Birmingham Safeguarding Children Board.

Radford, L. (2012) *Rethinking Children, Violence and Safeguarding*. London: Continuum.

Radford, L., Corral, S., Bradley, C. et al. (2011) *Child Abuse and Neglect in the UK Today*. London: NSPCC.

Ramesh, R. (2012) 'Council cuts "targeted towards deprived areas"', *The Guardian*, 14 November, 9.

Ray, L. (2011) *Violence and Society*. London: Sage.

Reading, R., Bissell, S., Goldhagen, J. et al. (2009) 'Promotion of Children's Rights and Prevention of Child Maltreatment', *The Lancet*, 373(9660), 332–43.

Reed, H. (2012) *In the Eye of the Storm: Britain's Forgotten Children and Families*. London: Action for Children/Children's Society/NSPCC.

Respect Task Force (2006) *Respect Action Plan*. London: Home Office.

Rhodes, R. (1997) *Understanding Governance*. Buckingham: Open University Press.

Roberts, D. (2009) *Social Harm and Crime at a Global Level*. London: Centre for Crime and Justice Studies.

Roche, J. (2008) 'Children's Rights, Confidentiality and the Policing of Children', *International Journal of Children's Rights*, 16(4), 431–56.

Rodger, J.J. (2012) '"Regulating the Poor": Observations on the "Structural Coupling" of Welfare, Criminal Justice and the Voluntary Sector in a "Big Society"', *Social Policy and Administration*, 46(4), 413–31.

Rohloff, A., Hughes, J., Petley, J. and David, M. (2011) 'Moral Panics in the Contemporary World' (guest editors), *Crime Media Culture*, Special Issue, 7(3).

Rowlands, J. (2010) 'Services are Not Enough: Child Well-being in a Very Unequal Society', *Journal of Children's Services*, 5(3), 80–8.

Rowlands, J. (2011) 'Need, Well-being and Outcomes: The Development of Policy-thinking for Children's Services 1989–2004', *Child and Family Social Work*, 16(3), 255–65.

Rush, F. (1980) *The Best Kept Secret: Sexual Abuse of Children.* New York: McGraw-Hill.

Rutter, M. (1990) 'Psychosocial Resilience and Protective Mechanisms', in J. Rolf, A.S. Masten, D. Cichetti et al. (eds) *Risk and Protective Factors in the Development of Psychopathology.* Cambridge: Cambridge University Press.

Rutter, M. (2006) 'Is Sure Start an Effective Preventive Intervention?', *Child and Adolescent Mental Health*, 11(3), 135–41.

Rutter, M. (2007) 'Sure Start Local Programmes: An Outsider's Perspective', in J. Belsky, J. Barnes and E. Melhuish (eds) *The National Evaluation of Sure Start: Does Area-Based Early Intervention Work?* Bristol: Policy Press.

Savolainen, J. (2000) 'Inequality, Welfare State, and Homicide: Further Support for the Institutional Anomie Theory', *Criminology*, 38(4), 1021–42.

Scott, D. (2007) 'Towards a Public Health Model of Child Protection', *Communities, Families and Children Australia*, 1(1), 9–16.

Scottish Executive (2002) *'It's Everyone's Job to Make Sure I'm Alright': Report of the Child Protection Audit and Review.* Edinburgh: Scottish Executive.

Scruton, P. (ed.) (1997) *Childhood in Crisis.* London: UCL Press.

Secretary of State for Social Services (1974) *Report of the Inquiry into the Care and Supervision Provided in Relation to Maria Colwell.* London: HMSO.

Secretary of State for Social Services (1988) *Report of the Inquiry into Child Abuse in Cleveland*, Cm 413. London: HMSO.

Seden, J., Sinclair, R., Robins, D. and Pont, C. (2001) *Studies Informing the 'Framework for the Assessment of Children in Need and their Families'.* London: TSO.

Seebohm, F. (1968) *Report of the Committee on Local Authority and Allied Social Services*, Cmnd 3703. London: HMSO.

Sefton, T. and Sutherland, H. (2005) 'Poverty and Inequality under New Labour', in J. Hills and K. Stewart (eds) *A More Equal Society? New Labour, Poverty, Inequality and Exclusion.* Bristol: Policy Press.

Segal, H. (1979) *Introduction to the Work of Melanie Klein*, London: Karma.

Segal, J. (2006) 'The Discipline of Freedom: Action and Normalization in the Theory and Practice of Neo-Liberalism', *New Political Science*, 28(3), 323–34.

Segal, L. and Dalziel, K. (2011) 'Investing to Protect our Children: Using Economics to Derive an Evidence-based Strategy', *Child Abuse Review*, 20(4), 274–89.

Shaw, I. and Clayden, J. (2009) 'Technology, Evidence and Professional Practice: Reflections on the Integrated Children's System', *Journal of Children's Services*, 4(4), 15–27.

Shaw, I., Morris, K. and Edwards, A. (2009a) 'Technology, Social Services and Organizational Innovation *or* How Great Expectations in London and

Cardiff are Dashed in Lowestoft and Cymtyrch', *Journal of Social Work Practice*, 23(4), 383–400.

Shaw, I., Bell, M., Sinclair, I. et al. (2009b) 'An Exemplary Scheme? An Evaluation of the Integrated Children's System', *British Journal of Social Work*, 39(4), 613–26.

Shearer, A. (1979) 'Tragedies Revisited 1: The Legacy of Maria Colwell', *Social Work Today*, 10(19), 12–19.

Shore, R. (1997) *Rethinking the Brain: New Insights into Early Development.* New York: Families and Work Institute.

Sidebotham, P. and the ALSPAC Study Team (2000) 'Patterns of Child Abuse in Early Childhood: A Cohort Study of the "Children in the Nineties"', *Child Abuse Review*, 9(5), 311–20.

Simon, C.A. and Ward, S. (eds) (2010) *Does Every Child Matter? Understanding New Labour's Social Reforms.* London: Routledge.

Sinclair, R., Hearn, B. and Pugh, G. (1997) *Preventive Work with Families: The Role of Mainstream Services.* London: NCB.

Skehill, C. (2007) 'Researching the History of Social Work: Exposition of History of the Present Approach', *European Journal of Social Work*, 10(4), 449–63.

Skehill, C. (2008) 'Socio-legal Practices in Child Welfare and Protection in Northern Ireland and the Republic of Ireland: Histories of the Present and Possibilities for the Future', in K. Burns and D. Lynch (eds) *Child Protection and Welfare Social Work.* Dublin: A & A Farmar.

Skinner, C. (2003) 'New Labour and Family Policy', in M. Bell and K. Wilson (eds) *The Practitioners' Guide to Working with Families.* Basingstoke: Palgrave Macmillan.

Smith, C. (2001) 'Trust and Confidence: Possibilities for Social Work in High Modernity', *British Journal of Social Work*, 31(2), 287–305.

Smith, R. (1991) 'Child Care: Welfare, Protection or Rights', *Journal of Social Welfare and Family Law*, 13(6), 469–81.

Smith, R. (2005) *Values and Practice in Children's Services.* Basingstoke: Macmillan.

Smith, R. (2008) 'From Child Protection to Child Safety: Locating Risk Assessment in the Changing Landscape', in M.C. Calder (ed.) *Contemporary Risk Assessment in Safeguarding Children.* Lyme Regis: Russell House.

Social Exclusion Task Force (2007) *Reaching Out: Progress on Social Exclusion.* London: Cabinet Office.

Social Exclusion Unit (2001) *Preventing Social Exclusion.* London: TSO.

Social Justice Policy Group (2006) *Breakdown Britain: Interim Report on the State of the Nation.* London: CSJ.

Social Justice Policy Group (2007) *Breakthrough Britain: Ending the Costs of Social Breakdowns: Overview, Policy Recommendations to the Conservative Party*. London: CSJ.

Social Services Committee (1984) *Children in Care*, the Short Report, HC360. London: HMSO.

Social Work Reform Board (2012) *Building a Safe and Confident Future: Maintaining Momentum. Progress Report from the Social Work Reform Board*. London: DfE.

Social Work Task Force (2009) *Building a Safe, Confident Future: The Final Report of the Social Work Task Force*. Nottingham: DCSF.

Soss, J., Fording, R.C. and Schram, S.F. (2009) 'Governing the Poor: The Rise of the Neoliberal Paternalist State', paper presented to the Annual Meeting of the American Political Science Association, Toronto, Canada.

Soss, J., Fording, R.C. and Schram, S.F. (2011) *Disciplining the Poor: Neoliberal Paternalism and the Persistent Power of Race*. Chicago: University of Chicago Press.

Squires, P. and Lea, J. (eds) (2012) *Criminalisation and Advanced Marginality: Critically Exploring the Work of Loïc Wacquant*. Bristol: Policy Press.

Stafford, A., Vincent, S. and Parton, N. (eds) (2010) *Child Protection Reform across the UK*. Edinburgh: Dunedin.

Stafford, A., Parton, N., Smith, C. and Vincent, S. (2012) *Child Protection Systems in the United Kingdom: A Comparative Analysis*. London: Jessica Kingsley.

Stedman Jones, G. (1971) *Outcast London*. Harmondsworth: Penguin.

Stewart, K. (2011) 'A Treble Blow? Child Poverty in 2010 and Beyond', in C. Holden, M. Kilkey and G. Ramia (eds) *Social Policy Review 23: Analysis and Debate in Social Policy 2011*. Bristol: Policy Press.

Surveillance Studies Network (2006) *A Report on the Surveillance Society*. London: Information Commissioner's Office.

Taylor, L., Lacey, R. and Bracken, D. (1980) *In Whose Best Interests?* London: Cobden Trust/Mind.

Taylor, M. (2009) 'Reflections on Social Evils and Human Nature', in D. Utting (ed.) *Contemporary Social Evils*. Bristol: Policy Press.

Taylor-Gooby, P. (2011) 'The UK Welfare State Going West', in N. Yeates, T. Haux, R. Jawad and M. Kilkey (eds) *In Defence of Welfare: The Impacts of the Spending Review*. Social Policy Association.

Taylor-Gooby, P. (2012) 'Root and Branch Restructuring to Achieve Major Cuts: The Social Policy Programme of the 2010 UK Coalition Government', *Social Policy and Administration*, 46(1), 61–82.

Taylor-Gooby, P. (2013) 'Why Do People Stigmatise the Poor at a Time of Rapidly Increasing Inequality, and What Can Be Done About It?', *The Political Quarterly*, 84(1), 31–42.

Taylor-Gooby, P. and Stoker, G. (2011) 'The Coalition Programme: A New Vision for Britain or Politics as Usual?', *The Political Quarterly*, 82(1), 4–15.

Theodore, A.D. and Runyan, D.K. (1999) 'A Medical Research Agenda for Child Maltreatment: Negotiating the Next Steps', *Pediatrics*, 104(1), 168–77.

Theoretical Criminology (2010) 'A Sketch of the Neo-Liberal State: A Symposium', *Theoretical Criminology*, 14(1), 58–123.

Thoburn, J. (2007) *Globalisation and Child Welfare: Some Lessons from a Cross National Study of Children in Out of Home Care*. Norwich: UEA.

Thompson, J.B. (2000) *Political Scandal: Power and Visibility in the Media Age*. Cambridge: Polity Press.

Thompson, J.B. (2005) 'The New Visibility', *Theory, Culture and Society*, 22(6), 31–51.

Thompson, J.B. (2011) 'Shifting Boundaries of Public and Private Life', *Theory, Culture and Society*, 28(4), 49–70.

Tickell, Dame C. (2011) *The Early Years: Foundations for Life, Health and Learning: An Independent Report on the Early Years Foundation Stage to Her Majesty's Government*. London: DfE.

Tilbury, C. (2004) 'The Influence of Performance Measurement on Child Welfare', *British Journal of Social Work*, 34(2), 225–41.

Tilbury, C. (2005) 'Counting Family Support', *Child and Family Social Work*, 10(2), 149–57.

Timpson, E. (2013) Edward Timpson Speaks to the NSPCC Conference: 'How Safe are our Children?', 18 April, www.gov.uk/government/speeches/edward-timpson-speaks-to-the-nspcc-conference-how-safe-are-our-children (accessed 27/11/2013).

Townsend, P. (1970) *The Fifth Social Service: A Critical Analysis of the Seebohm Proposals*. London: Fabian Society.

Townsend, P. (1979) *Poverty in the United Kingdom*. Harmondsworth: Penguin.

Toynbee, P. and Walker, D. (2001) *Did Things Get Better? An Audit of Labour's Successes and Failures*. London: Penguin.

Treneman, A. (2008) 'Shame, they cried. And they were right', *The Times*, 13 November, 10.

Tucker, S. (2011) 'Listening and Believing: An Examination of Young People's Perceptions of Why They Are Not Believed by Professionals When They Report Abuse and Neglect', *Children & Society*, 25(6), 458–69.

UNICEF (2005) *Council of Europe Actions to Promote Children's Rights to Protection from All Forms of Violence*. Florence: UNICEF Innocenti Research Centre.

UNICEF (2007) *Child Poverty in Perspective: An Overview of Child Well-Being in Rich Countries*, Innocenti Report Card 7. Florence: UNICEF Innocenti Research Centre.

UNICEF (2012) *Measuring Child Poverty: New League Tables of Child Poverty in the World's Rich Countries*, Report Card 10. Florence: UNICEF Innocenti Research Centre.

Utting, D. (1995) *Family and Parenthood: Supporting Families, Preventing Breakdown*. York: Joseph Rowntree Foundation.

Utting, D. (ed.) (1998) *Children's Services: Now and in the Future*. London: NCB.

Utting, D. (ed.) (2009) *Contemporary Social Evils*. Bristol: Policy Press/Joseph Rowntree Foundation.

Utting, D., Bright, J. and Henricson, C. (1993) *Crime and Family: Improving Child-rearing and Preventing Delinquency*. London: Family Policy Studies Centre.

Utting, Sir W. (1997) *People Like Us: The Report of the Review of the Safeguards for Children Living Away from Home*. London: HMSO.

Valentine, M. (1994) 'The Social Worker as "Bad Object"', *British Journal of Social Work*, 24(1), 71–86.

Veit-Wilson, J. (1998) *Setting Adequate Standards*. Bristol: Policy Press.

Wacquant, L. (2009) *Punishing the Poor: The Neoliberal Government of Social Insecurity*. Durham, NC: Duke University Press.

Wacquant, L. (2010) 'Crafting the Neoliberal State: Workfare, Prisonfare, and Social Insecurity', *Sociological Forum*, 25(2), 197–220.

Wacquant, L. (2012) 'The Wedding of Workfare and Prisonfare in the 21st Century: Responses to Critics and Commentators', in P. Squires and J. Lea (eds) *Criminalisation and Advanced Marginality: Critically Exploring the Work of Loïc Wacquant*. Bristol: Policy Press.

Walker, A. and Walker, C. (1997) *Britain Divided: The Growth of Social Exclusion in the 1980s and 1990s*. London: CPAG.

Walker, S. and Scott, J. (2004) *Implementing the Integrated Children's System: A Phased Approach: Briefing Paper 6*. London: DfES.

Warner, J. (2013a) 'Social Work, Class Politics and Risk in the Moral Panic over Baby P', *Health, Risk and Society*, 15(3), 217–33.

Warner, J. (2013b) '"Heads Must Roll? " Emotional Politics, the Press and the Death of Baby P', *British Journal of Social Work*, 40(4), 1035–45.

Wastell, D. and White, S. (2012) 'Blinded by Neuroscience: Social Policy, the Family and the Infant Brain', *Families, Relationships and Society*, 1(2), 397–414.

Wastell, D., White, S., Broadhurst, K. et al. (2010) 'Children's Services in the Iron Cage of Performance Management: Street-Level Bureaucracy and the Spectre of Svejkism', *International Journal of Social Welfare*, 19(3), 310–20.

Wattam, C. and Woodward, C. (1996a) '... And Do I Abuse My Children? No! Learning About Prevention from People Who Have Experienced Child

Abuse', in *Childhood Matters: Report of the National Commission of Inquiry into the Prevention of Child Abuse*, vol. 2: *Background Papers*. London: TSO.

Wattam, C. and Woodward, C. (1996b) *Childhood Matters: Report of the National Commission of Inquiry into the Prevention of Child Abuse*, vols 1 and 2. London: TSO.

Welshman, J. (2006a) 'From the Cycle of Deprivation to Social Exclusion: Five Continuities', *The Political Quarterly*, 77(4), 475–84.

Welshman, J. (2006b) *Underclass: A History of the Excluded, 1880-2000*. London: Hambledon Continuum.

Welshman, J. (2007) *From Transmitted Deprivation to Social Exclusion: Policy, Poverty, and Parenting*. Bristol: Policy Press.

Whitaker, D.J., Lutzker, J.R. and Shelley, G.A. (2005) 'Child Maltreatment Prevention Priorities at the Centres for Disease Control and Prevention', *Child Maltreatment*, 10(3), 245–59.

White, S., Hall, C. and Peckover, S. (2009a) 'The Descriptive Tyranny of the Common Assessment Framework: Technologies of Categorization and Professional Practice in Child Welfare', *British Journal of Social Work*, 39(7), 1–21.

White, S., Broadhurst, K., Wastell, D. et al. (2009b) 'Whither Practice: Near Research in the Modernization Programme? Policy Blunders in Children's Services', *Journal of Social Work Practice*, 23(4), 401–11.

White, S., Wastell, D., Broadhurst, K. and Hall, C. (2010) 'When Policy O'erleaps Itself: The "Tragic Tale" of the Integrated Children's System', *Critical Social Policy*, 30(3), 405–29.

WHO (World Health Organization) (2007) *Preventing Child Maltreatment in Europe: A Public Health Approach*. Copenhagen: WHO Regional Office for Europe.

Wiggan, J. (2011) 'Something Old and Blue, or Red, Bold and New? Welfare Reform and the Coalition Government', in C. Holden, M. Kilkey and G. Ramia (eds) *Social Policy Review 23: Analysis and Debate in Social Policy, 2011*. Bristol: Policy Press.

Wiggan, J. (2012) 'Telling Stories of 21st Century Welfare: The UK Coalition Government and the Neo-liberal Discourse of Worklessness and Dependency', *Critical Social Policy*, 32(3), 383–405.

Wild, J. (ed.) (2013) *Exploiting Childhood: How Fast Food, Material Obsession and Porn Culture are Creating New Forms of Child Abuse*. London: Jessica Kingsley.

Wilkinson, R.G. (1996) *Unhealthy Societies: The Afflictions of Inequality*. London: Routledge.

Wilkinson, R.G. (2005) *The Impact of Inequality: How to Make Sick Societies Healthier*. London: Routledge.

Wilkinson, R.G. and Pickett, K. (2009) *The Spirit Level: Why More Equal Societies Almost Always Do Better*. London: Allen Lane.

Williams, F. (1989) *Social Policy: A Critical Introduction*. Cambridge: Polity Press.

Williams, Z. (2013) 'Public sector outsourcing has created a shadow state', *The Guardian*, 7 February, 32.

Wintour, P. and Stewart, H. (2013) 'Spending review: George Osborne targets benefits and slashes public sector jobs', *The Guardian*, 27 June, 1.

Young, J. (1999) *The Exclusive Society: Social Exclusion, Crime and Difference in Late Modernity*. London: Sage.

Young, J. (2007) *The Vertigo of Late Modernity*. London: Sage.

Zelizer, V.A. (1985) *Pricing the Priceless Child: The Changing Social Value of Children*. Princeton: Princeton University Press.

Index